Norman Leys and Settler Colonialism in Kenya

Norman Leys and Settler Colonialism in Kenya

Colin Leys

Foreword by Paul Gilroy

Merlin Press

First published in 2025 by
The Merlin Press Ltd,
Central Books Building,
Freshwater Road,
Dagenham
RM8 1RX

www.merlinpress.co.uk

9780850367966
© Colin Leys
© Paul Gilroy

A CIP record of this book is available from the British Library.

All rights reserved. No part of this publication may be reproduced, stored in a retrieval system, distributed, or transmitted in any form or by any means, including photocopying, recording, electronic or otherwise, without the prior written permission of the publisher.

Printed in the UK by Imprint Digital, Exeter.

Contents

Foreword by Paul Gilroy ... i
Introduction ... 1
1: The making of an awkward customer ... 5
2: Encountering colonialism ... 17
3: Discovering settler colonialism ... 29
4: Exile, war and reflection ... 51
5: Brailsford ... 65
6: Writing *Kenya* ... 73
7: The problem of Phariseeism ... 85
8: The difficult years ... 103
9: The outcome ... 119
10: Intellectual legacy ... 125
11: The man himself ... 133
Annexes
   1. The letter to the Colonial Secretary, 1918 ... 139
   2. The Problems of East Africa ... 160
   3. Preface to the third edition of *Kenya* ... 168
   4. 'African Mentality' ... 175
Acknowledgements ... 185
Notes ... 187
Index ... 197

Foreword

The concept of settler colonialism has lately supplied valuable interpretative resources to the salons of twenty-first century radicalism. Outside that microclimate, the need to transform institutions by working through the enduring effects of departed imperial power has been widely accepted as urgent. The jargon of decolonisation is everywhere, however the detailed history of the notably transnational movements that opposed colonial government and statecraft remains little known. When those narratives do emerge, they are likely to appear as crude sketches or to be offered in nationally-differentiated chapters that are inclined to miss the larger resonance of solidarity articulated on a planetary scale. The political opposition to colonial power was dispersed and its actions multi-sited. They shaped a movement that had to be as complex and interconnected as the imperial systems it strove to overcome.

Today, the proliferation of extractive, neo-colonial economic relationships and the development of scholastic postcolonial criticism have demanded new historical approaches to anticolonial organisations and tactics. It now seems possible that struggles to rid the world of colonies and empires will define the political culture of the twentieth century, a period that W.E.B. Du Bois had prophetically dubbed the century of "the color line". That dawning will require the challenging figure of Dr. Norman Leys to be salvaged from the condescension of posterity and unearthed even from his own efforts to obscure the lasting and important contributions he made to the anticolonial movement. In the meantime, Leys has been forgotten, his books placed in storage and his combative activities conjured out of sight.

This valuable volume retrieves him and his various interventions from the archival shadows. It asks how his criticisms of empire developed during a long period of government service and what relevance they might still have for contemporary conflicts resulting from the distinctive pathology of settler colonial regimes: violent, racialised rule and brutal exploitation justified by eugenic assumptions. Beyond Leys' biography and evolving commentary on colonial politics and policy, important questions are raised about the movement that opposed and denounced colonial rule. What was its relationship to the organised Left, to feminist sensibilities, to humanist ethics and to religious belief?

The reader is invited to consider what might have motivated, leavened and maintained Norman Leys' intransigent criticism of imperial injustice and the racial order warranted by the incorrigible claims of white supremacy, ethnicity and nationalism? Leys did not employ the rhetoric of anti-racism, but it is abundantly clear that for him, visible and cultural differences did not amount to differences in human worth. His indictments of imperial injustice were incompatible with fixed notions of racial hierarchy. He was committed to the possibility of positive change rooted in access to the humanising power of education which he viewed as the best antidote to the violence that he saw exploding from the bloody machinery of colonial rule.

Leys' unlikely childhood and family formation is explored in a search for additional clues that can shed light on his moral and political perspectives. His Christianity and his experience as a medical practitioner yield further questions about the sources of his hostility to colonial power and his notable commitment to common humanity. The latter seems to have been reinforced by relentless exposure to a parade of human suffering for which his professional capabilities as a doctor – at home and abroad – offered nothing more than makeshift or piecemeal solutions. There was a religiously anchored counter-anthropological humanism pending in those serial encounters with a universal vulnerability touched by sympathetic, caring hands that were doomed to offer only limited and temporary kinds of relief.

Leys' Fabian socialism and his Scottish nationality were similarly implicated in the formation of critical and oppositional perspectives. Once his life as a disenchanted colonial functionary had been abandoned as a result of his protests and his health, he transitioned into a lengthy period of activism: writing, speaking and organising.

Building on earlier criticism of Europe's empires, he began to collaborate closely with the leaders of the pan-African movement and diverse elements of the Left to consolidate opposition to the thoughtless cruelty and chaos of colonial administration. Leys' advocacy in the anti-colonial cause brought him into close contact with a number pan-Africanist and socialist luminaries as well as a motley of angry moralists. He corresponded with Du Bois and addressed meetings alongside Casely-Hayford, C.L.R. James, and George Padmore. The latter two footnoted his work extensively, though by no means adequately, given the degree of their indebtedness to his insights and detailed knowledge of the practical operations of imperial power.

It is well known that East Africa has a peculiar history of colonisation by Scots, explorers, missionaries and military officers. Strange affinities must have arisen from the transposition of Scottish toponyms into an African landscape that had highlands, lowlands and lakes. Renaming is a feature identified by Benedict Anderson, as contributing to the fantasy of cultural continuity that underpins the absurdities of the colonial mentality. It fed the proposition that life in far flung pairs of places was somehow being lived in parallel.

Norman Leys' early time in what would become Malawi included a deeply formative encounter with the incarcerated associates of the radical, US-educated rebel leader, John Chilembwe.*

For Leys, Chilembwe personified and prefigured a new variety of anticolonial politics precisely because of his transnational formation and the level of education he had attained at the Virginia Theological Seminary and College, a black Baptist college located in Lynchburg, an area that was still reverberating with the aftershocks of the great battle to end enslavement. The resulting rebel outlook not only drew on biblical precedents, but also claimed inspiration from John Brown, the instigator of the raid on Harper's Ferry that heralded the US civil war.

Leys was also able to interview some of the survivors of the insurrection. That contact seems to have had a profound effect. His influential 1924 *Kenya* retold the story of the Nyasaland uprising as part of the cautionary note essential to the book's gloomy political thrust. The detail and sympathy evident in that section of Leys' argument endowed it with an impact that endures unacknowledged, even today.

Initially, his account was recycled without proper citation by C.L.R. James' in two 1938 publications *The Black Jacobins* and its less widely

---

* Norman Leys, *Kenya,* London: The Hogarth Press, 1924, p.327.

known companion volume *A History of Negro Revolt*. Later, Leys' observations were picked up from that source by the African American political theorist Cedric Robinson who, again without acknowledgement, made them into a cornerstone of his influential concept of "the black radical tradition".

Robinson's agenda linked the results of struggles against slavery in the Americas to the later movements that fought against colonial power, particularly in Africa. For Robinson—ever the idealist—the resulting network of contact and exchange yielded "a revolutionary consciousness that proceeded from the whole historical experience of Black people and not merely from the social formations of capitalist slavery or the relations of production of colonialism." He located the repeated refusal of mass or gratuitous violence at the centre of his influential attempt to specify where the boundaries between the peoples of Europe and Africa might fall.

Robinson was strongly attached to the idea that the resistance of the enslaved became more violent as they were acculturated. He did not deny that the rebels fighting for freedom were violent, but he was firm that, in contrast to the excessive, spectacular brutality of their captors and oppressors, freedom-seeking violence delivered from below was proportionate, even minimal, carefully targeted and combined with recognition of the vulnerabilities of "non-combatants", something that contrasts sharply with the exterministic mentality celebrated enthusiastically in the eugenic –nits make lice– prosecution of colonial, small wars.

Robinson's illustrations of that "wholeness" include evidence drawn from the rebel lives of Toussaint, Nat Turner and Dessalines. However, Norman Leys' report of the Chilembwe uprising has a fundamental importance for him. Chilembwe exhorted his eschatological rebel band to "strike a blow and die" in their militant opposition to being conscripted into WW1 by their colonial overlords.*

For Robinson, that slogan captured the profound contrast in political, ontic and epistemic differences evident between African and European cultures. It was not just that the Nyasaland uprising anticipated the path to be followed swiftly by a rising caste of African intellectuals and activists, but also that its patterning of insurgent violence and colonial brutality honed the contrast between the

---

* George Shepperson and John Chilembwe "A Major Chilembwe Letter" *The Society of Malawi Journal*, Vol. 68, No. 1 (2015), pp. vi, 1-2

opposed philosophical and theological resources animating the wider conflict over colonial and imperial domination. His proof of this difference was distilled in one startling image of Chilembwe's rebels. It appeared in *Kenya* as part of Leys' warnings about the likely future condition of conflict in colonial territories everywhere.

> ... wives and children were sent some miles away, hurriedly, but with no intentional unkindness. The rebels even paid women to get milk and eggs for the children, and to hold banana leaves over them on the journey to keep the sun off them.*

This picture presents care and humanity unfolding even from the epicentre of violent anticolonial resistance. Rebellion had been undertaken in a decidedly fatalistic manner that was philosophically eloquent by being attuned to the differences between historical and individual dimensions of being. It has proved deeply resonant for the radicals who followed in Norman Leys' footsteps towards "the black radical tradition", even when they did not know that he had made that path for them.

On his exit from the colonial service Leys sometimes employed the African pseudonym that he placed on the title page of *Kenya* beneath the English name that was his professional and political handle. It is 'Fulani Bin Fulani', which has been roughly translated from Kiswahili as "so and so, son of so and so". Nobody who has written about him has found that personal gesture to be significant or interesting. The achievement of this volume can be measured in the way it brings us closer to comprehending what it might mean, not for the past, but for the future.

Paul Gilroy

---

* Norman Leys (1924), p.329.

Introduction

From 1901 to 1917 Norman Leys was a doctor in East Africa; from 1918 until his death in 1944 he was a leading figure in the anti-colonial movement in Britain. He had gone to Africa hoping to do something to help Africans cope with the disruption of their lives by the arrival of capitalist commerce and industry, and believing that this aim was shared by Britain's colonial administrators. He found that in East Africa this was not the case, and that Kenya, in particular, was being developed as a settler colony in which Africans were effectively treated as slaves. He confronted the Governor of Kenya and was punished by being demoted and transferred out of the colony.

Back in Britain from 1918 onwards he threw himself into campaigning to end settler colonialism. He corresponded with W. E. B. Du Bois and spoke at the second Pan-African Congress in London in 1921. In 1924 he published a book called, simply, *Kenya*, which explained what settler colonialism meant for Kenya's African population. *Kenya* made a deep impression on liberal opinion in Britain. In collaboration with Leonard Woolf and McGregor Ross, a former government official in Kenya, Leys also persuaded the leadership of the newly-formed Labour Party to adopt a 'pro-native' policy for the African colonies, and campaigned tirelessly to educate MPs and the media. These efforts played a major role in thwarting the ambition of the Kenyan settlers to get political control of the colony.

Between them, Leys and Ross made Kenya the focus of debate about colonial policy between the wars to a degree out of all proportion to the colony's significance in the Empire. Virginia Woolf complained to a friend that her house had become 'a mere ante room to the House of Lords', in which her husband Leonard was 'caballing about Kenya day and night'. One of the caballers, she added, was 'a fiery and intractable Scotchman called Norman Leys, a perfect saint and martyr, but not altogether easy company about the house.' Leys made many people uncomfortable. He was single-minded and relentless, and wouldn't let anyone get away with professions of support for African liberation while doing nothing about it – an attitude he called 'Phariseeism'.

Leys' ideas are now so familiar – supposedly they are what everyone now thinks – that it is easy to forget how far ahead of his time he was. When he arrived in Kenya in 1905 the territory had been under British 'protection' for just ten years. Its inhabitants were seen as savages who needed to be taught obedience and the value of work. Leys saw them instead as human beings, entitled like all others to equality and liberty – a 'uniquely unpopular idea', as he called it ironically in a letter to his friend Winifred Holtby. A second unpopular idea came from his attention to what was happening to ordinary people and what they thought about it. He saw settler colonialism through the eyes of its victims and analysed its defining features a quarter-century before they were made widely known by writers such as Karl Polanyi and Frantz Fanon. His writing could be compelling. He wrote three books and numerous statements and reports, most of which are not widely available. Extracts from some of these have been included here as annexes.

What made Norman Leys such an early champion of African liberation and racial equality, and one of the earliest analysts of settler colonialism, would be a story worth telling even if settler colonialism had not abruptly become a defining issue of our own time, with the Hamas attack on Israel in 2023 and the subsequent genocide in Gaza. Leys saw that settler colonialism in Kenya was bound to end in violence. He ended his second book, *A Last Chance in Kenya*, published in 1931, with this warning: 'The terrible truth is that no nation or race or caste has ever won its liberty, whether in Ireland or Poland or any other country, without either the use or the threat of violence.' He campaigned with increasing desperation to try to avert violence in Kenya, or at least to mitigate it.

But public opinion had been shaped by fifty years of imperialist propaganda and was deeply racist. In 1924, the year *Kenya* was published, the British Empire Exhibition opened at Wembley, in London, and by the time it closed in 1925 it had attracted 27 million visitors. When the 'Mau Mau' rebellion eventually began in Kenya in 1950 it was repressed with a savagery that Leys had foreseen and feared, and the British public still sympathised with the settlers. It was only after African nationalists broke free from imperial control and established independent states that racism in Britain began to be seriously challenged. Then Leys' work was recognised afresh. A fourth edition of *Kenya* was published in 1969.

Half a century later the lesson taught in *Kenya* needs to be learned again. The authorities in Britain, and throughout the 'West', support the settlers in Palestine and discipline and punish people who sympathise with the natives. Norman Leys' example as a public intellectual is as important here as his writing: someone able to compel attention to principles and facts that the authorities want the public to forget, and ready to pay the price of doing so.

It is this, as much as what he wrote, that prompted me to write this book. My connection to him is through my father, his much younger half-brother. I read *Kenya* when I was a student and it had a lot to do with my spending many years working in and on Africa, including three in Kenya. This is not a full biography. It is doubtful that a full biography could be written, since Leys destroyed all his own papers; nor is one really needed, since his impact on contemporary events has been recorded by several excellent historians. But it is possible, and thought-provoking, to look at the way events made Leys the remarkable man he was. He was not religious, but he had a strongly religious upbringing, and he was driven by a profound conviction of the rightness of Jesus' ethical teaching. This is the story of how his experiences in Africa refined and toughened that conviction and shaped his thinking and actions.

1: The making of an awkward customer

Most people who have written anything about Norman Leys mention that he was the subject of a famous custody case brought by his father against his grandfather, who had abducted him to the United States. How did this strange Victorian melodrama come about, and what did it mean for Norman Leys?

He was born in the village of Willaston, in the Wirral, in June 1875. His father, John Leys, came from Strathaven, a small textile town south of Glasgow, but he had studied for the English bar and was practising as a barrister in Newcastle. A second son, Kenneth, was born just over a year later, in October 1876; but two weeks after Kenneth's birth their mother died. John was suddenly left alone, with a child barely one year old and a newborn infant. He wasn't making much money and couldn't look after them himself. Kenneth, the newborn, was taken in by a Mrs Lang, a friend of his wife, who lived near Dollar in the Scottish Lowlands. In later life Kenneth remembered 'a dog called Mullin, and a pony', but little else from that time, except that 'he had been happy there, and free'.[1]

What happened to Norman at this point we don't know, but it seems likely that he was initially taken in by his mother's parents, Mr and Mrs Munsie, who also lived in Scotland; but after two or three years he was transferred to the home of his paternal grandfather – John's father Peter Leys, a Presbyterian minister in Strathaven, to be looked after by John's two unmarried sisters who were still living at home.[2] There is no record of what, if anything, Norman remembered from these early years.

Early in 1880 the arrangement with Mrs Lang came to an end. John now tried to provide a home for his two sons by renting a house in Sunderland, from where he could commute to his work in Newcastle; and Agnes, the older of his two sisters, came with him to look after the boys. But he soon found he couldn't afford it. In September 1880 the boys and their aunt went back to live with Peter Leys. John moved to lodgings in Newcastle.*

By now Norman had lost his mother and, in effect, his father. From the age of one he had most likely been cared for by two grandparents, the Munsies; at age three or four he found himself living with two other grandparents (Peter Leys and his wife), two aunts, and three adult uncles, who were all still living in their father's house; at age five he was joined there by a brother he had not previously known. On top of all this strangeness Peter Leys' household was not a happy one, as we will see. Kenneth, certainly, did not feel 'happy and free' in Strathaven.

At some point after this John Leys left the bar, moved to London, and began to make a living from writing popular novels and books for children; and in about 1884 he met and became engaged to a fellow evening class teacher called Ellen Holligan. But before marrying they both converted to Catholicism; and in the course of their conversion John received an offer of two years' free education for his sons at Mount St Mary's, a Catholic boarding school near Sheffield 'in return for literary services which he was to render'.[3] Shocked by his son's conversion, Peter Leys was even more outraged when he learned of this proposal; and in December 1885, when John asked for the boys, he refused to hand them over. In May 1886 John sued him for custody, and in July the case reached the court in Edinburgh. Peter maintained his refusal to return the boys, or say where they were, declaring that his obedience to 'a higher law' would not allow him to do so, and was accordingly sent to prison for contempt of court. The case attracted a lot of attention, and most people supported Peter.[4] The intensity of anti-Catholic feeling in those years is difficult to credit now, but it was widely shared, especially in Glasgow, where an influx of Irish immigrants fleeing the famine of 1847-52 had created a large minority of desperately poor Catholics.

After a month, knowing his father's character, and that he would die in prison rather than obey the court order, John withdrew his case. He didn't give up his demand for custody but said he was unwilling to see his father imprisoned indefinitely, and the old man was released. In the meantime the two boys, now aged eleven and nine, had sailed, in the care of Agnes, the older of their two aunts, to New York, and from

---

* Why John Leys took a house in Sunderland is a mystery. At the court hearing Peter Leys said it was because he had 'no employment in Newcastle', but John moved back there to work after sending the boys to his father.

there travelled to Northfield, Massachusetts, the home of the evangelist Dwight Moody. Moody, with his musical collaborator Ira Sankey, was a star of the 'revivalist' movement of the late nineteenth century: he preached and Sankey sang, attracting huge crowds on tours across the United States, and also in Britain.

According to a fictionalised account of their arrival at the Moodys' home, based on the recollections of Moody's daughter, Emma Fitt, they arrived unannounced. The boys' aunt explained why they had come and declared that she had done it without her father's knowledge 'to protect him, should he be questioned, or should my brother make trouble'.[5] Moody asked if he had ever met her in Scotland; she replied that he had not, but that she had sung in the choir at more than one of his 'wonderful meetings' in Glasgow. Moody had spent five months preaching to sometimes huge crowds in Glasgow and Edinburgh in 1873, and a whole year preaching in both Scotland and England in 1882-83.

The memoir has Agnes adding that after one of those meetings she had told her father that 'if she ever got into trouble it is to Mr Moody I would turn'. This seems rather unlikely – what sort of trouble could she have had in mind at that time? What contact, if any, Peter Leys had with Moody in Scotland we don't know, but as Agnes was wholly dependent on her father financially it is impossible to believe that he didn't plan and finance the trip, and subsequently pay for their living expenses and school fees in Northfield, for what turned out to be the next four years. But a single woman in her thirties who could make the journey with two small boys from Glasgow to Northfield Massachusetts in 1886 was not lacking in determination, so perhaps it was a well-rehearsed story and she told it the way Moody's daughter remembered it.

Moody evidently accepted the risk involved in being complicit in the abduction. He had recently opened a boys' boarding school, Mount Hermon School for Boys, on a large campus near his house. According to Emma Fitt, 'Father asked four of the Mount Hermon students to form a secret bodyguard and to plan that all four of them should never leave the hill at the same time, but one or more always be watching over the Scottish lads'. After a few weeks the two boys moved with their aunt into one of the 'cottages' on the school campus – actually substantial houses, which are still in use. They would stay there for the next four years and would not see their father again until they were in their late teens.

John Leys seems to have made no further effort to get them back. The court order for their return to him was still in force, and even in 1886 it couldn't have been too hard to find out where they were. But he barely knew his sons: they hadn't lived with him, except for a fraught few months in Sunderland, almost from the moment his wife had died; and after moving them to his father's house he had moved south, and only saw them on visits to Scotland, which Peter Leys told the court were at 'distant intervals'. By 1886 he was making a modest but steady living as a writer.* He may have felt unhappy about not having paid his father all he had promised towards the boys' costs – 'not even a third', Peter Leys told the court; and he couldn't consider marrying again, and starting a new family, unless he first provided for his sons. The offer of free school places would have solved this problem, and it may be significant that even after the court hearing he didn't remarry for a further three years, perhaps waiting until his financial situation had improved (he went on to have five more children). The loss of his sons may have seemed just another episode in a life-long struggle with a censorious father which had led him to seek a career at the English bar rather than the Scottish. His sister Agnes, whom he had trusted with the care of his sons, had made off with them with the connivance of all his other siblings, and he was surely tired of it all. A volume of children's stories which he published in 1886, the year of the court case, was dedicated simply 'To Norman and Kenneth Leys'.

Back in Massachusetts, Moody's Mount Hermon School had only been opened five years earlier. It aimed to give disadvantaged but God-fearing boys, mostly sponsored by their churches, a Bible-based but broad education, chiefly with a view to producing ministers and missionaries.[6] In other ways it was unusually progressive: manual work on the school grounds was part of the curriculum, and the student body was multiracial. One student who was there at the same time as the two Leys boys was an African-American called Thomas Nelson Baker, who had been born in slavery.

Because they were not supposed to be there the Leys boys were never formally admitted as students, and their situation was peculiar in other ways as well. For one thing, they were much younger than the other boys. When Norman and Kenneth arrived the minimum age of

---

* He published altogether 19 novels and at the court hearing in 1886 he said he had earned £174 in the previous year, equivalent to about £28,000 in 2024. His father, however, maintained that this was not true, and that John had debts of £2,200 and so couldn't afford to keep his sons. The court was unmoved by these claims, which did not affect John's obvious right to his children.

admission was sixteen; most of the boys were in their late teens and some were in their twenties. But the two brothers studied along with the others and seem to have done remarkably well, enabling them to fit back successfully into the Scottish school system when they returned to Glasgow four years later.

But not only were they so much younger than the other students, their aunt also never left them alone, apparently in constant fear that their father would find out where they were and seize them. Sixty years later a former teacher who had lived in the same house on the campus remembered them as having 'perfect manners' and said she had 'loved the little fellows very much, Kenneth especially – such a little fellow', adding that their aunt 'couldn't bear to have them out of her sight for fear she would lose them', even for a walk in the fields near the school.[7] An older student recalled that 'they wore Eton collars and their aunt had them in tow'.[8] What kind of a life they had outside the classroom we don't know. A close friend of Kenneth's from his student years in Glasgow wrote after his death that he couldn't remember him ever speaking about sports, or companions, or holidays away, while he was in Northfield. It seems likely that the only fun they usually had was the walks with their aunt near the school. Kenneth remembered liking the fall colours, 'the kindly New England farmer folk', skating in winter, and that Moody himself was 'splendid in pillow fights' (an endearing and slightly surprising fact, since Moody was famously fat). As if marking a very unusual event, the school magazine for 25 June 1888 records that the two boys had gone with their aunt to Connecticut to visit Mr Harris, a rich trustee of the school.

What they felt about being sent to live as refugees among strangers thousands of miles from home, hovered over by their aunt, we don't know; nor what they felt about never getting letters, let alone visits, from their father. In court Peter Leys painted a picture of John as uncaring – visiting the boys infrequently in Strathaven and not keeping his promises to pay for their upkeep;[9] and since their aunt Agnes was complicit in their abduction she must have told them the same story. Peter Leys also told the court that the boys were 'in great terror' of being sent to the school their father had in mind, which may well have been true if it was represented to them as terrifying. But since both were intelligent, as the years passed in Northfield did they find all this a good enough reason for what had been done to them?

There is an expression in the note on Kenneth's life, written by his widow after his death in 1950, which may offer a clue. After the boys returned to Scotland, she wrote, their father 'never again attempted to interfere in any way' – a curious description, one might think, of the role he had been able, or allowed, to play in his sons' lives up to that point.[10] It seems possible that even in later life Kenneth, at least, saw his father as the guilty party.

The boys must sometimes have felt that no one except their aunt really cared about them. Their father had been relieved of the cost of looking after them. Their grandfather still had a house full of his own adult children and may well have been glad to have them out of the way (and his wife even gladder, to judge by her behaviour after Peter died, mentioned below) – all of which Norman, as a teenager, could have deduced for himself. The only sustained affection he had known after his mother died was from his aunt Agnes; but she had also been the means of separating him from his father.

When she died, in 1900, Kenneth grieved for her. Norman's only references to her that I have found are that she was 'the aunt who brought me up', and that for the last six years of her life she was 'markedly neurasthenic'. He had good reason not to attach much weight to love, of which he had known so little, and none from the age of one that was unconditional. But in 1905 he named his first child (as it turned out, his only child) Agnes.

In 1890, aged fifteen and fourteen, the brothers sailed with their aunt back to Glasgow. Probably they wanted to go back; it also seems likely that Moody had not undertaken to look after them into adulthood. So, they re-entered Peter Leys' household (it was now in Glasgow, the old man having been forced to retire by ill-health) and attended Albany College. They were quick students and did well.

But they were now old enough to see the narrowness of their grandfather's outlook. Life in America, and not least at Mount Hermon School, had offered a sharp contrast with life in Glasgow. In his surviving letters Norman never refers to their time at Mount Hermon, but Moody's evangelical 'revivalism' has strong echoes in his later thinking about religion, and especially about the New Testament. It is also hard to imagine that seeing Afro-Americans like Thomas Nelson Baker getting an education and excelling at it (Baker went on to Harvard and became a well-known minister in Pittsfield, Massachusetts) didn't play a role in his later rejection of racism.

Life in Northfield had been isolated and peculiar, but it had not been miserable; in contrast, life in Peter Leys' household was. Aunt

Agnes and her sister Eliza were not happy, Kenneth recalled: there were 'constant rows'. Norman once described one of his aunts by marriage as 'the best hand at family rows I have ever known',[11] and said his Glasgow relatives had provided him with 'a museum of neuroses'.[12]

As for their father John Leys, Kenneth had some contact with him after they returned to Glasgow. Jack Lochead, one of his two close friends during his student years in Glasgow, recalled that his relationship with his father had been 'cordial, but could not after the lapse of so many years be very close', adding that Kenneth seemed to find him 'likeable, interesting and an object of some amusement'.[13] After John Leys died in 1909 Kenneth supported his step-mother and her family, especially by paying for his three young half-brothers' school fees. Norman seems to have had little if any contact with his father or his new family before he went to Africa.

We can only speculate on the way this disrupted and largely unloved childhood shaped his later life. But it seems clear that by the time he left Northfield he had realised that he needed to make up his own mind about everything.

In 1892 Peter Leys died. His widow was now in charge and was, Kenneth later told his wife, 'in all things directed by the worst of her five sons' (perhaps the one who had had to help Peter Leys pay for the two boys' education and clothing).[14] Aunt Agnes and her younger sister Eliza were now 'not wanted at home' and were sent to live 'in lodgings on a very small pittance', where they became chronic invalids. Norman and Kenneth were sent out to work. At age 17 and 16 respectively this was not unreasonable, but both of them wanted to go to university and had the brains for it but not the money. Kenneth 'always hated the very thought of his grandmother who, unfortunately, had the money'. He was set to become a chartered accountant, beginning as a clerk in an accountant's office 'at one and a quarter pence an hour'. Norman was found a job in a millinery shop.

Given his education and brains it is unlikely that he would have remained a shop assistant for long, but it is also unlikely that he would have become a doctor without the intervention of Miss King, a great-aunt on his mother's side. Like something in a Victorian novel Miss King left each of the boys £350 (equal to perhaps £60,000 today), to be theirs when they turned twenty-one. Kenneth stuck to his five-year training as an accountant, qualifying in 1897, when he was 21 and came into his inheritance. He immediately dropped accountancy and enrolled in the University of Glasgow to study humanities. Norman had already entered the university in 1894, when he was only nineteen. How he paid for his first two years before he was 21, during which he was registered in the Arts faculty, we don't know. He may have worked part-time, or had some help from one of his uncles (one of them later lent him money to help him become a GP, and to publish his first book). He also, significantly for his future plans, secured two small grants from the Foreign Mission Committee of the United Presbyterian Church.[15] In 1896 he came into his inheritance and transferred to the Medical Faculty.

When they were sent out to work the two brothers rented rooms in the university's 'Settlement' in a slum area of Glasgow. Known to students as 'the Creeperies', on account of its lack of hygiene, the Settlement gave them cheap accommodation in return for undertaking social work in the surrounding area. We have a glimpse of life in the Settlement in the recollections of Kenneth's friend Jack Lochead which are worth quoting for the light they shed on some of Norman's formative years.

> Most of us were pretty poor and 12/- to 15/- [shillings] a week was as much as we could afford to pay for our board and lodging. What we got for this was far from luxurious. Food and furnishings were of the plainest. A row of narrow bedroom studies, separated by thin wooden partitions, opened onto a long corridor. The only heating was by gas fires, which smelled abominably. The evening meal consisted of nothing but tea, bread and butter and jam... Whoever poured tea at the end of the table was duly admonished to 'water early and often' and he did... There was no paid warden and the social and religious activities we carried on were organised and shared out in haphazard fashion. But somehow they succeeded. To each of us was assigned the visiting and befriending of about a dozen poor families. The stench and overcrowding of some of these single and two-roomed homes was appalling.[16]

Seeing the wretched lives of Glasgow slum-dwellers was an obvious source of Norman Leys' firmly held socialism, and life in the Settlement was educative in another way too. The residents went in for practical jokes and played games like 'hunt the slipper' and 'blind man's bluff', but they also spent a lot of time discussing national and international issues and ethical questions, or what they called 'cosmogony'.[17] Imperialism, the Boer War, and race and racism in the US, were all headline news in those years, and must have been discussed. Norman Leys' decision to go to abroad when he qualified as a doctor looks like a natural result of the mission-oriented teaching at Mount Hermon and the financial support he got from the Foreign Mission Committee in Glasgow, but the intellectual life of the Settlement gave his decision more political depth.

Lochead and another student came from middle-class homes in Bute, a short ferry trip from Glasgow, and escaped there as often as they could at weekends. 'In an afternoon', Lochead wrote, 'to pass from the noise and dirt and smells of the Settlement to the sweetness of shore and heather was always a thrilling experience'. They invited Kenneth to come with them, and he became a frequent and welcome visitor in both of their large houses. He later told his wife that 'these two families showed him what happy family life was like – for he was never happy, as he grew up, in his grandfather's house, whatever he may have been when he was quite a small boy'.[18]

It seems telling that Norman didn't make these friendships. This could have been partly due to the heavy demands of his medical training, which involved working at the Glasgow Western Hospital as well as attending 100 lectures per subject, in accordance with the university regulations then in place, although he only switched from Arts to medicine in the summer of 1895. Lochead's memoir of Kenneth mentions Norman only once, as someone 'with more apostolic intensity than any of us'.[19] It sounds as if he wasn't open to the kind of social life that Kenneth enjoyed so much, and needed it less.

At the turn of the century the lives of the two brothers diverged sharply. On graduating from Glasgow University Kenneth won a scholarship to Oxford, returned to Glasgow as a history lecturer, and finally became a fellow of University College, Oxford. He was much loved by his students, helped to look after the College's investments, and became an expert on Irish history, but never published a word. Even in the Oxford of those years this was unusual, although it should be added that he suffered a double blow: his first wife was killed in a traffic accident and their daughter had a severe mental disability. Norman, by contrast, qualified in medicine in 1900, obtained a certificate in public health from the brand-new Liverpool School of Tropical Medicine in 1901, and by October the same year was working as a doctor for the African Lakes Corporation in the British Concession in Chinde, on the coast of Portuguese East Africa (today's Mozambique), and starting, within months of his arrival, to formulate the critique of colonialism that would become his life's work.

Although he didn't make close friends at the university he did form one important personal relationship there, with the youthful professor of Greek, Gilbert Murray, which lasted for the rest of his life. Leys had studied Greek at Mount Hermon and presumably also at Albany College, and he had to study *Antigone* for his degree; but he didn't study Greek at the university, and he never heard Murray lecture.[20] Murray's wife Lady Mary Murray, however, belonged to a rich, titled and influential Liberal family, the Howards of Castle Howard. She was active in hosting students in their house, and Leys evidently made a mark there. Murray himself was already well known as a scholar, but he was only nine years older than Leys, having been appointed to the professorship when he was just 23. He made himself accessible and found the younger man, with his unusual background and independent mind, worth spending time with. In January 1899 he wrote his wife: 'I had Leys the Christian Socialist to lunch; an interesting and most attractive fellow. We went for a walk in the afternoon and lost our way on Dowan Hill!!' (Dowan Hill was a few hundred yards from the university).[21] It also seems likely, to judge from the way Leys referred to the Settlement in his letters to Murray, that Murray knew it at first hand; he served on the university committee which supervised the Settlement and its finances and was very supportive of it.[22]

Murray was the first mature intellectual Leys got to know personally, and his impact was profound. Murray was keenly interested in world events, in war and peace, and relations between white and black; above all in what he called the 'great things' that people should be concerned with – the core moral issues at the heart of classical Greek drama. Leys saw him as a friend of the ordinary students, concentrating on 'men who would have to earn their bread', as opposed to Honours students, those who had independent means. He complimented him for not being 'afraid of being popular', and not hiding behind jargon and esoteric knowledge, as he thought most professors did.[23]

Murray became something of a father-substitute. Leys felt understood and encouraged by him and wrote to him throughout his life, beginning in his final year of medicine and continuing, though at increasingly long intervals, until shortly before his death in 1944 – letters in which he probably revealed more of his innermost thoughts than to anyone else except his much later friend Winifred Holtby. As with any father-son relationship it is touching, and slightly amusing, to see how his early reverence gave way, as he gained confidence, to seeing Murray as a sometimes-useful ally in high places, but also as someone with whom he was not afraid to disagree. In 1930 Murray must have written something to the effect that the fast-growing discipline of anthropology was making people readier to support liberal policies in Africa.* Leys, on the contrary, thought that anthropologists' tendency to celebrate tribal cultures had the effect of buttressing the belief that Africans had a different 'mentality' from Europeans, and so were unsuited for 'western' freedoms and rights. His response was short and sweet:

> I knew anthropology was all the vogue and believe it will have a permanent though small place in the field of knowledge. But I didn't expect that people like you could be persuaded that it can provide a clue to right policy.... The danger lies in regarding Africans as specimens instead of human beings who react in certain circumstances just as we should if born to their heritage and placed in the same circumstances. Why suppose anthropology to touch the central problems of the native African any more than it touched those of the native Irish? It is truly hard to keep people to the point about Africa.[24]

This was typed, with a couple of mistakes, on a post-card.

---

* Murray did say this in a letter dated 2 July 1941, thanking Leys for sending him a copy of his new book (*The Colour Bar in East Africa* came out that year). He wrote: 'Don't you think there has been an enormous advance in public opinion about colonial questions since the days when you were fighting on behalf of the Masai and the Kikuyu? It is partly due to your work and the work of others like you, but very largely to the remarkable spread of anthropology'. Murray's view that anthropological writing had been more important than the work of Leys and other activists in changing public opinion might well have accounted for Leys' unusually blunt reply; but although the Bodleian has archived this letter together with Norman's 1930 post-card it can't have been what he was replying to. Murray must have said something similar eleven years earlier. Leys' reply is repeated more or less word for word in the chapter on 'African Mentality' in *A Last Chance in Kenya*, published a year later, and included here in the Annex.

Norman Leys in Chinde

2: Encountering colonialism

In February 1900, a few months before he graduated from medical school, Leys told Gilbert Murray: 'I still mean to go abroad, the general idea being that a man ought to do what most needs doing. And what I imagine the black and yellow people need most is not so much treatment for dyspepsia or rheumatism as something to make them stand up to the circumstances of the new civilization that I suppose is coming to them'.[25] How exactly he might help to give them that he had no idea, he admitted, but it was presumably part of the Empire's responsibilities, and he assumed he would find a way.

His first step was to enrol at the newly-established Liverpool School of Tropical Medicine, completing a certificate course in the spring of 1901. Malaria and other tropical diseases were now taking a heavy toll of Europeans in East Africa as well as in the West African colonies, and the mission of the new Liverpool School, and its counterpart in London, was to do something about this (improving Africans' health only became government policy much later).*

Within two months of completing the course Leys became an employee of the Glasgow-based African Lakes Corporation, and sailed via Cape Town to Chinde, at the mouth of the Zambezi on the coast of Portuguese East Africa (Mozambique).** The Corporation had originally been set up in 1877 to supply the Scottish missions in Nyasaland (Malawi), moving goods and passengers between Chinde and Nyasaland on shallow boats up the Zambezi and Shiré rivers and on larger steamers north on Lake Nyasa (now Lake Malawi). By the time Leys arrived the company had branched out into general trading

---

* Leys thought that a further qualification in public health, which the Liverpool School went on to provide, would prove especially relevant to the needs of Africans, and he devoted part of two subsequent leaves in England to studying for a Diploma in it. He was proud of his DPH, insisting that it should be included after his name on the frontispiece of his first book when his publisher, Leonard Woolf, proposed, for some reason, to leave it out.

** His contract was for three years from 1 April 1901 at an annual salary of £350, the equivalent of about £55,000 today – perhaps not as high as it might seem for a newly qualified doctor if the long absence from home, and the health risks posed by the job, are taken into account.

and land speculation, and was even being subsidised by Cecil Rhodes for its possible use in furthering his ambition to make Africa British 'from the Cape to Cairo'. It had a substantial European staff. Leys' job was to look after their health from the Corporation's base in Chinde. The British Concession in Chinde, on a 25-acre spit of sand at the mouth of the Zambezi, was a free-trade zone serving British interests in the landlocked British territories inland – Northern and Southern Rhodesia (Zambia and Zimbabwe), as well as Nyasaland. It took Leys eight weeks to get there.

His letters to Gilbert Murray from Chinde, like those he wrote later from Nyasaland and Kenya, never describe his working day. But reading between the lines, and remembering that the Europeans he had to look after in Chinde, other than the Portuguese, who had their own doctors, numbered little more than a hundred, it is clear that he had time on his hands. After five months he reported to Murray that he was teaching two English children daily, running a discussion group for Europeans on Sundays, and hoping to set up 'a small school and a meeting on Sundays for the mission boys [mission-educated young men from Nyasaland who were working in Chinde] when I have learned more of the native languages'. But, he added, 'I confess I find the place depressing. If there was somebody else of similar aims it would be better.'[26]

Life inside the Concession was claustrophobic and unpleasant, populated by people who didn't read and were uniformly racist, which was depressing enough; but life outside it was degenerate. Unlike Britain and Germany, which had only recently established themselves in East Africa, the Portuguese had dominated the coast for five centuries. The carve-up of Africa at the Berlin Conference had awarded them the huge area that is now Mozambique. But since the seventeenth century Portugal's wealth and power had been in decline; its colonial officials were too few in number, and too poorly funded, to establish control in the interior. Apart from Catholic missions, the Portuguese presence inland consisted of large private estates, called *prazos*, mainly located in the Zambezi valley. In return for rent paid to the government the *prazos* were left free to use forced labour procured and policed by private armies, while the officials at the coast grew lazy and corrupt (in the view of the *Encyclopaedia Britannica* of 1911, 'they and the small body of planters led in general a life of indolence and debauchery'). 'Perhaps you don't know', Leys added in his letter to Murray, that before Columbus discovered America the country [Mozambique] was as firmly held as now, and in parts more prosperous. From canoes on the river one sometimes hears, sung to the measure of the paddles, a hymn to the Virgin taught to the ancestors of the present generation by Jesuit fathers hundreds of years ago. As far as I can make out the Portuguese race as a whole must steadily have deteriorated… The strongest language cannot describe the depth of corruption and folly of Portuguese politics.

This long letter set out to give Murray a considered account of what life there was like. Above all, he was shocked by the arbitrariness and cruelty of Portuguese rule. 'The law of the land is as little respected as the law of Moses… Every industry breaks the law whenever it touches it … the laws are unjust and they are not enforced'.

… a [British] government official landed at Chinde, on his way to British Central Africa [present-day Zambia and Malawi], ill with enteric fever. With the British Consul's permission I took him into my house to nurse him. The Portuguese heard of it and insisted that he should go to a death trap they have that they call a Sanatorium. I refused at first. Suddenly my boy [his house servant] disappeared. I heard the same evening that he was in jail, offence unknown. I got him out after 3 days by paying 30/-. The poor chap was arrested simply because he was my boy, so the Consul says. Neither he nor I know what he was charged with. The Portuguese are adepts at these petty persecutions.

Their treatment of the natives is even more insane. I don't suppose all of them are cruel. But a boy who has served a Portuguese can always be told by a servile manner that annoys a child of democracy. My house boy is a Portuguese boy. When I first had him, at the least fault he would shrink as from an expected blow. In fact when he found I wouldn't strike him, he grew careless till I found my weapon unfailing. It was simply to utter a few unknown words in a loud voice with a stern face …

The Portuguese are uniformly disliked by the natives. I know of two reasons. One is their sheer rapacity. Taxes are farmed. You know what that comes to mean. A Portuguese court of justice has two peculiarities. A native is never acquitted and he always is given the option of a fine. Explanation obvious. Punishment of offences against white men is given with a 'palmatorio', a sort of 'cat' with bits of iron in it, that cripples the boy for weeks. The second reason … is their treatment of native women. Of course, as in every other similar country it is the rule among all Europeans to keep a native woman. Comparatively few, chiefly 'Puritanical' Scots, can show a clean record. But the English almost invariably use no force. Whereas the Portuguese simply go to a village, choose the girls they want and carry them off. From my own verandah I have seen *an official* in uniform having a girl dragged off to his house with the husband following behind, protesting and pleading.

I came here determined to think well of the Portuguese, but I find they deserve all the cursing they get. I can't help thinking that there are stormy times ahead for this and other similar parts of the world.[27]

If Leys had landed in King Leopold's Congo he would have encountered a still more depraved example of European colonialism, but not much more. In Portuguese colonies all able-bodied native men were legally required to work, and the authorities could use force to make them. The result was 'akin to slavery'.[28] Leys was shaken, and lonely. 'The continuous sight of cruelty and lust, and the absence of intimate friends, are dulling to mind and soul', he admitted. 'To a man in my place the memory of clean straightforward lives of friends and relations is as the breath of life. Letters from home are like bread to the starving.'

Seven months later he wrote to Murray again, acknowledging his continuing loneliness. It was 'the absence of wise and good', he said, that made him 'unproductive'; 'life often takes on a dirty drab colour, clearness of mind goes and the greatest things in the world' – a phrase Murray would recognise – 'are for the time uninteresting. The nightmare of slipping away from all that sometimes visits me'. 'But', he added, 'I am certainly not sorry I came here. Within the last year my ideas of the cosmogony as we called it in the Settlement have got more coherent. And the few things worth while trying to do before Charon paddles me over, grow clearer, on the whole.'[29]

There were numerous ideas and formulations in these letters that he would soon drop – he wrote of 'races' and described 'the natives' as 'uncivilized' and 'naturally cruel'– and several attitudes that he would also abandon, though more slowly. One of these was his initial 'horror' of mixed races. He saw that racial equality, to which he was committed, must mean mixed marriages, but he confessed that he found the 'mulattos' in Chinde 'pitiable' – which indeed they were, pitiably poor, and unloved by both Europeans and Africans. This prejudice he decisively overcame. In 1941 he wrote that if black and white were given equal educational opportunities, prejudice against mixed marriages would 'fade away'. 'Even as things are now', he added then, he 'would rather his daughter married one of several black men he has known than one of many white men he has known, though if she did, her countrymen, and especially her countrywomen, would give her a hard time'.³⁰

By the end of his first year in Africa he had identified many of the key elements of the critique of colonialism which two decades later would make him briefly well known. Later experience would show him how much of what he was seeing was peculiar to Portuguese colonialism and how much was common to all colonies (most of it was inherent, though not always so crude). He noted that new arrivals from Britain quickly adopted the prevailing racism and habitual abuse of Africans. 'I want to find a way', he told Murray,

> of convincing the average Britisher, emigrant to the tropics, that it is better not to treat black men under him, subject only to the restrictions of the law, as his own private property. The rough difference between the Portuguese and the English is this. Both treat natives pretty much as they do livestock, i.e. practically as private property. But as a rule British men do not treat either livestock or natives with the callous cruelty of the Portuguese. In any British community of any size there is always a minority to enforce a certain amount of humanity in respect of giving pain at least.'

Leys catalogued and assessed the various classes of people he encountered, both African and European, in Nyasaland as well as in Chinde. At some point in 1902 he travelled up the Zambezi and Shiré rivers to Nyasaland and visited the missions there, and met some of the colonial officials, of whom there were just a hundred in the territory all told. 'In the case of the organised non-conformist missions particularly', he wrote, 'the men are of a high average ability. Most of them have the democratic spirit and a few, in their self-denying lives, are the salt of the earth.' The officials were a different story:

> At present the Englishman governs black races much after the style of tossing for drinks at a bar.* (That of course is 2/3 untrue. I speak from knowledge of the BCA [British Central Africa – i.e. Nyasaland] administration alone. Its men enter without examination and on the average are a poor lot.)

---

* This slightly obscure remark probably refers to the closed culture of the whites-only clubs around which social life tended to revolve in small colonial communities, limiting officials' contact with the native population and reinforcing their prejudices. The theme recurs in Leys' later writing.

He would pass the same judgement later on the administration in Kenya. But what already preoccupied him most was not the question of how Africans should be treated – plain humanity demanded that they should be treated honestly and with respect – but whether they would be capable of self-rule. At the end of his first long letter, he added a postscript:

> I reopen the letter to add a reservation and a question. Will a race that has tamely submitted to Portuguese oppression for 500 years ever be fit for a share in government? Will they ever ask for it? What can education do for so spiritless a people? How much education will they be found capable of? I am aware that nobody can answer the last question till a limit is found by experiment.

Several of these formulations jar on us today. But what stands out is the independence of his thinking. Hardly anyone in the colonial administration in Central or East Africa before 1945 – or for that matter in Whitehall – saw African self-rule as even a long-term possibility, whereas in 1902 Leys saw preparing Africans for it as the purpose and justification of colonial rule. And although he was still thinking in terms of separate races, he had no truck with the idea that they had intrinsically different capacities. If the Africans under Portuguese rule were 'spiritless', it was because they had been brutally oppressed for five centuries, and there were contrasting cases to consider. Notably, 'boys' who had been educated at the Scottish missions in Nyasaland were 'cleaner, better clothed and better set up generally'. 'They generally know something of a trade, all of them speak some English, and most of them can read and write. Some at least have their natural cruelty partly removed.' 'But', he added, 'by the ordinary Englishman they are not liked even when they are most useful'.

> The mere fact that they are beginning to compete with him is a great deal. And then they are 'cheeky'. The effect of Christian teaching in dissolving class and racial divisions is astonishingly great. The mission boy will not stand a blow. He is quite ready to take his master up before the court. Or if particularly dignified he will simply go away with some such remark as 'God will not love you'. That sort of thing is infuriating to the buccaneering devil that frequently represents civilization in these parts.

What infuriated other Europeans Leys saw as grounds for hope, and over the ensuing years his hope changed to a conviction that with education Africans could and would excel in every field.

In his disgust with the rampant racism he found in Chinde it is easy to see the deep impression made on his thinking by Scottish non-conformism, reinforced by the non-racist culture of Moody's school at Mount Hermon and by his encounter with the Scottish missionaries in Nyasaland. There is also a passage in his second letter to Murray from Chinde about what slavery means for individuals that makes one think that his own lack of a settled and caring family life may also have played a part in his response:

> Since I came to Chinde natives have come down by the river who go by the name of slaves. Chiefly children, they are the spoil of a recent war by the Portuguese against a tribe that refused to pay taxes. They are brought up by their masters in ignorance of their native home. They have no conception of their position except as being their masters' servants.

He himself was offered a boy for £2.[31]

Leys' third and last letter to Murray from Chinde, written just a few months later, was very different. Its subject was not Chinde but Glasgow University, prompted by news of some changes being made there of which he disapproved, and its tone was cheerful. He wanted to thank Murray, on behalf of many students besides himself, for 'not being afraid of being popular', for being 'the friend of the common man', unlike most professors, 'who put fences of technique round their gardens and grow hothouse useless plants'...

> The glory of the Scotch University System ought to be that a large number of very ordinary men with bread to earn are taught that there are 'things' (as you would say) in the world less material than ledgers or engines or even flying machines. Instead nowadays apparently the Scotch Universities are pretentiously emulating Oxford in the attempt to produce exact scholars. Is there a greater need in the country than to give to ordinary men some clear vision of the main issues of life and some instruction on the way to use our minds on them?

He runs on about Euripides – his favourite Greek dramatist, and perhaps Murray's too – and a book project he has in mind for a friend – at a guess, his brother Kenneth, who he thought was capable of doing something great; and then abruptly ends by saying: 'I mean to come home next year, marry, and probably come out again. At a next attempt I will make fewer mistakes.'

We can deduce what this meant from what happened next. When he went out to Chinde he was engaged to a nurse he had met while working as an intern at the Glasgow Western Hospital. Chinde was no place for a wife, but his contract with the African Lakes Corporation was due to end in 1904 and his visits to Nyasaland had opened up the possibility of a job in the government medical service there which would make it possible for them to get married. It all panned out as he had hoped. In June 1904 he was on leave in London, making a social visit to the Murrays. In August he married Jane ('Janey') Donald, in Renfrew. They had a brief honeymoon on the Scottish island of Arran, where they were visited by Kenneth, their father, John Leys, and two of their young half-brothers. By early October they were in Nyasaland, where Leys had been appointed a government medical officer, living on the shore of Lake Nyasa near the remote government district office at Karonga, close to the border with German East Africa (today's Tanzania).

In 1904 Nyasaland's population was perhaps 800,000.* The government medical service consisted of about ten doctors and as many European nurses, plus local assistants. Although their main task was to treat the white population of some 6-700, including the 100 officials and their families, they were also deployed to prevent or control outbreaks of dangerous infections among the native Africans, from smallpox and plague to sleeping sickness. It was not risk-free. The first medical officer, appointed in 1891, had been killed. Another, appointed in 1895, 'arrived on a Friday and died on the following Sunday'. In 1901, of some sixteen doctors appointed over the previous decade, 'four were dead, nine remained, and the rest had left'.[32]

But unlike Portuguese East Africa, in 1904 relations between the colonial administration and the African population in Nyasaland were reasonably good: after a decade of intermittent warfare, slave raiding by the local African agents of Arab slave traders had eventually been bloodily suppressed and a decade of peace had followed. The country was landlocked and poor, and various companies, including the African Lakes Corporation, had been granted vast areas of land, much of which became European-run

---

* The entry on British Central Africa in the 1911 volume of the *Encyclopaedia Britannica*, written by the former Commissioner of British Central Africa, Sr Harry Johnston, 'estimated' that in 1907 the population was precisely 927,335. It added that 'The history of the territory... is recent and slight...the real history of the country begins with the advent of David Livingstone ...'.

plantations growing tobacco and other crops for export. But there was no significant settler population – people intending to live and die there; and the Scottish Protestant missions, especially, with their comparatively democratic culture, played an important role in shaping the country's culture, especially by providing Africans with extensive school and medical services which the government failed to provide. By comparison with Chinde, life in Karonga was decent and congenial.

In February 1905 Leys reported to Murray: 'It is lonely here, 8 weeks from home, but my wife and I are happy and busy… Curiously out of the ten white people all told in this place, eight are Scots and one of them, a doctor in the Livingstonia mission, was an old classmate in Glasgow.' This led to a fresh appreciation of the transformative power of mission education:

> The Livingstonia Mission U[nited] F[ree] Church goes in strong for education. They have nearly 400 schools in their 'sphere', an area containing about 200,000 people. These schools are most furiously hated by most of the Administration officials. Even a very little education is a magical thing. It is amusing to find in some outlying village among the hills, a native teacher with his shirt tails hanging *outside* his loin cloth as the mark of his profession, who speaks curious grammatical English with an Aberdonian accent, preaching from a text in a Fifth Standard English Reader, on the nature of lighthouses or the wonders of the steam engine. It is all like Arabian nights to them, only doubly wonderful because they know it is true. Tho' a great deal more than amusing. Still it is amusing. And part of the joke is that the precious administrators of the people would gladly put it down if they could.

He added:

> The natives of this country pay 3/- [shillings] a head and for this sum they get fairly efficient magistrates and police. They get nothing else. Even if we doctors attend natives we have to pay for the drugs ourselves! The height of absurdity is that the country would support itself if it were not for the two battalions of native troops, who are not and never will be of any use in the Protectorate. The country is as peaceful as an English market town… And still they can't afford a penny for education.

The kernel of Leys' later critique of colonialism is contained here. He kept himself busy studying the local languages and reading world history ('I had no idea Gibbon [*The Decline and Fall of the Roman*

Empire] was so good', he told Murray), but he was plainly feeling restless. 'I hope your health is better', he wrote:

> Why not try Karonga, restful and cheap, the very place for a – what shall I say? Fowls 6 a shilling, eggs 5 a penny, bananas a penny a bunch. No trains. A steamer once a month or so. A brilliant lake, mountains 7000 feet high and eternal green. Many of these things don't suit me but I'm sure they would suit you.

But a few months later, when he next wrote to Murray, it was to report how his thoughts were turning to what he could do to end the abuses of colonial power. What he saw in Nyasaland disturbed him, even if it was much less crude than what he had witnessed in Chinde.

> One can't live long in Africa without taking sides. I got into trouble a couple of months ago by protesting against the local magistrate's action in confining several women, the relations of an escaped prisoner, in the hope of his being so soft-hearted a criminal as to come back for them and get caught. I appealed to the judge of the High Court and was told 'not to expect a more perfect judicial system than is possible in the latitude of the Protectorate' [Nyasaland only became a colony, with a Governor instead of a Commissioner, in 1907]. But the magistrate got a wigging all the same. The judge told me privately (he is something of a friend) of far greater injustices, which owing to their support in high places, he is powerless to stop. If I ever come to first hand knowledge of one of these I think I'll make the thing public if I can learn how to. The great thing the Commissioner and his party dread is a question in Parliament with a public enquiry to follow. The threat of it always humbles them.[33]

He could act anonymously, he said, through the Aborigines Protection Society, but he 'wouldn't like to': what he would later call 'the mechanical part of my brain', i.e. his sense of what it was proper for a government officer to do, made that unattractive – a scruple he would later qualify, although he would continue to be troubled by it. But the alternative of speaking out openly would mean resigning. 'That wouldn't matter much except for the pension. I may leave in not so long in any case' – an indication of his sense of being under-employed, perhaps. 'But really, the fact is that neither the British people nor their representatives have any control at all over their dependencies. And nobody in the Colonial Office cares for a little Protectorate like this.'

He then added, almost as an aside: 'My wife and I were made very happy three weeks ago by the birth of a daughter. The joys of fatherhood are greater than I had thought'. (Later, when practising as a GP in England, he would tell mothers whose babies he had just delivered, 'This is the best *second class* baby I have ever seen', and then explain that the only first class one he had ever seen was his own.) He added a PS: 'If you know anybody who wants facts – by the bushel – about B.C.A. [British Central Africa] let me know'. This might seem to contradict the principle mentioned above, but as he would later explain, he meant facts that were in the public domain and known by everyone in the Protectorate, and which people in Britain were also entitled to know.

It was not just his 'cosmogony' that was becoming clearer, but also how he might go about furthering his purpose in coming to Africa. Nyasaland was a land-locked rural backwater, with no settlers. The injustices that came to his attention in Karonga were few and minor, compared with those he had witnessed in Chinde. But after barely a year in Karonga, in 1905, he was transferred to British East Africa (later Kenya Colony), to be a medical officer in the fast-growing port of Mombasa.

Given his habit of always speaking his mind, his colleagues in Nyasaland must have known he was already critical of colonialism, but evidently no one in the Colonial Office in London, or in Nairobi, knew it, or could have imagined the problem they would have as a result of posting him to one of the two remaining settler-dominated colonies in Africa (the other was Southern Rhodesia) still subject to control by the British Parliament.

3: Discovering settler colonialism

How Kenya came to be a settler colony, and what that meant in practice when Leys and his wife and daughter landed in Mombasa in 1905, needs to be briefly explained. Ten years earlier the 'scramble for Africa' had not been quite over. Britain was effectively in control of Uganda and Egypt; between them lay Sudan, nominally a dependency of Egypt within the Ottoman empire, but increasingly challenging Egyptian rule. France wanted to push east into Sudan from its holdings in West Africa. To prevent France from challenging British control of the Nile, which ran from Uganda to Egypt through Sudan, the government in London financed the building of a railway from Mombasa on the coast to Lake Victoria, 600 miles to the north-west, from where troops and supplies could be shipped to Uganda. Begun in 1896, the railway was completed in 1901. By then, however, a British army had defeated the Sudanese Mahdists and the French threat had also been repelled. The question now was how to make Kenya profitable enough to recover the cost of building the railway.

The railway's first 300 miles ran through largely arid land but then climbed up into a countryside that was over 5,000 feet above sea-level, well-watered, forested, and attractive to European eyes. These 'highlands' were sparsely occupied, the population having been severely reduced by crop failures and diseases in the previous decade. Sir Charles Eliot, the Commissioner of the British East Africa Protectorate from 1901 to 1904, adopted the view that the colony could and should be developed by Europeans with capital, using African labour. The Europeans' enterprise would make the railway profitable and produce urgently-needed tax revenue. The Colonial Office accepted this advice, and advertisements appeared in newspapers in Britain inviting applications for land. 'We must picture, accordingly', Leys wrote later, 'a steady stream of more or less wealthy people arriving from England, travelling in the country, fixing upon the areas they wished to possess, and opening up negotiations with the Land Office and Government House…'[34]

Most of the land had not yet been surveyed, so provisional grants were made. The land rights of the local inhabitants were largely ignored, since their role was in any case to be labourers on the settlers' estates. The upshot was that more than half of the best land in the colony was eventually 'alienated' (i.e. not initially sold, since most early settlers were granted land for next to nothing) to white settlers (always officially called Europeans, although a significant minority came from South Africa). The individual holdings were often enormous – 5,000 acres or more was common – so that the number of land-holding settlers was small. By 1924, when Leys wrote *Kenya*, there were still just 1,893 registered European landowners, occupying 5,000 square miles of land – land that would later be restricted to Europeans, and become known as the 'White Highlands'. Some of the settlers were very rich and very well-connected in London. Some lived in London and employed managers on their estates. Some were members of syndicates based in London. Collectively, their interests dominated policy-making in Nairobi and in the Colonial Office.

When Leys arrived in Mombasa the process of settlement was in full swing and the town was being transformed. Prospective settlers looking for land disembarked from every ship, along with big game hunters and other wealthy tourists, and left for the interior on the train, while a gradually increasing flow of agricultural produce came back by train from the interior to be shipped to markets abroad. But the nature of the emerging settler-colonial economy was not immediately visible from Mombasa, separated as it was from Nairobi and the settler highlands by 300 miles. Mombasa was changing fast, but what was driving the changes lay in the interior. The drivers of change would only become fully clear to Leys after he was transferred, three years later, to Nakuru, in the settler heartland.

In Nakuru he learned how what he called 'the settler system' worked. It was also while he was there in 1910 that he learned of a plan to move the Maasai out of their last remaining land in the highlands, which they had been promised would be theirs forever. For his efforts to prevent this Leys was eventually demoted and transferred out of Kenya. These experiences put what he had seen in Mombasa in a new perspective, and an unexpected temporary posting back there in early 1911 as Acting Medical Officer of Health (MOH) gave him an opportunity to write about it in a report full of controlled indignation resulting from his up-country experience, a report he could never have written during his first years there. Indeed, if it hadn't been for this report we would know almost nothing about his life during that time: his letters to Gilbert Murray stop when he left Nyasaland and only resume in 1910 when he sought Murray's help in publicising the Maasai affair. But to appreciate what he wrote in his report we need to know something about what had happened to him in the meantime.

The punitive expedition

Returning to Kenya from leave in Britain in January 1908, Leys had no sooner got off the train in Nairobi than he was informed that on the following day he was to join a 'punitive expedition' against the Kisii (now Gusii) in the remote south-west corner of the country. He hastily found somewhere for his wife and daughter to stay in Nairobi and left with the expedition. On his return he sent home an account of it in the form of a letter to his family and friends. The Kisii, he explained, had not yet got used to paying hut tax (this hated tax was first introduced in 1901 and gradually extended to more outlying areas). One day the European tax collector had been speared in the back. Leys commented:

> ... certainly there was dissatisfaction over the hut tax. The resentment was probably no greater than is felt by many European taxpayers. But Africans are unfortunate in the way they show resentment. They have not the custom of constitutional agitation. Just what kind of agitation would be constitutional in their case, I find it hard to imagine. Their resentment is shown by the killing of the people judged responsible. A certain woman of the Kisii is said to have made herself the popular champion, and preached war... During the next week [after the collector was attacked] about ten men were killed by the Kisii, two police, one or two Indians and several porters from a neighbouring tribe of traditional unfriendliness who were carrying either government stores or trade goods, and were unarmed. In the opinion of the collector (who had recovered within a month) the Kisii 'thought the hut tax money went into his own pocket and that if he were got rid of, their old ways would not again be disturbed...' They particularly objected to the stone house that was being put up for him, as the sign of a claim to a permanent hold on the country... Northcote [the tax collector] says an impersonal government is beyond their limits of the conceivable. I wonder what they conceive now.[35]

'To resume', Leys continued, 'this that I have described constitutes a rising. So … a punitive expedition was decided on'. Three hundred troops and two hundred police, commanded by a colonel with a dozen European officers, including Leys, plus several hundred porters, travelled by train to Kisumu, and then on barges south on Lake Victoria, and finally on foot into Kisii country. There they met virtually no opposition but burned all the huts except grain-stores, and rounded up all the livestock. Leys mocked the elaborate and largely ineffectual attempts by the colonel to make the expedition orderly, the ill-planned feeding arrangements in the open amid the noise of the thousands of confiscated cattle, sheep and goats, and the exaggerated estimate of Kisii killed, for the loss of only two members of the expedition (both by what we would now call 'friendly fire', including a police corporal 'who was shot dead in action, probably intentionally, by one of his own men'). The Kisii wives they spoke to said 'they didn't know where their husbands had gone to and gave us to understand that they didn't care'. The expedition finally went home because the enemy had all run away, and the rains were starting.

But Leys' account concluded with a defence of punitive expeditions in general that has attracted a lot of criticism. 'Punitive expeditions are abominable things', he wrote, in a different tone. Very few Kisii had been killed, he thought, probably no more than had been killed by the Kisii themselves before the expedition arrived, but a great deal of misery had been inflicted, and almost entirely on people who had nothing to do with the crimes that had provoked the expedition. Yet he thought the expedition was justified, and he defended it in two ways. First, he asked: 'What else could have been done? Granted the existence of British East Africa, to do nothing would have been as unjust as what we did. Traders and officials have to be protected. And I have no doubt that their lives will be much safer than before, for many years to come.' Second, the punitive expedition 'and all that it is typical of', was justifiable if it served the purpose of bringing people into a genuinely Christian civilisation. But then, acknowledging that this seemed too large and problematic a justification, Leys asked again, 'What else are we your servants to do?'

It was a fair question: having sanctioned the imposition of British rule on East Africa, how else did people in Britain think it could be maintained? The hard *raison d'état* of this conclusion has upset some of Leys' most sympathetic readers, and some of the things he says in passing also jar on our sensibilities today: for example, a casual reference to the punishment of soldiers on the expedition by flogging, or the remark that 'A hut only takes a week or two to build up and these people have years of time on hand.' But more than anything it is the tone of the whole account that is disconcerting. It is unlike anything in Leys' letters before or after this date, and as different as could possibly be from the tone of his later writing for publication, or of what he would write in 1911 in his official report on Mombasa.

I think the explanation is that none of his previous experiences in Africa had prepared him for what he encountered in Kisii. Chinde was old and decadent. Nyasaland had been rescued from slavers and was deeply influenced by the Scottish missions. Mombasa was an old and relatively sophisticated port town. In contrast, the country of the Gusii was still at the frontier of colonisation. Leys' encounter with it, straight off the boat from England, was disorienting. He accepted his fellow-officers' view of the expedition as an unavoidable evil, but he was made very uneasy by it. The self-conscious style of his account betrays this. He added a postscript: 'the Kisii are to have all their cattle returned to them on condition that they make roads through the country'.

In fact, there had been another expedition against the Gusii three years earlier, and there would be a third in 1914; there was more to the challenge to British authority than opposition to paying hut tax, as Leys' allusion to a woman leader suggests. The expedition was one of fifty recorded 'incidents' of its kind between 1894 and 1914 in western Kenya alone.[36] Beside the threat to British control, almost all of the punitive expeditions also involved local conflicts between tribes or sections of tribes, which the British settled by force, or the threat of it, enlisting the support of one or more nearby tribal groups against the one that offered the most serious challenge: thus the Kisii expedition's advance guard consisted of fifty Nandi spearmen, traditional enemies of the Gusii. Using the official reports, the historian John Lonsdale found that the 1908 expedition was the second most deadly in the history of the region, with 240 African deaths.[37] Leys thought the much lower figure given to the officers by Colonel Mackay at the end of hostilities – 160 – was itself far too high, being based on the unverified claims of numbers killed made by each military unit in the expedition. (He also recorded two deaths of members of the expedition, whereas the official report listed none.) It was his first, and as it turned out only, experience of a punitive expedition, so he was not qualified to evaluate the official figures; but he was a stickler for facts, and as the expedition's doctor his assessment of the casualties seems likely to have been better grounded in evidence than the others.

This point needs making because once he became an open critic of the administration Leys was often charged with inaccuracy. In 1986 the historian of the Gusii, Robert Maxon, who seems not to have known of Leys' first-hand report but had access to many other documentary sources, confirmed his account remarkably closely.[38] He also found Leys' scepticism that there had ever been 'a rising' that needed to be put down was fully justified. The report of the large numbers killed upset Winston Churchill, the Colonial Secretary at the time. A former military officer attached to the Colonial Office was asked to review the evidence and concluded that 'The whole episode betrays a degree of administrative ineptitude and a vicious misuse of force on the part of the Administration which deserves the gravest censure'.[39]

The historian John Cell saw Leys' account – calling punitive expeditions 'abominable' but necessary – as evidence of 'an ambiguity that he never overcame'.[40] But it seems more a matter of ambivalent feelings than ambiguity. In Leys' view, the British East Africa Protectorate existed, like all the European colonies in Africa, as a result of the overwhelming power of European commercial expansion and industrial and military superiority. In the international conditions of the time, colonial rule by one or another European power was inevitable. What mattered was whether it was exercised in the interest of Africans, and it could not be exercised at all if tax collectors were liable to be murdered. But that didn't mean he had no negative feelings about punitive expeditions. His thinking was clear enough, but his feelings pulled in a different direction.

Nakuru and Fort Hall

Leys wrote his account of the expedition in March 1908 at his new station in Nakuru. There his official duties were to look after the health of European government staff and their families, and, increasingly, their employees, which he evidently did well: the annual report for Nakuru in 1910 said his 'constant attention and devotion to the end in his endeavours to resuscitate [an employee of the railway] who succumbed to the scourge [plague] at the risk of his own life is remembered by all with a deep gratitude and pride'.[41] But he also supervised the network of mainly mission-run 'dispensaries', offering elementary medical services to Africans. This involved safaris, sometimes lasting several days. He learned enough Kikuyu to follow the gist of a conversation, and these safaris were the basis of his later remark that to know what Africans really thought you had to overhear them talking: 'The only way to learn, discreditable as it may appear, is to listen unseen, when one is supposed to be asleep in a tent, for example, while the porters talk round the campfire. On such occasions a listener hears about himself things that are more salutary than amusing'.[42]

In 1912, after his temporary posting back to Mombasa, Leys was posted to Fort Hall, a settler enclave in the Kikuyu heartland, from where most of the labourers on the settler farms around Nakuru were drawn. Here he saw at first-hand how Africans were being driven to leave their homes and work for the settlers by the need to earn cash to pay the hut or poll tax,* but also by the threat of force. Family life was broken, and in the absence of so many men the reserve no longer produced enough food for people to eat. Colonial rule was proving as calamitous as the slave trade. In less than a decade, between 1902 and 1911, hunger and diseases (of both people and livestock) had reduced the African population of Kenya from four million to three (and thanks to the first World War it would fall by another 500,000 between 1911 and 1921).[43] Leys now saw what had driven a party of twenty Kikuyu, who had been brought 'dead and dying' to the Native Hospital in Mombasa in 1911, to make their fatal 300-mile journey. He was also learning from his travel around the district and from talking to district officers and missionaries, the best of whom were similarly unhappy with government policy. He talked with Africans at missions and on safaris, and with settlers. His personal relations with most settlers were good, but he also witnessed crude settler racism – settlers beating their employees and settler juries refusing to convict whites for murdering Africans, and he became aware of the sadistic use of flogging in the Nairobi prison and the close ties between the administration in Nairobi and the settlers' political leaders that allowed these things to be condoned.**

At Nakuru in 1909 he wrote an appendix to his annual report about what had also been one of his major concerns in Mombasa, an

---

* A poll or head tax was introduced when Africans took to reducing the impact of the hut tax by crowding into fewer huts.
** Leys got Edmund Harvey MP to ask questions about the routine flogging of prisoners in the Nairobi and Mombasa jails. The Administration reported that in 1911 'there were over 180 floggings in Nairobi Jail for offences against prison discipline, all inflicted by visiting justices. In Mombasa Jail during the same period, with rather more prisoners, there were 17! These are the official figures and do not include what the Nairobi head jailor does on his own.

'epidemic' of venereal disease among the African population.[44] Wage workers were on labour contracts of three to six months and could be punished by law if they went home before their contracts were up, so they used prostitutes or formed temporary sexual relationships, and then carried venereal diseases back to the reserves. In Nakuru the only solution he could see to the spread of venereal disease was to raise wages enough for workers to be able to have their wives with them – which would, of course, have made settler farms uneconomic. The epidemic was another of the prices Africans were paying for the maintenance of the settler economy. During all this time he was studying 'the settler system'. His curiosity was boundless, and it was combined with an unusual need to systematise what he learned: 'I wonder where you put certain things', he wrote to Murray, 'where you fit them in. Perhaps you don't fit them. I can't help it. They rattle about if I don't.'[45]

In this respect he was evidently alone among the two dozen medical officers working for the government.[46] By this time candidates for the medical service were being selected by interview in London in the same way as administrative officers, with an emphasis on having a personality 'such as to command the respect and trust of the native inhabitants of his Colony as well as the confidence of the local European community' (and explicitly *not* on being outstanding doctors).[47] The selectors preferred men who had been to public school (i.e. private fee-paying school), which, Leys noted, produced men who were usually honest but rarely intellectually curious. His letters never mention another doctor. He had been recruited into the colonial medical service in Nyasaland before selection by interview in London had been established. One wonders if he would have been accepted.

What he learned in Nakuru about how the settler system worked made him angry, and the Maasai affair provoked him into confrontation. But in 1911, before this confrontation came to a head, he was, as mentioned earlier, transferred temporarily back to Mombasa as Acting Medical Officer of Health. His friend McGregor

---

The Governor issued an angry circular saying that the Sec. of State was smelling about, and prohibiting floggings for such execrable crimes as cigarette smoking in the sacred building of the prison, but so far as I know neither the prison staff in Nairobi - obviously at fault for letting discipline become so lax, nor the Justices themselves have been visited by punishment or rebuke. That is the usual way - put the blame on home sentimentalists for any interference with brutality. Nevertheless some backs have gone unscarred because you made enquiry. And for that we should be thankful.' (Leys to Harvey, 11 March 1912).

Ross, the Director of Public Works, wrote to his mother: 'Dr Leys is back at Mombasa, still very mutinous'.[48] As Acting M.O.H. he had a duty to make an annual report. He seized the opportunity: instead of producing the usual anodyne statistical update he wrote a blistering criticism of the government's failure to take even the most elementary steps to look after the town's native inhabitants.

Mombasa

Mombasa had been an ancient Arab harbour town serving the dhow traffic between East Africa and Muscat. Now it was a rapidly growing international port. As Acting M.O.H. Leys was responsible for patients in the European Hospital, the Native Hospital, and a municipal dispensary; for the health of prisoners in the prison; and for examining migrant labourers coming from the interior, applicants for the police force, and passengers arriving on ships. He told Murray that the last of these responsibilities often involved getting up at dawn: 'You would like to come. The world is cool and clear and steady then – obviously ready for a better kind of human creature than it gets.'[49] He was also responsible for the town's public health.

His 74-page report, entitled 'Memorandum on the Sanitation, economic and social condition of the people of Mombasa' was his first piece of writing on Africa other than letters to friends and family, and a reminder of why he had gone to Africa in the first place – to do what 'most needed to be done' to help Africans cope with the changes that colonialism was bringing to them. It was a case-study of what the changes meant for the population of Kenya's oldest, and at the time its most important, town. The report began, without any preamble:

> The existing sanitary law of Mombasa is contained in the Township rules of 1904. Their deficiencies may be variously illustrated. Under them it is lawful to allow filthy water to discharge from a house so as to accumulate and become putrid – anywhere except in a street or in a drain: it is lawful to erect a house in any position and of any height the builder pleases over the greater part of the native town; it is lawful to build a soakaway cesspit as near a well as the owner wishes – many are actually built within 10 yards of a well. On the other hand for the Medical Officer of Health to enter any house against the wish of the occupant, even after giving notice, to investigate a nuisance, is unlawful: sanitary arrangements in new houses are never submitted to him… attempts to extirpate mosquito breeding places or to get filth cleared away are ignored or resisted – frequently by other government departments.[50]

The reasons for this situation were to be found, Leys wrote, partly in weaknesses in the legislation, and lack of interdepartmental cooperation, but also in the challenges posed by the very different conditions of life in the European, Swahili [i.e. Muslim Afro-Arab] and Native sections of the town. From a sanitation perspective only the last two were of interest, the European section 'being composed of villas and gardens with ample space' (such as he and his family occupied). The other two sections presented different problems. The old Swahili quarter close to the port was overcrowded and filthy; the newer and expanding native section (mainly housing migrants from the interior) was much less crowded but desperately poor and lacking in basic infrastructure. Leys' memorandum covered each of them, in terms of housing conditions and standard of living, with careful statistics and some striking details (such as the fact that a party of 20 Kikuyu had come to Mombasa the previous year to find work – presumably on foot, a distance of over 300 miles, without a corresponding food supply – and had been taken to the Native Hospital 'dead or dying').

But it was the social effects of rapid change that concerned him most. For example twenty years earlier prostitution had barely existed; now there were at least 150 prostitutes working in Mombasa. Marriage had given way almost completely to temporary unions.* 'No false shame in such matters hinders [women's] acceptance of a custom so obviously suited to the precarious economic standing of the new generation', Leys pointed out, but it meant that venereal disease was becoming 'almost universal'. Public leisure activities had disappeared. Swimming in the sea, which had once been popular with all communities, and competitive outdoor games, and even chess and equally challenging board games, had gone. Koranic schools, which used to be of some quality, had severely declined. As for government schools, a school capable of holding a hundred students had been built two years earlier but still stood empty, even though people 'thirsted' for education. Two major features of what had happened stood out. The first was 'levelling':

> The old aristocracy of land and birth is broken, the new aristocracy of money awaits recognition. Swahili [the Afro-Arab coastal population]

---

* Diana Wylie has expressed a reasonable doubt about any port at any time having barely any prostitutes (personal communication). But Leys was careful about facts and had good informants.

recognise the fact themselves and have a proverb to express it in current speech that I have roughly translated in the last sentence… We, our industrial and legal system, and our way of treating all alike who are not Europeans, are making them for the time being astonishingly homogeneous in speech, knowledge, feeling.

The second was that the changes had been exclusively economic and external.

By the people concerned in them they were not sought after – not even expected. Whatever good might have been gained from them has been largely lost by the almost complete lack of mental preparation. In most countries great economic changes are only part of a larger movement of human life, religious, political, scientific. It all goes on together. Increasing knowledge leads to social rearrangements, which themselves again acquire a religious sanction. Or, conversely, a new quality of religious belief may lead to material regeneration. In any case it is a natural process.

Not so here. The unprecedented development in trade… has been a devastating flood. It is little that old land marks have gone. Sentimental regret for the past has in it little that is of service for the future. It is more that there is no sign of new human enrichment. I doubt if there are half a dozen natives in Mombasa whose education Government has ever done anything deliberately to help.

… When the [British East Africa] Company came to the coast people were assured that everything would remain as before. In these 20 years, nevertheless, there is not a corner of industrial, social, political life that has not been transformed. No people could stand it all without disorganisation, and no people in the midst of disorganisation could feel anything but regret for the changes.

Coming back to sanitation, all this meant that the public understanding and trust in public officials that had made possible the sanitary revolution in European cities was lacking in Mombasa.

I do not know of one native of Mombasa who is glad that their Sovereign in Zanzibar gave the country to the British. I do not believe there is one, though I know a few who have hope that the future may belie the promise of the present. One expects an alien government to be unpopular. Ours is mistrusted, in every act.

And the mistrust was aggravated by the systematic incivility shown to

Africans by almost all Europeans. 'Those [Europeans] who came first, as invited guests, did usually try not to offend. Now Europeans feel the country to be their own, and Africans to most are menials. It is becoming bad form to drink tea or shake hands with a Swahili or an Arab.' The result was predictable: 'Money is being raised for a kind of club for well-to-do Swahili. Its purposes are educational and political. So far, the rights of man are not familiar to the Swahili. Ten years more and that will probably be no longer true'.

If the Principal Medical Officer, to whom the Memorandum was presumably sent, got this far, he will have found, next, a set of practical proposals to remedy the situation – proposals some of which would undoubtedly have confirmed his opinion that Leys was not just a loose cannon but a deluded dreamer, or worse. For example, there should, Leys argued, be a Municipal Committee, open to the public, so that people could learn what the government was doing; and as if that wasn't a shocking enough idea, he further proposed that the residents of the European section should pay 'rates' (property tax) towards the cost of running the town, from which they were currently excused. The government should also buy enough cheap land to meet the foreseeable needs of Africans for rented housing; and so on. Leys even suggested that the plantation agriculture that existed at the coast (for crops such as cotton and rubber) should be replaced by independent peasant production, which would be more efficient as well as much better for the workers. His thinking was running in precisely the opposite direction to that of the government in Nairobi.

As for the memorandum's conclusion, if the Principal Medical Officer was still reading he will have had a foretaste of what would make Leys' writing so uncomfortably compelling once he had left the medical service and was back in Britain. 'On the last day of the year', Leys wrote, switching without warning to more fundamental issues,

> there landed in Mombasa a coast Arab on the way home from the Mecca pilgrimage, one of about forty by the same steamer. He was very old, he had put the journey off too long. He had thought his journey of devotion, the first to take him from the country of his birth, would have given him the special blessing that all who die on pilgrimage obtain. He had been content to reach the holy places and now was doubly content to reach home again.
>
> For generations his ancestors had been the principal family in the island of Wasin, 60 miles to the south, an old settlement, Arab, Portuguese, then Arab again, and always African, always with African

slaves to do the work. The place is much decayed, though I fancy its only glories take colour and romance when ready to be cast off from the tree. A predecessor describes the people as degenerate, and so they are, poor and lazy, building little shelters inside the older better houses, beggars and untruthful. Sheikh Rashid himself is simple and kindly, no honester than the rest or more truthful – they don't admire our laws of the game at all, in fact they feel certain we make them up as we go along – and being African as well as Arab, is not impressively dignified. He used to be nervous and shuffling, but now his face has the open, slightly surprised look of old age. As he lay on the deck – their tickets were all 'deck without food' – with someone holding an umbrella over his face, one saw how spotlessly clean his clothing was, and his skin. Without the strength to rise, he shook hands with civil interest. His friends were more concerned. The Indian Immigration Clerk had been for forbidding him to land, the reasons given being that he was sick and had no money. The clerk was wrong, of course. The law can keep out no native of the country. His intention was simply to prove his eagerness to discover undesirables, all with empty pockets being so described.

One's mind went back to days, not so far distant, when he [Sheikh Rashid] and his kind were courted by the first agents of our country, when from them these agents got land, houses, slaves for our caravans to the interior, were given in short those weapons of peaceful penetration that have gone right through to the other side. And one remembers, too, a cherished dispatch of Lord Salisbury's which enjoined the continued observance of the salutes our men of war gave to the more important of these old Governors and Judges. One never hears them. The prime minister when he signed the minute could not possibly understand. What unreason to fire guns in honour of men with whom most Europeans in the country would decline to sit at food. So this old man, easily delivered from the zealous immigration clerk, was welcomed by his sons and other younger relations, one a bumboat man, another an office boy, the others I know not what.

It is all a huge mistake. The crew is worth more than a ship, much more than the cargo. With land gone, and occupation and honours gone, we offer them the sanitary bucket, the registration of deaths, the hut tax, courts to enforce laws they neither trust nor understand, and we complain of the religious prejudice with which they resent our benevolent regulations, which blinds them to the blessings we have brought, of peace and the prosperity of trade…

Not just the anger, but the foundations of Leys' critique of settler colonialism, are all in evidence here. He concluded:

To disregard for them the common attributes of political and economic justice is the height of childish folly. To treat a protectorate as an estate to be developed and its population as labour thereon, to judge the conditions of that labour by reference to its efficiency as a wealth creator, is not only to plunge the country into that quagmire from which the older countries of the world are struggling to be free, but is to court the opposition, ripening in years to come, of what marks the human in every race. Our failure on this coast is due, and will be due, not to the poor price of cotton in Manchester nor to the rainfall being deficient for ceara rubber trees, but to our having held human life and endeavour cheaply. The art of Government of such a people as the Swahili consists, not only in such matters as channelling the free flow of merchandise and investigating parasitic diseases, but in the enrichment of human relations and in the encouragement of human knowledge and achievement. And the measures of its success are not trade returns, nor the rate of interest on invested capital, but the closeness and strength of our relations with the natives of the country, the extent and thoroughness of our instruction and help.

The fate of Leys' Memorandum is interesting. When he was writing it his involvement in the Maasai affair was at a critical point. Thanks to his actions in opposing the move, which he had made little effort to keep secret, he kept being told by various people in the administration that the Governor was angry at his 'disloyalty'. He eventually wrote to the Governor saying he was willing to tell him face to face exactly what he had done. Not getting a response, in order to raise the ante he sent the Governor his Memorandum on Mombasa. 'As M.O.H.', he told Edmund Harvey, a sympathetic Liberal MP, 'I had to write [a report] but in this report I travelled far beyond my subject and described the appalling condition of the coast and the faults of Govt. as frankly as I ever have in letters to you. I know as a fact that he read the report. I had hoped to be asked (?) to withdraw it. I should then have sent it to the Sec. of State. But they took it and said nothing.'[51] Later on he asked the administration in Nairobi if any part of it could be published, and was surely not surprised to be told it could not.[52]

The Maasai move

Back to Nakuru in 1910. If Norman Leys is remembered at all in Kenya for what he did while he was living there it is as a whistle-blower in the Maasai affair. The Maasai were a small pastoral tribe in west central Kenya, who had once grazed their immense herds of cattle, sheep and goats across most of the Rift Valley and much of the highlands, and dominated the surrounding peoples. Their young men were organised in warrior groups, called *moran*, who raided other groups and tribes for their cattle (usually with prior notice). They were interested in cattle, not cash, and before the British came they were much feared.

The completion of the Uganda Railway cut their land in two. In 1904 an agreement was signed between them and the government. Under duress the Maasai accepted being confined to two 'reserves', one to the north and one to south of the railway, in return for a declaration that this land was reserved to them for ever. In 1910, however, responding to pressure from some settlers who coveted land in Laikipia, the northern reserve, the Governor, Sir Percy Girouard, decided to move the northern Maasai into the southern reserve. Officially this was done with the consent of the northern Maasai leaders. In reality, it was forced. It was exactly the kind of scandal that Leys had envisaged using to expose the abuse of imperial power.

The affair left a deep mark on Leys' thinking, as well as costing him his job. His role in it consisted chiefly of writing letters, first to Gilbert Murray, and then, especially, to Edmund Harvey MP, and to Ramsay MacDonald, the chairman of the Labour MPs in parliament, setting out the facts of the Maasai affair as accurately as he could.[53] He urged them to ask parliamentary questions, and/or to talk to the senior officials in the Colonial Office. He thought the British public were entitled to know what was common knowledge in the colony. He hoped that if the facts were known the move would not be allowed.

He accepted that government inaction had made the position of the northern reserve problematic. Europeans wanted the land, which was some of the best in the country, while disease control was beginning to lead to a potentially exponential growth of the Maasai herds; the result was that they were increasingly grazing on adjacent land outside the reserve that now belonged to Europeans, although they were not yet farming it. Disputes were likely and the Maasai *moran* were a force to reckon with. Given that the settlers were not going to be moved, moving the northern Maasai to the southern reserve made sense. The southern reserve could be extended to accommodate them. But the additional land in the south was largely waterless and much of it was infested with tsetse-fly, the bearer of *trypanosomiasis*, and with the tick that caused East Coast Fever, both of which were then major killers of cattle. The government needed to prepare for the incoming

Kenya in 1913

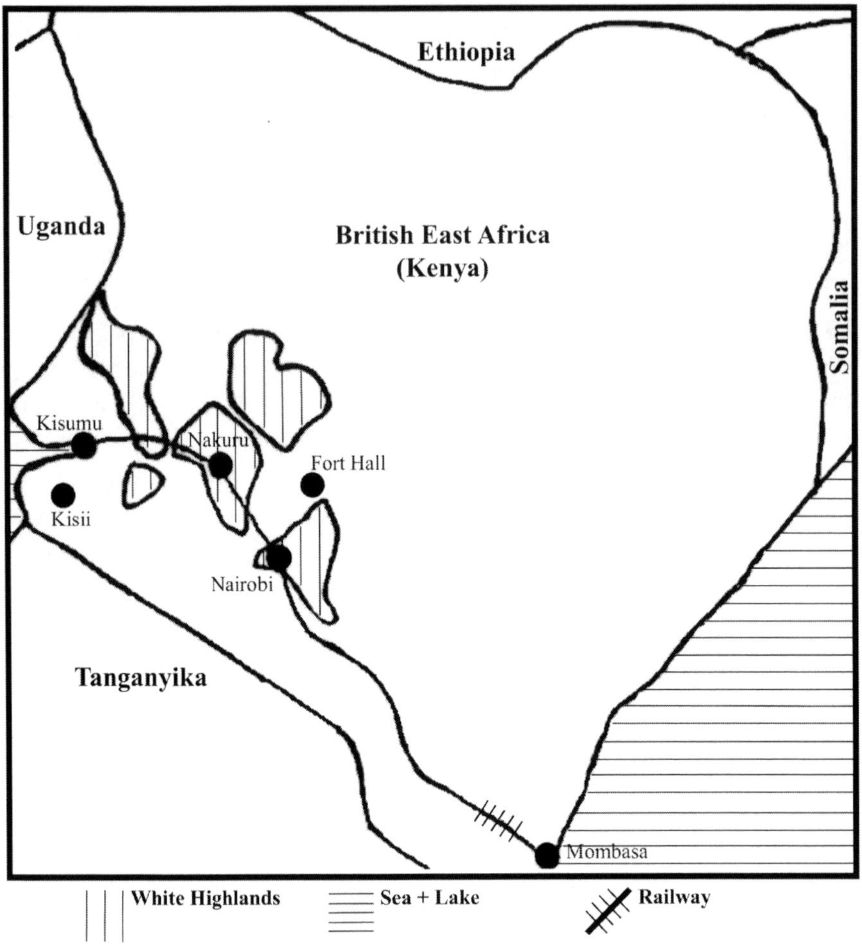

The Masai Reserve before and after 1913

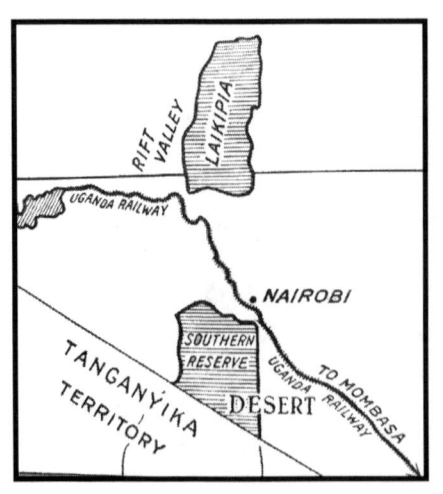
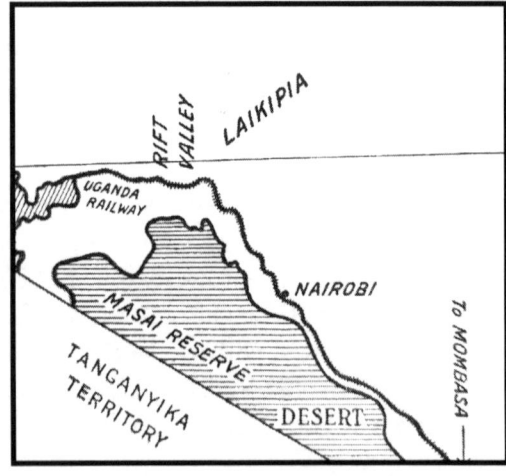

herds by putting in water supplies and other infrastructure, but made no serious attempt to do this. Much of the additional area had not even been surveyed.

Leys suspected, correctly as it turned out, that Girouard was not telling the Colonial Office the whole story. In his first letter to Murray he said he could use his name if it would help, although it would probably lead to his dismissal. Murray passed a copy of the letter, minus the author's name, to the Colonial Office. It would be interesting to know how much of the letter Murray left out, since the last few pages of it could hardly have been written by anyone else. But the administration in Nairobi was probably reading his letters by now anyway (they certainly were soon after this), and his views were in any case already well known. They would have had no doubt about who was causing the trouble. He knew he was risking his career.

He didn't think moving the Maasai from Laikipia was necessarily wrong: sooner or later there would be conflict with settlers on the boundary of the northern reserve, with disastrous consequences for the Maasai, and the Maasai way of life was in any case doomed, being incompatible with capitalist development:[54] 'Now the reason the Maasai refuse to dip their cattle', he later explained to people in Britain,

> and to spend money on irrigation, is simply that they have little or no use for money and what money buys in Africa. What was a virtue in Diogenes is a vice in the modern world. The cure of that vice, the only cure, is education of the kind now fashionable. Its great object is to create new appetites, for tea, and cigarettes, and gramophones… all the innumerable objects with which modern civilization has enriched the world. Many of us are gravely dissatisfied with that civilization. But with all its crimes and follies it is better than Maasai civilization. And there is no room for both in the same world. That statement is impossible of proof. Some gentle readers will dispute it. One can only advise them to live for a year in Kenya Colony and they will be convinced that the only alternatives for the Lumbwa, Nandi and other tribes as well as the Maasai, are civilization or destruction.[55]

If the move was well managed, Leys thought, and if the southern reserve was made large enough and safe enough, it made practical sense. What was absolutely wrong was to break the 1904 treaty. 'The importance of the question is not the possible harm to the Masai', Leys told Murray:

> The abomination is that the Government is going to break its word. A

year or two ago Winston Churchill came out and made speeches to Natives telling them the reserves were theirs for ever. Now we are going to break for our own advantage the only written treaty ever made in this country with a purely native tribe ... If this scheme to move the Masai succeeds it will be proof to every intelligent native that the profit of the European immigrant is the government's main object. So to break our word is more than criminal. It is madness.[56]

It was also another case of modern economic forces overwhelming a group of Africans, whom Leys had seen it as his job to help. Like the people of Mombasa, the Maasai needed to be shown how to adapt, and assisted to do so. So far the government had done nothing to help them.

Alerted by MPs to whom Leys had written, the Colonial Office refused to sanction the move until they had a full account of the case from Girouard, who was summoned to London; and before he left in 1910 he gave Leys an interview. Girouard was not a typical Governor. A French-Canadian military engineer, he had used his family connections to get transferred to the British army, where he quickly proved himself an outstanding railway engineer in Kitchener's regime-change campaign against the Mahdist state in Sudan in 1898, and again in Kitchener's campaign to subdue the Boers in South Africa. For this he was knighted, at the unusually early age of 33. He lost his French-Canadian accent. In 1906 Churchill, who had seen his work in Sudan, appointed him as High Commissioner for Northern Nigeria, from where he was moved to Kenya as Governor in 1909. But the self-assurance and impatience with lesser mortals that had got Girouard to the top in the army made him unsuited to govern a colony. His betrayal of the Maasai seems to have been due as much to a drive for tidiness as to a wish to give their land to the settlers, who did not particularly like him.

But when they met Girouard seemed, to Leys' surprise, to share his views on 'native policy', and gave him the impression that the move was not going ahead. At that point Leys actually hoped that Girouard would stay on as Governor, as he recognised that he was far abler than any typical replacement was likely to be.[57] But in April 1911, while he was temporarily back in Mombasa, he learned that the move was on after all. Girouard had 'diddled' him, he told Murray. 'He diddles everybody'.[58] The administration had made a new agreement with a group of the northern Maasai leaders, and claimed that they were now willing to leave Laikipia. In May the Colonial Office sanctioned the move. The operation was botched; many cattle and some of the Maasai died on the high ground that had to be crossed to reach the southern reserve. Many turned back and refused to leave again. These ones were finally induced to leave a year later, by the threat of armed force. And it turned out that their leaders' signatures to the new agreement had been secured by intimidation.

In 1912 the leader of the northern Maasai, Ole Gilisho, started legal action to have the new agreement declared invalid, and to seek compensation. Leys, who had previously thought the Maasai too ignorant to go to law, recommended them a lawyer whom he considered the best in the country. The administration in Nairobi did everything possible to block the Maasai's case, refusing to let the plaintiffs leave the reserve to meet the lawyer, or to let the lawyer enter it, or to allow Ole Gilisho to sell cattle to pay the lawyer's fee. They only stopped when told to by the Colonial Office, which by then was under constant pressure from MPs and press coverage, prompted by Leys. But they need not have worried. When the case finally came before a judge in Nairobi, he ruled that both the 1904 and the 1911 'agreements' were treaties, and that no court in Kenya could rule on a treaty between Britain and another sovereign body. The Maasai appealed, but the appeal court in Kenya said the same. A further appeal to London was considered but abandoned. The pressures on Ole Gilisho were too great, and the prospects of success looked more and more dim.

So while the Maasai had been induced to make agreements with the government, the courts held that they couldn't hold the government to them because they were agreements between Britain and another government, over which the courts had no jurisdiction. On that principle the Maasai were foreigners. On the other hand the British government had taken them under its protection in the East African Protectorate ((Kenya was not yet called 'Kenya Colony), in return for which the courts held that they owed obedience to the British government, which had the right to appropriate their land and enforce whatever laws it liked on them. Or as Leys summed it up in a letter to Murray: 'It works out that they are foreigners, all these tribes, who have to pay prodigious annual sums to a British Government for stealing their land and harrying them without cessation. They form an enslaved community since, in law, they are governed by the purest form of despotism.'[59]

In August 1912 Girouard was on leave in London. The Acting

Governor urged the Colonial Office to dismiss Leys, and sent him a message telling him to 'refrain from any further interference, either directly or indirectly, in political matters outside the scope of your official duties'.[60] But by now Leys was angry and reckless. His friend McGregor Ross, the Director of Public Works, reported that Leys had 'written a final counterblast to Sir Percy ... he says it is none of the "timid slush" that he wrote to Sir P. two years ago ... [this seems likely to have been Leys' memorandum on the condition of the people of Mombasa which he had sent to the Governor in March]. He says he expects to get the sack for it but that he will refuse to go! Talk about stormy petrels! ... I believe that H.E. [the Governor] and Hollis [the second in command] are trying to get him the sack before the new Governor comes. Fools.'[61]

Perhaps because Girouard was away, and the issue had become so public in Britain, Leys was left in his new post in Fort Hall until he too went on leave early in 1913; it was Girouard who was forced to resign for having concealed from the Colonial Office that land in Laikipia had already been promised to some settlers. But while Leys was on leave in London he was told he was to be transferred to Nyasaland. The officials in Nairobi believed, wrongly, that he had advised the Maasai to go to court, when all he had done was put them in touch with a lawyer, although his role in informing MPs was insubordinate enough in itself to make them determined to get him dismissed. But given the connections he had made in London it may have seemed easier to muzzle him by keeping him in the colonial service, but out of Kenya. He was sent back to Karonga. Leys was fatalistic about it. From Karonga he wrote to Murray, 'So it seems there is nothing to do but wait till Africans prove themselves men, as they certainly will.'[62]

By this time his understanding of settler colonialism had advanced a great deal. Before his posting to Nakuru his thinking about it had been primarily historical and ethical. By the time he left Kenya it had become economic and social as well. Yet he still seems to have seen the system as remediable. For example, in July 1912 he told Murray he was 'strongly tempted to take up a still more scandalous business than the Masai – the condition of contract labour'.[63] Here was another scandal, another stick to beat the authorities with. Leys had not yet reached the point that would lead him to conclude, by the time he left Africa, that it was a system 'incapable of reform'.[64] It would take four years of corresponding and reflecting in Nyasaland to knit everything into a coherent whole.

But the components of that analysis were assembled during Leys' years in Kenya. One component was a deeper knowledge of Africans in the interior, especially the Kikuyu, who in Mombasa had been in a minority, chiefly migrant labourers he had treated in hospital or at the municipal clinic. Now he met them as staff and patients at dispensaries, as porters on safaris, and above all on mission stations where they mostly spoke English. (Leys estimated later that he had spent a total of six months altogether at missions, including those in Nyasaland). He also got to know settlers, and mostly got on well them, as opposed to their political leaders. And he got to know the administration. In a letter to Edmund Harvey in March 1912 he described its class character:

> This country affords a good illustration of the bad results of a nominated civil service [i.e. chosen on the basis only of interviews, not by examination]. It is staffed by the less intelligent kind of public schoolboy – the brothers and cousins of fashionable London Society. The one creditable quality leading to advancement is business capacity. But other qualities weigh more heavily, birth, social popularity, the favour of financial interests, of the planters and settlers. Under the present regime knowledge of native life is no aid to a man who aims at high position.
>
> … What makes the evil so much worse in this country is the rigid line between gazetted officers and subordinates, almost military in its severity. As a result, in some departments, 'gentlemen' learn their work from subordinates who have no chance to prove their own capacity for direction. There is no provision in the railway for instance for engineers and traffic superintendents rising from the ranks. And much of the most important work is done by men whose social position keeps them down.
>
> In practice the system of nomination results in restricting Govt. Service to one class, with great virtues – honesty the chief of them. But the best of the class go elsewhere where the pay is better and those we get have scanty natural abilities. They are uncomprehending and very simple things are misunderstood because they were unfamiliar in childhood. I honestly believe better results, even at present rates of pay, would come from recruiting men by examination. But this view is dreadful heresy with most men out here.[65]

Given the deceptions practised by the authorities in relation to the Maasai – the forced signing of the 1911 agreement, and the deceptive half-truths told to London – Leys' statement that the administrative service was honest might seem odd. But his point was that men who started out honest had to be ready to compromise if they wanted promotion. It was 'the men at the top not the underlings' who were to blame.[66] 'Most of the rank and file of the officials in the Province feel as I do, though few of course are inclined to "make trouble"', he told Murray in 1910.*[67] Even small-scale honesty could be fatal to your career.

A cautionary tale cited by Leys in his 1931 book, *A Last Chance in Kenya*, illustrated this. A District Officer, whom he called A, took over a district from another District Officer, B. On inspecting the jail, A found several prisoners doing hard labour who had not broken any law, but who had 'not given their masters the satisfaction they desired.' A set them free. The employers protested. A ignored them. One of them, a leading settler politician, then complained to the Governor, adding that A had been disrespectful. The Governor sent A 'a letter of reproof'. A demanded an inquiry and, rather unusually, got one: the judge found that he had done nothing wrong. But A was transferred to a remote unhealthy station and kept at the bottom pay grade, while B was promoted to near the top of the service.[68] Leys added:

> The punishments that behaviour such as A's disregard of the wishes of the settlers receives, are those he received – unhealthy stations, withholding of promotion and increments of salary, posting him to stations in charge of his juniors, and in addition compulsory transfer with loss of seniority to less healthy Dependencies where there are fewer settlers or none at all, and compulsory retirement as soon as the regulations allow the Government to require it. Those who dare to expose, either instances of injustice or the political and economic system that makes injustices inevitable, take their reputations in their hands.**

---

* Several examples of District Officers who wanted to promote peasant commercial farming and resented the way the government consistently blocked it are given in Michael Thomason, 'Little Tin Gods: The District Officer in British East Africa', *Albion, A Quarterly Journal Concerned with British Studies* Vol. 7, No. 2, pp. 145-160.

** It was actually Leys himself, not A, who had been transferred out of Kenya to a less healthy colony with no settlers. McGregor Ross provided more details of the incident, including the names of those involved: A was a Mr S.V.Cooke, B was a Mr Oldfield, and the leading settler who had had his workers illegally imprisoned, and who complained that A was rude to him, was Mr C.K.Archer, the chairman of the settlers' party, the Convention of Associations. Cooke's alleged rudeness consisted, Ross explained, in not having been willing to interrupt a court hearing he was conducting in order to listen to Archer's complaint. He was sent to Wajir, in the Northern Frontier District, 'a desert region, low and unhealthy' (McGregor Ross [1927], pp. 113-14).

4: Exile, war and reflection

Leys went on home leave in late 1912, well aware that the administration in Nairobi wanted him dismissed. He pleaded to be allowed to stay in Kenya, but knew he was lucky when the Colonial Office decided only to transfer him back to Nyasaland. He had a wife and daughter to support, and no money except what he had saved from his salary, and needed the pension, for which he needed to do another seven years of service. The Colonial Office's decision was influenced by discovering that the Governor, Girouard, had not informed them that some settlers had been promised land in the northern Maasai reserve. Leys was only transferred, while Girouard had to resign.

Exile in Karonga was a painful experience for Leys. His aim was now the ending of settler colonialism in Kenya, but he couldn't do anything from within the medical service in Nyasaland. On top of this he had forfeited his seniority and was kept at the lowest pay grade ('as a further lesson to others', he later noted) and given only routine work to do.[69] In June 1914 he was assigned to spend five months 'hunting out Sleeping Sickness – a perfectly beastly job, because the poor wretches will consider me worse than a slave hunter. The whole outfit of police and gland puncturing [a painful diagnostic procedure]… makes them bolt into the bush'.[70] Worst of all, the Nyasaland administration, evidently including the senior medical officers there, saw him as a traitor. He became 'sick to loathing of living and working with the brand of disloyalty on me, accused of encouraging sedition, reckoned unfit for responsible work that my juniors are given.'[71] The moral support he had found in the relatively congenial community in Karonga in 1902 had gone.

But what might have defeated many people seems only to have strengthened his determination. Distance gave him space to reflect, and under-employment gave him time. As early as 1914 he was beginning to think of writing a book, though he doubted that rational argument could overcome imperialist attitudes among the British public. 'If I were to write a book', he told Gilbert Murray, and make it clear that the natives of the 'Protectorates' are debarred from the Courts of Justice, that their land has by a few strokes of the pen been made 'Crown' land, that discontent on these and other grounds is widespread and growing, the public of Britain would answer partly by pointing to rapidly increasing trade and revenue and partly by disclaiming the wisdom of admitting rights to these people. So it seems there is nothing to do but wait till Africans prove themselves men, as they certainly will.[72]

'But', he wondered, with his usual realism, 'what kind of men will a generation of commercialism produce?' At a time when hardly any other European in East Africa believed that Africans had the capacity to rule themselves, Leys was now sure that they had. But he didn't think they would necessarily do it well.

The battle of Karonga

Gathering materials and ideas for a book may have looked like the only way for Leys to use his exile, but his time back in Nyasaland was not exactly a writer's retreat. In August 1914 Britain declared war on Germany and on 7 September, in one of the first battles of the war, a German force of 400 Africans and thirteen European officers crossed the border from German East Africa (Tanganyika) and attacked the district headquarters at Karonga, opening a military campaign which would lead to a death toll in East Africa on a barely conceivable scale. Leys and his wife Janey – their daughter was now of school age and had been placed in a boarding school in Scotland – found themselves trapped in a compound next to the district office, treating wounded officers under heavy fire.

Two weeks after the battle Janey Leys sent an account of it to her sister in Scotland which would have done credit to a war correspondent. The colony's hastily mobilised troops had been sent north towards the border, where the Germans were thought to be camped, leaving for the defence of the boma about 50 African policemen and some African soldiers, most of whom 'were either very old time-expired soldiers or raw recruits just taken on who could hardly hold a gun properly'; and about eight Europeans of varying degrees of competence – the commander was a Canadian Marine Transport Officer. The German force had evaded the troops sent to meet them and lay in the bush, raking the boma with machine gun and rifle fire. The idea was, Janey reported, that we three women [there were two other nurses from the mission hospital] should take shelter in the rice store, but somehow things happened so quickly that we never got there. First of all we sat on chairs in the shelter of a wall of the rice store; when the bullets began to get a bit thick we sat on the ground with our backs to the wall; when it began to get rather exciting we lay flat on the ground. The Germans had three Maxim guns, two of which were in action nearly all the time; the third they turned on the Lake or I don't think anything could have saved us… We were besieged for about three and a half hours and during this time the firing never ceased. Sometimes it died down for a few seconds and then started again with renewed vigour. The bullets went whizzing and screaming in all directions, sometimes there was a long drawn out ping, something like the wind in a telegraph wire. This was caused by bullets ricochetting I think… the branches were falling from the trees in all directions and little clouds of dust rose up where the bullets fell… We had the occupants of the native hospital lying beside us, four pneumonia and a man with a crushed foot. They had refused to be left behind in the hospital! After a bit a wounded Askari [policeman] was brought up, only flesh wounds in the thigh where a bullet had passed in and out. The sisters dressed it and made him lie down beside us. Later on another bullet grazed his elbow, and that had to be seen to… We were just beginning to get anxious about the outcome of all this when relief came about noon.[73]

The main British force had circled back, and the Germans withdrew. The next day a much bigger battle took place outside Karonga, filling the boma with more wounded Europeans. 'Two of the wounded died almost at once, making five dead of our white men altogether. We had four of our wounded left, and two wounded Germans.' The surviving Germans finally retreated back across the border.

The next morning all the wounded Europeans were being well looked after, but at the native hospital things were different.

There was plenty going on there and confusion indescribable. About forty wounded had been brought in and more were coming at intervals. There were only one or two beds, they simply had to be laid in rows on the ground, without in many cases even a mat or blanket underneath… Some of the wounds were horrible, specially the face ones, where the poor wretches had been shot through the mouth or the jaw. One seems to have had the whole roof of his mouth shot away. There were three frightfully bad compound fractures, and nothing suitable in the way of splints to do them up with… [The Germans] have probably nine Europeans killed.. They must have had about one hundred and twenty natives killed and wounded, of which about twenty-five are our prisoners, and we have of our natives about eight killed and twenty-five to thirty wounded.

Janey Leys at least mentioned the Africans who had died and was concerned for the wounded. The official despatch sent to London by the Nyasaland government made no mention of them at all:

> Whole force engaged yesterday at Karonga. Enemy fought with great determination and had to be dislodged by repeated bayonet charges but ultimately fled towards Songwe. German losses eight officers killed, two wounded and captured with Medical Officer...British losses – killed, Caldicott and Ascott; since died of wounds, Manning and Merriman; seriously wounded, Garnett, Muirhead, Mason, Sinclair; slightly wounded, Barton and Ness; missing, Williams and Harvey. All reports speak highly of gallantry of all engaged.[74]

Leys' view of things, in a letter to Gilbert Murray written two months later, was predictably different:

> Here in Africa natives kill their own fellow tribesmen at the order of strangers from Europe. They have nothing to gain, no gain or motive or quarrel whatever. This whole district has been devastated by raids. The people are living half starved in shelters of leaves in the reeds by the lake shore, flooded out by the rains. Schools are all broken up. The troops, black and white, bribe women, spread disease, create anarchy. I know my world is of a small minority. Perhaps in Belgium and Poland things are no better. Death and pain and sickness are little. War here in this corner has meant the destruction of the tissues of human life itself.[75]

The Germans never entered Nyasaland again but fought on in the surrounding territories and only surrendered two weeks after the armistice had been signed in Europe, having inflicted as much suffering on the region, in relation to the size of the population, as the German army had in Europe, if not more. Over the four years of war 11,000 (9%) of the 120,000 African soldiers who were recruited to fight for Britain in East Africa died, and some 95,000 (also about 9%) of the one million Africans who were conscripted to serve as porters. Some 200,000 of the conscripted porters were from Nyasaland – a good half of the colony's adult male population. Famines caused by the absence and loss of so many men led to widespread sickness and deaths, aggravated in 1918 by the global flu epidemic. Leys later remarked that 'war is a word which Europeans in Eastern Africa should never mention in the hearing of Africans without shame'.[76]

The Chilembwe rising

The onset of the war was the context of a second event which had a major impact on Leys' thinking. In January 1915 an American-educated minister called John Chilembwe, the founder and leader of an independent church in the south of Nyasaland, organised a revolt against the government. The impact of the war on the population was one trigger for this: Chilembwe wrote a letter to the *Nyasaland Times* protesting against the loss of African lives at Karonga (the letter was censored). A longer-running cause was the abusive treatment of the workers on the tobacco plantation at Magomero, next door to Chilembwe's church, one of the many vast tracts of the southern highlands of Nyasaland that had been given to European planters and corporations in the 1890s. Alexander Bruce, who owned several of these estates, opposed education for Africans and would not allow any schools or churches to be built on the Magomero estate. The estate manager also exploited the workers, cheating them in various ways, and beat them. A third factor was the manager's racist hostility towards the relatively well-educated and 'westernised' Chilembwe, an attitude shared by the administration and other whites.

Chilembwe decided that a revolution was needed and in late January 1915 launched an attack on the estate; the manager was decapitated and four other employees were killed. Attacks were supposed to take place simultaneously on other estates, and were to have led to a general rebellion, but this failed to materialise. After preaching a sermon, with the manager's severed head displayed to the congregation on a pole, Chilembwe fled, but was hunted down and shot dead, along with many of his followers, in the reprisals that followed. Some fifty suspected participants were shot out of hand; thirty-six were hanged after 'summary' trials, some in public; 300 were sentenced to long prison sentences and flogged; villagers' huts were burned, and a collective fine was imposed.[77]

Leys went to Zomba, then the administrative capital, and interviewed some of the survivors in prison there. Nine years later he included a short account of the rising in his book, *Kenya*. He identified four related causes. The first was 'the existence of Africans with knowledge and ability' who were denied a chance to play a role in public life that matched their influence on African opinion. 'It is unreasonable', he observed with his trademark irony, 'to expect that missions can protect all these men [their educated graduates] from the vice of ambition'.[78] Worse still, 'many Europeans in Africa think it good form to be rude to educated Africans'. In a letter Leys sent to the Colonial Secretary in 1918, discussed below, he added a story that linked this behaviour directly to the Chilembwe rising:

> A certain officer once told me that he had had a correspondence with John Chilembwe. Misled by the style of the letters, he at first answered them as he would have answered the letters of a European. But, as he told me, when he learned who his correspondent was, he soon put him in his place. That officer had his share in the rising.[79]

The second cause was 'the ignorance and lawlessness' of Chilembwe's followers, who were ignorant because they were denied schooling. The owner of the Magomero estate was opposed to education for Africans and would not allow schools on the estate. From his earliest days in Chinde Leys had seen that education was the key to enabling Africans to adapt to modernity; now he saw that unless it was provided on a large scale, and soon, the educated minority was liable to lead the uneducated majority in uprisings that could only end in disaster.

The third cause was economic injustice:

> The great majority of those concerned in [the rising] were serfs surrounded by people living rent-free [the European land-owners]. Chilembwe no doubt dreamed of an Africa for Africans, but the bait he tempted his followers with was land of their own, and release from the necessity of work without wages in order to pay rent and taxes.[80]

The fourth cause was 'the kind of treatment given to the Africans on the estate by the European staff' – i.e. routine brutality, which a subsequent official inquiry documented, but did nothing to stop.

Leys' analysis has been confirmed by later research.* He thought Chilembwe's rising represented a new phase of African resistance, quite different from what he had witnessed in Kisii. Later scholars and activists have agreed. And although Leys may not have known it, his account of the rising in *Kenya* was included word for word by C.L.R. James in his 1938 book, *A History of Negro Revolt* (republished after the war as *A History of Pan-African Revolt*), a founding text of Pan-

---

* Shepperson and Price concluded in 1958 that Leys' 'pioneer analysis' was 'in many ways still the best'(pp. 253-54), and treated it as a primary source. Landeg White's 1987 oral history study of the village on the estate also seems to confirm it (*Magomero*, Cambridge: Cambridge University Press, 1987.)

Africanism, and so passed into the historical memory of anti-racists generally.[81] In Nyasaland the rising became the founding event in the ideology of the Nyasaland African Congress, which in 1959 broke the grip of the settler-controlled Central African Federation and won independence for Malawi. Chilembwe's portrait is on Malawi's banknotes today.

Leys saw that the rising was a predictable response to rule by foreigners founded on racism and injustice, and letters he was receiving from friends in Kenya reinforced his fear that risings were already brewing there. He came to think that it might be only through violence that Africans could win their right to self-rule, but he hated violence, and had seen the price they would have to pay. For some time he continued to hope that a better-informed and wiser government in London would avert it.

The letter to the Colonial Secretary

In late 1917 Leys was on leave in Britain, waiting to hear whether he would be going back to Nyasaland, or be invalided out; he had had a second attack of Blackwater fever, and had also developed a chronic lung problem. While he was in London he learned that the Kenyan authorities had received warning of growing discontent and were making a large permanent increase in the strength of the King's African Rifles (an East Africa-wide standing army of African troops with white officers) so as to be able to crush any rising.[82] He talked with a number of well-connected people who urged him to share his analysis and fears with the Colonial Office. Since the senior officials in Nairobi identified closely with the settlers and were unlikely to tell the Colonial Office how things looked from the standpoint of the Africans, he felt he must try, so he spent the next three months composing a 45-page analysis of the situation in Kenya in the form of a letter to the Secretary of State. He finished it in February 1918 and sent it to Gilbert Murray, asking him to send it on to the Colonial Office for him with a word of endorsement. It is not certain that it reached the Colonial Office at the time – in the 1970s John Cell found that there was no official record of it. In due course the officials did read it, but as Leys later remarked, it had 'as little influence on the Colonial Office as an incantation'.[83]

But almost everything Leys wrote in *Kenya*, published six years later, the book which more than anything else made settler colonialism in Kenya the focus of anti-colonial activism in Britain in the 1930s, was prefigured in the letter to the Colonial Secretary in 1918. In fact, it prefigured everything he wrote for the rest of his life. The three books, dozens of articles and pamphlets, and hundreds of letters, that he wrote between 1918 and his death in 1944, were all essentially restatements, for different audiences, of the ideas he had crystallised during his exile in Nyasaland, and which he summed up in the letter. On the other hand there is also little in the letter that was not itself prefigured in Leys' Mombasa report, and in his letters to Gilbert Murray. His thinking continually evolved, from his arrival in Africa in 1901 until 1941, when he wrote his last book. His belief that Africans had the same capacities as other humans gradually developed into certainty, and his initial belief that the Empire was meant to help them gave way to the realisation that it served only the interests of the colonisers. But the moral premises and the central themes of his thinking stayed constant.

John Cell thought that the compressed form of Leys' letter to the Colonial Secretary made it 'more powerful and incisive' than *Kenya*. What strikes me, rather, is that it is so finely attuned to the readers Leys wanted to reach – namely, the senior civil servants in the Colonial Office. The Permanent Under-Secretary, Sir George Fiddes, was an Oxford-educated classical scholar, and Fiddes' immediate subordinates had similar backgrounds. The letter was really written for them, not the Colonial Secretary of the time, an ardent imperialist called Walter Long, who would never see it. Every sentence is in tone and style what these civil servants would have found familiar and legitimate. Far from being always concise, parts of it, such as a disquisition on the role of Christianity and Islam, have a quite leisurely philosophical quality, reminiscent of passages in the works of John Locke or J. S. Mill. But other passages are succinct and direct. Like Gilbert Murray and R. H. Tawney and the other people in London who had urged Leys to write it, the civil servants in charge of policy in Kenya would have found the letter's argument hard to resist. It politely rubbed their noses in what life was really like for Africans under settler colonialism in Kenya. It was nothing like what their colleagues in Nairobi told them, and it suggested that their Kenya policy was bound to end in disaster. It must have made some of them very uncomfortable. But what did this disgraced doctor from Nyasaland really know? The Colonial Office never acknowledged receipt of the letter. After some months Leys raised the stakes by asking if he could publish it. The answer from the Assistant Under-

Secretary was that he should first submit it to the Governor of Nyasaland, whose servant he still was – in other words, no.[84] The Colonial Office had read it and they found it dangerous.

The letter noted that the government had been warned that 'disturbances' were feared, and set out to try to make the officials understand the causes of the discontent by telling them things that were never mentioned in the dispatches they received from Nairobi; both because the Governor and his senior officials were committed to supporting the settlers, and because hardly anyone in the senior administration in Nairobi had a really close knowledge of the people they governed. It also set the Kenya situation in a broad historical context, including parallels between British rule in Kenya and Rome's management of the Roman Empire, which would be familiar and persuasive to the classicists in the Colonial Office.

The causes of unrest were discussed in eight 'chapters'.[85] The first was economic: Africans' lack of sufficient and secure land, and forced labour.

> There is no slavery under our flag. But labour is performed under conditions which produce and even exaggerate some of the evils of slavery... It is most important to realise that we are dealing with men as moved by impersonal economic forces and not by either philanthropy or cruelty. The motive of the West African slave trade was not race hatred but profit. Three generations ago it was believed that by preventing the ownership of the person slavery would be abolished. Servile conditions of a new type have arisen, in consequence of new and unforeseen factors. These new factors are the ownership of immense areas of land by Europeans in tropical Africa, the adoption by Government of the duty of helping European owners to develop their land, and the system of direct taxation.

Africans were compelled to work for European landowners to get cash to pay a tax based on their family homes (the 'hut tax'). When that didn't produce as much labour as the settlers needed, magistrates (who doubled as District Officers) and the chiefs (the District Officers' agents) 'encouraged' men to go to work, which in reality amounted to an order with serious consequences if it was not complied with. Wage labour was also unregulated, so that the working and living conditions of the labourers on European farms were wretched; 'the physical condition of unskilled labourers when they return home is markedly inferior to their condition on leaving home.

One can always tell in which direction men are going when one meets a gang resting on the road from the appearance of the men'. And labour procured in this way was mostly 'of poor quality. Many go to work with the intention of doing as little as possible… Hence frequent fines and floggings… I have never met anyone in British East Africa familiar with native opinion there who knew of any tribe that would not prefer to see all Europeans leave the country…' If serious trouble was to be avoided in the next few years it was necessary 'at once to make labour free in fact and everywhere; to forbid and strictly enforce the prohibition of every kind of influence by magistrates and other government agents over the free choice of natives'.

But, Leys argued, while economic injustice and hardship was the simplest factor in causing unrest, it was not the most important in the long run. More important, and more calculated to touch a nerve in the Colonial Office, which was running an Empire that was expected to last for generations, if not for ever, were larger historical forces that were rapidly destroying all social and religious institutions and ties in Africa, and undermining the essential foundations of the Empire's stability.

> When barbarians are turned by the hundred thousand into a vagrant proletariat, when not only the deliberate influence of Europeans, in religion, in government, and in industry, but even every meeting point between men of different tribes and traditions destroys superstitions that gave security to property, when the new conditions of life make thousands every year forget their families forever, the cement that makes government of any kind possible, is being dissolved… Society becomes atomic, a mere aggregation of individuals enslaved by instincts and appetites, and the social virtues which alone make men good subjects of the state disappear…

The governments in the British colonies in East Africa recognised the danger of social disruption, Leys acknowledged, but their response was always to try to preserve the tribal system, and strengthen the power of chiefs. That was worse than useless. In areas where chiefs had existed before the British came they now served as government agents and had less and less popular support; while the Kikuyu, accounting for about a third of Kenya's population, had no chiefs before the British came. Their chiefs had been created by the British and enjoyed no traditional authority. Giving chiefs more powers just made them even more unpopular. And tribal life itself was fast dissolving. Leys saw no reason to regret this. It had offered social cohesion, but at the price of conformity and superstition. 'The old order', he wrote, is already in many tribes moribund, and is everywhere doomed. It deserves a euthanasia'.

Another section of the letter was devoted to the Chilembwe rising, to illustrate the way in which anomic conditions predictably bred insurrection. But all the remaining sections were devoted to what he insisted – in terms that would have been very familiar to his readers from the recent and continuing struggles over the franchise in Britain – were the essential foundations of political loyalty: religion, education, and, in all spheres, government policies closely attuned to the needs and feelings of the people.

> The loyal are those who feel their government, even if they think it a bad government, to be their own, whether made by them or for them; the disloyal those who feel they are governed by strangers, however wisely they may govern… the aim of governments in Eastern Africa must be one of acclimatisation, of adaptation of feelings and beliefs widely different from those natural to a governing race or caste [such as the one his Colonial Office readers belonged to]. Governments must do more than take directly on themselves the duty of sharing the knowledge and the arts and the instruments of civilized life according to the measure of the capacity of their subjects. All that they must carefully undertake. But in addition the spirit of government must be African… in the sense that there must be as instant and intimate a response to the states of mind of the governed as in the case of governments by the governed themselves. If governments cannot be by the people they must be with and in the people.

In East Africa this principle was being wantonly disregarded. In one of several prescient passages Leys argued that unless it was followed, colonial rule would give way to nationalism:

> No alien bureaucracy [i.e. no empire] has ever inspired gratitude or loyalty. Yet without such a basis of loyalty government is in a condition of permanent estrangement from its subjects. Elsewhere, in the result, the bureaucracy is superseded [a reference to the Austro-Hungarian, Russian and Turkish empires, which had all just collapsed]. In Africa, so far as our vision goes, it must persist. It must find its own escape from the riddles of nationalism, an apparition that always takes a bureaucracy by surprise. It is certain that national feeling will pervade all the tribes from Kenia [sic] to the Zambezi during the next generation. Presuming that the solution

of self-government is impossible, how are we to meet that African nationalism?

Did Leys really presume self-government was impossible? He was beginning to think it was not only possible, in the sense that Africans were fully capable of it, but inevitable, and sooner rather than later. But it was a fair presumption that the Colonial Office thought it impossible, and he wanted his analysis to be taken seriously. So he urged the need for local councils to be set up, open to everyone in a district, where people could express their opinions and through which they could take on the management of local public health and other local issues (as he had recommended in his Memorandum on Mombasa seven years earlier). The 'inevitable alternative' to such 'embryonic bodies of local government' was secret societies.

> These already exist. They are probably always seditious. They are certain to spread and multiply until an alternative means of expression is provided. It is only through such local bodies that Government will become native to the soil. It is through them alone that the more intelligent, who are also the most restless, of natives will find their place of natural responsibility and a bond both to their own people and the Government. And if they are set up without delay, they will be channels, dug before the flood comes, through which the Government may lead the developing sense of race and nationality.

This sounds more like Margery Perham, the leading British authority on colonial administration in the 1940s, than Leys in 1918 – a sketch of how the Empire might wind itself down peacefully, a sketch that he knew the Colonial Office – not to mention 'Nairobi' – would say was 'idealistic' and impractical. He put it in to sound reasonable. What he really wanted was for the officials to understand what was at stake, and this was also why he disavowed having any position on the issue of self-rule:

> My argument is based on no presumption of what the future may bring. The African may or may not prove to be capable, in the phrase of the day, of self-determination. He is certainly capable of protest by insurrection against what he conceives to be wrong determination. Both the religions he is absorbing [Christianity and Islam] teach him that he is capable of more than a mere political equality with Europeans… In a standard book upon Nyasaland the native is described as a person most wisely treated

like a dog to which one has the friendliest of feelings, wayward, quarrelsome, but happy when fed, obedient under discipline, submissive to direction because incapable of self-direction. It would be hypocrisy to pretend that such a conception of native mentality has not been influential and even prevalent among those who have hitherto had the direction and shaped the policy of our governments. In permitting it to continue to influence events our country encourages the one means that, unfortunately, man can always use to prove that he is not canine but human, and not slave but free, the murder of his master.

This, he added, was already a real danger in Kenya. And the murders happened as he had predicted. In 1952-54 a total of 32 Europeans were murdered, in several cases by their own servants.

Some things in the letter to the Colonial Secretary were exaggerated – for example the suggestion that migrant workers in Kenya tended to forget their families for ever, like the children taken captive down-river to Chinde – and things on which Leys' views were already changing, such as Africans' capacity for self-rule. A few expressions, such as referring to Africans as 'barbarians', may have been sops to his intended readers in the Colonial Office; a few months later, in a letter to Gilbert Murray, he was using the term very differently, to describe the incoming Kenya Governor, General Northey: 'a pretty typical regular soldier, a barbarian. He will do what he can to make the damned niggers work in spite of the obstruction of the sentimentalists….'.*[86] Or perhaps these expressions indicate that he still had some imperialist assumptions to shed. But the substance of the letter to the Colonial Secretary expressed as clearly as he could the position he had arrived at, and that he would lay out again in *Kenya* six years later.

---

* True to Leys' expectations, the following year Northey issued a notorious circular obliging all administrative officers and chiefs to use all their power to get Africans, including women and children, to go and work on settler farms. It was later withdrawn thanks largely to a campaign against it in Britain, prompted by Leys and organised by J.H. Oldham.

5: Brailsford

Gilbert Murray praised the letter to the Colonial Secretary warmly, calling it 'persuasive'. Leys replied: 'You can have no idea how your word of commendation has cheered me'.[87] He would like more than anything to write a book. To turn the letter into a book, he thought, 'perhaps nearly as long again, would take three months more'. But while he remained in the colonial service it was impossible: 'the kind of man I would have to submit my writing to – and I can only write one kind of stuff – would think it horrible blasphemy'. He could resign, and 'it wouldn't be funking, because in the Service I am damned for good and all. I am not wanted. I am kept at prentice work'. But he had no money, and he was still seven years short of being eligible for a pension.

The dilemma was resolved by what he called his 'damaged lung' (probably tuberculosis), and the fact that he had twice been dangerously ill with Blackwater Fever during his last posting in Nyasaland. In the spring of 1918, the Colonial Office doctor gave him a further six months' leave, during which he took a summer job as a locum for a GP in Scotland who had been called up to serve in France; but before the six months were up he was allowed to retire, with a pension of £200 a year. With £500 he had saved, and with loans from friends, he was able to buy a small general practice in Brailsford, a village near Derby – 'an England I always had thought existed only on Christmas cards', he told Murray.[88] The practice income plus his pension would give him and Janey enough to live on, and put Nanice through university, but still leave him time to write.

So began the second half of Leys' working life. For his years in Africa we have to imagine everything – the government housing with the servants' quarters at the back, the mission stations in the bush, the heat at the coast and the cold in the highlands, the dusty red earth roads, the Indian *dukas*, and the whole peculiar, alienated life of 20,000 expatriate whites among a population of two and a half million Africans subject to their control. His years in England are also remote now, but easier for a reader in Britain, at least, to envisage, and slightly better documented than the African years, since some people who knew him in England have left some records; and a few, including his daughter Nanice and his brother Duncan, and some of his Brailsford patients, were still alive in the 1970s, and talked to the historians John Cell and Diana Wylie. We can imagine the doctor's large, comfortable, (rented) house in Brailsford, with a side entrance to the surgery; the cottage in the grounds where Monica and Fred, the cook and gardener, lived; the twice daily visits of the postman, delivering bundles of letters; the occasional visits of a message boy with a telegram (none of Leys' letters ever mentions phone calls).

He still wanted to write a book, but it would take him four years from the time he and Janey settled in Brailsford to start writing it. At first the practice demanded a lot of work. The previous GP had run it down: in the first six months Leys' net income from it was £50 (equivalent to about £13,000 in 1924).[89] Even when he had built it up it was never lucrative, thanks to his socialist politics. He would give his patients, who were mostly farm labourers covered by the limited health insurance system introduced in 1911, a pamphlet, written by himself and published by the Independent Labour Party, called 'Why the Land Worker is Poor'. Not surprisingly landowners and farmers went to doctors with sounder politics. And the work could sometimes be demanding: on one day in 1931, he reported in a letter to his friend Winifred Holtby, he had 27 houses to visit.[90]

His feeling that the situation in Kenya was urgent also clashed with the plan to write a book. He spent most of his free time agitating: writing articles for any publication that asked – he wrote at least forty between 1919 and 1938[91] and a steady flow of letters to editors; getting questions asked in parliament; and, above all, trying to influence the Labour Party, which he was sure was going to come to power soon: 'In Glasgow 80% of manual workers and 50% of small business people will vote Labour next election', he told Murray in 1918. 'So far as Scotland goes I doubt whether anything the Labour Party can do will prevent them from winning most of the seats in Parliament in a few years – anything except timidity' – which proved accurate.[92] Working with Leonard Woolf and Arthur Creech Jones (later the Colonial Secretary in the post-war Attlee government) on the party's Advisory Committee on Imperial Questions, Leys and McGregor Ross, the former Director of Public Works in Kenya, succeeded in getting the Party officially committed to a radical change of direction in colonial policy. Leys stopped writing frequently to Gilbert Murray and began a voluminous correspondence with a range of people who were active on colonial issues. In 1921 he helped W. E. B. Du Bois find a venue in London for the second Pan-African Congress, and spoke at it himself.

The formation of the Congress excited him intensely. He told the Liberal MP Borden Turner: 'So far it is only educated negroes who are attached to the movement. But plans are being laid for a new liberation campaign, to be preached to Africans, not to Europeans, and to every African. The twentieth century will find the African no longer the patient docile drudge he has been.'[93]

He told J.H. Oldham, the Secretary of the Conference of Church Missionary Societies: 'I wish you could have been at the Pan African. I was more deeply moved than ever in my life since boyhood'.[94] He made monthly visits by train to London for meetings of the Advisory Committee, and, less frequently, for the Mandates Committee of the League of Nations Union, and occasionally for other groups too – although only if he thought his views had a good chance of being accepted. In September 1920, responding to a request from Oldham to meet the Bishop of Zanzibar and other churchmen to discuss forced labour in Kenya, he said such meetings meant 'a day in London, nine hours in a train, an expenditure of 50/-, no other work done that day' and cost him £40-50 a year. 'If I was rich… I would gladly accept your invitation. As it is I am afraid I would find myself imperfectly in agreement with others present'. And then his usual sticking-point: 'The B. of Zanzibar's articles don't express my mind at all. He attributes to the African a different nature from the European's. I find it hopeless to look for a common policy for Africans with those who think so.'[95]

Leys' resistance to collaborating with people to try to achieve changes within the framework of the existing system was reinforced by his experience on the Mandates Committee of the League of Nations Union at about the same time. His draft for a new policy for the former German African colonies that were now British mandate territories was unanimously accepted by the Committee. But it was then 'emasculated' by the League's Executive, to make it something that the British and French governments could agree on. Leys told Gilbert Murray, who was also on the Committee: 'I would never have wasted my time and money in these visits to London if I had thought the mandates we were to draft were to be conditional on what the British and French Govts. of the day would approve. They are governing Africa now in the way they think wise and right. The mandate we were told to draft was to describe quite another way'.[96]

His medical practice was relatively small but it formed the structure of his working week. His patients were spread over a six-mile area, and he used to visit them on a motorbike until 1923, when he had an accident and broke his thigh, leaving him with one leg shorter than the other. He also had a car, in which he gave rides to children in the village on Saturdays. Former patients remembered his socialism ('If you talked to him about politics you'd have Labour drummed into you') and approved of it when it was a matter of local class relations: thirty-five years later they still remembered that he had once told a 'county lady', who had come to the house for medical advice, to come back in his office hours, saying 'only friends of my wife come to the door'.[97] Except for having to send bills out every quarter, which he hated doing because so many of his patients were poor, he seems to have enjoyed the work.

He treated many of his patients' families for nothing, since only employees, and not their dependants, were covered by the state health insurance scheme at the time; he gave them medicines free, and never sent a bill if a patient died. His half-brother Duncan, who had acted as a locum for him in 1924, thought he was 'probably not a very good doctor but infinitely conscientious and human'.[98] His daughter Nanice remembered that 'old men and women would come out to receive remedies and painkillers for their chronic complaints'.

> He knew them all well and many of their problems apart from the medical ones and came to have a very intimate knowledge of the lives of the rural poor. He said that they were very like Africans, both being at that time a deprived and inarticulate people with their potential abilities stunted and discouraged.[99]

A case in point is mentioned in a letter to Holtby written in 1932. One of his patients had new-born twins.

> One day I was talking to their father about the difficulty of waking every two hours at night to feed them. He took me up wrongly, thinking I was concerned about his wife's rest and said with a laugh that I needn't worry as nothing would ever disturb either of them at night. In the end it was Sunday morning before I got the unworthy parents to let me take the little girl to the hospital where she died in a few hours. And I took the little boy yesterday. This morning the sister agreed with me that he is moderately

safe to live. So helpless are the parents that they asked me to bring home the dead body of the girl, which now lies on my usual chair in our sitting room.[100]

He thought he was disliked, on account of his impatience and brusque manners, whereas Janey was well liked.[101] But he seems to have been well enough liked, as well as respected; his feeling that he was disliked seems likely to have reflected his unhappiness about charging for his services. His bluntness, and his impatience with muddled thinking, did put some people off, but he got on well with intelligent people of all classes. Mrs Meynell, a 'county' lady whose servants were his patients, became a good friend, as did George Rodgers, a former drover, interviewed by Diana Wylie in 1973. He was good with old ladies, Nanice said, in her more sceptical way, 'and with children before they began to think for themselves'. He kept a bottle of sweets in his car to give to his patients. He also loved animals. A dog or a cat features in several of the few surviving photos of him.

His marriage was not ideal. Janey would have preferred to spend her life as the wife of a medical officer in Africa, rather than of a driven political campaigner.[102] She wasn't his intellectual companion, but nor was she a self-effacing drudge, and he never forgot how she had supported him emotionally through the years of his exile in Nyasaland, but there was a lack of deep rapport. She read all his letters aloud to him over breakfast, which no doubt served as kind of guarantee of trust. They shared the pleasure of Nanice's visits from London, where she was a hospital social worker, and they had quite frequent visitors, including Paul Robeson and the socialist journalist Leonard Barnes, among other notables. Even Bishop Willis of Uganda, who at one time had been seen by Norman as anything but a supporter of African liberation, stayed with them in Brailsford.

They had less help than they had had in Africa, but they had two servants, Monica and Fred. Having a cook/housemaid and a gardener was normal for a professional family at the time, but Monica, especially, was very much part of the household. In August 1931 Leys reported that 'Monica's mother paid us a visit for a few days. She had nine children. When two had come her husband had 19/- a week and when the youngest had come he had 28/-. Yet Mrs Shaw is withal a dignified old dame who might be a peeress.'[103] In a studio portrait of the family taken around 1930 Monica and Fred are included, in their Sunday best – Fred wearing a jacket he has long grown out of and looking very determined to live up to the occasion.

In Brailsford Leys had, for the first time since he left Glasgow, some continuing family contact. Kenneth was in Oxford. Norman admired Kenneth's disinterestedness, and his scholarship, and was always conscious of his generosity in sending him books throughout his time in Africa. Kenneth also did some research for *Kenya*, and read and commented on the drafts of both *Kenya* and Norman's second book, *A Last Chance in Kenya*. In the preface to *Kenya* Norman wrote that he had wanted Kenneth's name to be on the title page. Yet they were not close. He thought that Kenneth had become a different, unknowable, person. Kenneth's wife died in a road accident, leaving him with a severely mentally disabled daughter whom he persisted in believing, against all the evidence, was not really disabled. Norman found this painfully irrational. Then, in 1933, Kenneth surprised him by announcing that he was getting married again, to Agnes Sandys, a much younger, beautiful and vivacious history don who had tutored Nanice at Oxford. Rather than being happy for Kenneth, Norman was worried. He foresaw the new wife sacrificing herself to Kenneth's irrational and obsessive system of care for his daughter. He wrote to Holtby:

> I am terrified for the poor woman. It isn't merely that K. though younger than me is far more completely dried up and ancient. The greater trouble is that he is an actor. As our sister Helen [his half-sister] once said, he never does anything else so that the real K. is undiscoverable. First he set himself to become a don and at 25 spoke behaved and thought quite differently from what he did at 20. At his wife's funeral he wore a mask so complete it was almost hilarious. But the child is the terrible problem. Driven from one fantastic theory about her condition after another by patent facts, he now tells people that she has aesthetic sensibilities greater than normal! ... My one hope is that Miss S. who is a delightful person may turn K. into yet another personification.[104]

He soon decided that his fears had been unjustified: Kenneth's new wife Agnes seemed to be in charge, he wrote. And Kenneth did take on a new persona. He took Holy Orders and became the vicar of a remote Church of England parish in the Lake District, with a tiny mediaeval church. But Agnes did look after him and his daughter in the large, barely heated Georgian rectory across the river from the church, until he died.

Leys' relationship with his half-brother Duncan was very different. When Leys was back in Britain in 1918, Duncan was on sick leave from the front in France suffering from shell-shock. Norman did what he could to help him and Duncan, aged 21, found in his 43-year old half-brother something of a father-substitute, much as Norman had found one in Gilbert Murray. Norman was a socialist, and Duncan had come out of the war a socialist, and no longer a Catholic. There was a strong meeting of minds. Duncan married in 1928 and from 1932 to 1938 he and his young family lived in Birmingham, just fifty miles from Brailsford. They remained close, and Norman took a keen interest in Duncan's children until 1936, when he retired and moved with Janey to Yalding, in Kent.

It was in this much more supportive setting that Leys eventually got down to writing the book he had been contemplating ever since his exile to Karonga in 1913. In the preface he said it had been in preparation for fifteen years – i.e. since his arrival in the settler heartland of Kenya in 1908.

Norman Leys in Brailsford

6: Writing *Kenya*

Perhaps what delayed the writing of a book more than anything else was that Leys had been out of Kenya for so long. He knew quite enough to write short pieces: by April 1919 he had already published articles in the *Manchester Guardian*, *Truth*, the *International Review*, *New Europe*, the *Round Table*, and two missionary papers.[105] But for a book he needed more, and more up-to-date, information, which he had to get by writing to people in Kenya, which took time and didn't always yield usable data. One of the friends on whom he relied for accurate information was McGregor Ross, the Director of Public Works in Kenya, whom he had known since 1907 when he had treated him for malaria in Mombasa. Ross was very well informed and in 1923 he was unexpectedly back in England.

Ross had been a good ally in Kenya. A fellow Scot, an engineer, he had been promoted very early to become an extremely successful Director of Public Works. This gave him an ex officio seat on the Legislative and Executive Councils, where his stern opposition to land grabbing and other questionable transactions relating to public property, combined with a sure grasp of detail and a sharp tongue, made him increasingly unpopular with the kind of settler whose financial interests were hampered by town planning and land transaction rules. After one unsuccessful attempt to remove him, in 1923 the settlers on the Legislative Council passed a vote to cut his salary. The Governor failed to defend him, so Ross left.

Leys proposed that they write a book together over the summer, with a September deadline for a first draft. Ross was to cover the economy, production, and the settlers. Leys would draft chapters on the missions, the Maasai, the Chilembwe rising, and native life, custom and belief.[106] His half-brother Duncan, whom he had encouraged to study medicine, had recently qualified and was available to act as a locum for him ('encouraged' is actually not quite the right word. When Duncan asked for Norman's opinion on medicine as a career the characteristic reply was that it was 'a trade like any other'). Leys got down to work and by early September he was 'nearly up to programme'; but he had heard nothing from Ross, who had in fact not written anything. Why Ross failed to do what they had agreed is fairly clear. He had felt it was a good idea but he had had second thoughts, especially when Leys sent him what he had written so far and he realised that their views were too different (Leys said later that Ross had 'violently disapproved' of what he had written).[107] Ross had been part of the system in Kenya, as Leys later reflected, socially as well as professionally, in a way that Leys had never been. The Department of Public Works had a large workforce; Ross' job made him part of the administration, and the administration was committed to the settler model of development of Kenya. He saw the problem as one of a minority of greedy and unscrupulous settlers, not as a fundamentally unjust and unsustainable economic and social system. He may also have felt that he would not enjoy arguing with Leys, whose intellectual strength he was well aware of, and have begun to think of writing a different kind of book himself. But instead of writing to say he had had second thoughts he went on holiday, leaving his wife, Isabel, to respond to Leys' initially baffled inquiries and subsequent angry reproaches. By the middle of September it was clear to Leys that he was on his own. His readiness to risk friendships for what he saw as principle, and the tone of self-righteousness that sometimes went with it, are evident in his last letter to Isabel Ross. She had declared that the work would be bad for Ross's health. Leys replied that in his medically qualified opinion it would be good for him, but that if there was any cost it was worth paying. He himself would willingly give 'both my legs or life itself as the price of making the book as good as it might be':

> My wife knows that, regards me as unfit to do the job, believes, quite possibly correctly, that doing it will mean 5 hours sleep a night all winter instead of 7, and has quietly opposed the scheme all through. I have given in on most occasions when my wife and I have differed during the last 20 years. I only once regretted doing so afterwards. She is nearly always right. This time I have resolutely held out. I tell you that to explain what a gulf there is between your ideas and Mac's and mine. I blame myself of course for taking it for granted that you and he would attempt the job regardless of what it would cost. What <u>does</u> it matter what happens to us?[108]

He ended by saying that they must 'just make the best of what each can do and ignore everything personal' – including asking her not to care about 'the fact that I don't admire the way Mac made a promise and how he kept it'. Forgiveness was not one of Leys' strong points. On the other hand he didn't bear grudges; he made it up with Ross and continued to treat him as a friend, or at least an ally.

Leys' letters to Mrs Ross complaining about her husband's failure to do what he had promised are interesting for the light they shine on how he saw the project. Unlike the officials in the Colonial Office, to whom his letter to the Colonial Secretary had been addressed, and who knew a good deal about East Africa even if their knowledge was incomplete and biased, the readers of the book he and Ross were going to write would need a lot of additional background information. It had to be 'more of a picture, less of an argument', as he had envisaged it in a letter to Murray in 1918. It also had to engage the reader's interest, and this was extremely difficult. 'The only thing for us both to aim at', he told Isabel Ross, when he still had some slight hope that Ross would come round,

> is to give a perfectly accurate picture of the facts in their true proportions. And to use words successfully to that end is just as difficult as to use paints and brush to describe a face… I have wearied you both by trying to explain all this before. Let me try to define once more and for all what making such a book demands. It demands a holding of the facts clearly before the mind, so that every activity of the mind when engaged on the task is <u>solely</u> directed to seeing the truth of things. No sentence should ever be written that isn't as true as it can be made. And truth means both perfect clearness and perfect unity of all the elements in the attempt to depict it… Writing well isn't a thing for leisure moments.

Ross could well be excused for thinking this was sanctimonious nonsense, and for feeling he was well out of it. The curious thing was that in spite of having written what sounds like a formula for unreadability Leys went on to write a best-seller. Cell's verdict was correct: 'Literary skill and not, as Leys supposed, mere exposure of the facts made *Kenya* a commercial success in its own day and a classic worth reprinting in ours'.[109]

Leys worked through the winter and by the spring of 1924 had a reasonably complete draft which had been closely edited by Kenneth. Now he needed a publisher. He entered into negotiations with Allen & Unwin and asked Leonard Woolf, whom he had got to know through their joint efforts in the Labour Party's Advisory Committee, whether he should accept Allen & Unwin's offer. At that time unknown authors were expected to put significant sums of their own money into the cost of publication, getting it back with a profit if the book sold well, and losing some or all of it if it didn't. Woolf thought the terms Allen and Unwin were proposing were unreasonable (they included a commitment from Leys of £350, equivalent to about £27,000 in 2024) and proposed instead that *Kenya* should be published by the Hogarth Press, which he and Virginia had set up in 1917. Leys was surprised, though delighted. The Hogarth Press had never published a political book before: it had mainly published Virginia's novels and rather high-minded literary and philosophical works by their intellectual friends. 'I fear I had the idea', Leys told Woolf, 'that the publishing firm you have some connection with publishes only the kind of book that corresponds with olives and artichokes in diet'. (This was a measure of his closeness to Woolf. He only made jokes when writing to trusted friends).[110]

His friendship with the former Cambridge 'Apostle' Leonard Woolf, with his network of brilliant friends, from Lytton Strachey to Maynard Keynes, is at first sight surprising. True, both had first-hand experience of the Empire – while Leys was in Kenya, Woolf had been an administrator in Ceylon (Sri Lanka)– but what each got from their experience was different. Woolf came to despise his fellow administrators and the artificial life he and they had led, and to feel cynical about colonial rule; but unlike like Leys in Kenya he didn't research and analyse colonialism as it operated in Ceylon. It was only later, through meeting E. D. Morel and Leys and other anti-imperialists, and writing about imperialism for the Fabians, that he became an active anti-imperialist himself. But he and Leys had other things in common. Woolf was a Jew, while Leys was a poor country doctor; in different ways both were socially marginal in establishment circles. Woolf was adaptable, moving easily among the intellectuals and artists he and Virginia socialised with so energetically while being privately critical of their affectations. Leys was not adaptable, but he was no respecter of status and was quite at ease in Woolf's world, regularly making other people in it uncomfortable. They were both socialists, and like Leys Woolf had no illusions that significant changes of government policy could be achieved by private lobbying.[111]

When Woolf offered to publish *Kenya* he knew what he was doing, and Leys knew he could trust him. An edition of 1,000 copies was published in October 1924 and was sold out by the following April. A second edition was published in 1925 and a third, a cheap paperback edition, in 1926. That edition was still selling when Leys died in 1944. A fourth edition was published by Frank Cass in 1969.

A new form of slavery

Kenya was seven times as long as the letter to the Colonial Secretary, not twice as long, as Leys had once imagined it would need to be. The book was aimed, he told Woolf, at members of the Labour Party's Advisory Committee on Imperial Questions (of which Woolf was the secretary); at officials in London and Africa, at MPs, at some missionaries, at the editor of the *Manchester Guardian*, C.P. Scott, at experts like Woolf himself, and at friends: 'The book's chief purpose is to convince these various groups. Everything else is secondary'.[112] Kenya Colony was then little known – until 1920 it had been called the East Africa Protectorate – and to the extent that it was known it was as the home of a handful of British settlers struggling heroically to develop the country's potential, which its native population were seen as incapable of doing. This impression needed to be displaced by careful reframing. So the book opened with the observation that 'Near the beginning of the age of discovery a Papal Bull divided the countries then unknown between the kings of Spain and Portugal' – and reached the beginnings of Kenya's colonisation only sixty pages later. Happily, they are sixty beguiling pages, informative and sometimes moving, describing the European exploration of East Africa, African traditional society, and the devastation of the slave trade, before the arrival of European colonists imbued with a belief in racial superiority.

I'm not sure if *Kenya* is less powerful than the letter to the Colonial Secretary, as John Cell thought. It seems to me, rather, that it is equally well adapted to its different task. What it lacks, by comparison, in concision, it makes up for with pithy sentences and shafts of irony and satire. The style is sometimes faintly archaic, but somehow all the more engaging for it, and it achieves the author's fundamental aim – to establish inescapably in the reader's mind what Kenya Colony really was: 'an unprecedented economic system' that was nothing less than a new form of slavery:

> In our age alone has it been found possible for an oligarchy to obtain the profits of the labour of the governed of a different race, without creating property rights in their bodies. That is the unique feature of society in

Kenya… In a sense, the essence of the economic situation in Kenya is that it is the full and perfect expression of the capitalist system.[113]

It was quite an achievement to make liberals like Gilbert Murray and J. H. Oldham read this blunt assertion and come away not only convinced of its truth, but also feeling, as Leys insisted, that they were responsible for it. When he called what was happening in Kenya 'capitalist' it seemed no more than the correct name for the forces he showed to be at work there, and didn't incline them to dismiss the book as a communist tract. *Kenya* described how a good half of the country's productive land had been given to Europeans, and how the native population had been confined in 'reserves' which could be, and were, periodically reduced in size. It explained that all native men aged 16-30 (later raised to 40) had to pay either a hut or a poll (head) tax, in cash, which could only be earned by working for a European employer because alternative ways of raising the cash, such as by selling crops or livestock, were blocked by the shortage of land and the lack of roads in the reserves; moreover the production of high-value crops such as tea or coffee was explicitly reserved for Europeans. The book described how it had been made a crime, punishable by prison, for Africans to 'desert' before the end of their labour contracts; how they had to carry a certificate signed by their employers, which had to be produced to the police on demand and ensured that deserters were identified, caught, and jailed.* Wage levels were fixed by agreement between the settlers in each region; when too few Africans came looking for work on settler farms, instead of wages being raised, district officers and 'chiefs' were instructed to get men to go to work, which in practice meant using force, or the threat of it. The order given was that 'while no compulsion was to be used, "moral suasion" was to be resorted to', and chiefs were to be 'encouraged' to persuade their people to leave home to work for Europeans. 'How Mr Pecksniff would have enjoyed himself in Kenya in those days!', Leys remarked. 'With what a blessed unction would he have discoursed of encouragement and moral suasion!.. To the chiefs an order was an order and their salaries depended on their obeying orders'.[114]

An additional feature of the system was that not only were the settlers provided with the cheapest possible labour, but the workers'

---

* In 1923 the law was changed to make desertion a civil, not a criminal offence, one of the few positive reforms that were adopted in response to the critical view of Kenyan affairs that he and Ross had aroused in Britain (Norman Leys (1924) p. 207).

tax payments, plus their payment of the duty levied on imported goods such as hoes and blankets, accounted for two thirds of the colony's revenue, almost all of which was spent on services and subsidies to Europeans alone. And all this was justified in terms of the supposed ability of the settlers to out-produce peasant production, and the general superiority of the white race.

It was a perfect closed system. The settlers enjoyed 'all the advantages of a system of slavery with none of its disadvantages':

> The State sees to it that the bulk of men available as labourers seek employment, and both prosecutes and punishes them if they desert employment. The employer need neither buy his workmen, nor feed their dependants, nor support the workmen themselves in old age or sickness – all of these obligations which, under slavery, the slave-owner cannot escape. Instead he merely buys labour at his own price – wages being an unfortunate necessity to the revenue of the colony – and is perfectly sure of getting the labour so long as the Government remains under his control.[115]

Such was the core message of *Kenya*, by any measure a remarkable piece of political-economic analysis. But Leys was at pains to insist that the settlers were not evil men. 'It is necessary to state', he wrote,

> that the Europeans who live in Kenya are just ordinary people. Eager reformers at home may naturally assume that they are specially bad, or at least have more bad people among them than usual. They themselves think they deserve to have an influence in the colony... out of all proportion to their number. Both views are false. The great bulk of the Europeans in Kenya are neither more nor less virtuous, neither more nor less well educated, neither more nor less intelligent, than the people in any area in England or Scotland with a population of 10,000 souls [in 1921 the total white population of Kenya was 9,651]. One does not expect to find many people of exceptional ability in a town or district in England with a population of 10,000, and one does not find many in Kenya.[116]

It was the system that was evil. Brutal crimes were routinely committed against Africans. In 1907, while Leys was still in Mombasa, three Europeans seized three Kikuyu rickshaw drivers in Nairobi who two European women claimed had 'insulted' them, dragged them to Government House and flogged them in front of a crowd of cheering white onlookers. When they were brought to trial one of them explained that 'it has always been a first principle with me to flog a nigger on sight who insults a white woman'.[117] Murders of Africans by Europeans were not entirely uncommon, and were rarely punished. But Leys refused to see outrages of this kind, which aroused public opinion in Britain when they were reported there, as the central problem. He restricted himself to just two examples – without names – of murders of Africans by Europeans for which, as usual, all-white juries had refused to convict the murderers.. He had chosen these particular cases out of dozens, he wrote, to refute the idea that such crimes were committed by 'the less reputable kind of European'.

> It is not so. On the contrary, the more wealth and authority a European has in Kenya the more likely is he to fall to the temptations they bring. Of the two men whose cases have been described, one was the son of a bishop, the other the son of a peer. They had every advantage that birth and education can give. In fact they were not specially bad men. Some will regard that statement as preposterous, others as offensive. It is absolutely true. Their crimes, it is true, were revolting. The stain these crimes have left on the honour of the colony and the Empire is so dark that no man should read of them without vowing to make their repetition impossible. That is the motive of their inclusion in this narrative, perhaps the only justifiable motive.
>
> But the emotion that outrages arouse is by itself powerless and valueless…we shall not face the facts squarely unless we realise that the reason these crimes happen in Kenya and do not happen in England is not that Europeans in Kenya are by nature specially cruel, or unjust, but that they live under conditions that thrust such crimes into their minds and drive them to commit them. In a word, many such crimes are inevitable wherever men are given both political control over a subject people and the opportunity to profit by their labour.[118]

If *Kenya* marked a further development in Leys' thinking, it was most obvious in the chapters that he had expected Ross to write. He now linked the economic with the political elements of his analysis, showing that it rested on a contradiction:

> The very reason that was held to justify the alienation of land to Europeans was the fact that the country was half empty of people… There really was more land than the Africans of Kenya could use. But that very land that was in excess of their needs is precisely the area which the government has for twenty years by every means in its power been trying to make them work upon for the profit not of themselves but of European

grantees... And now, after twenty years, the 7487 square miles of alienated land are occupied by, and 335 of them are cultivated by, no more, and by now probably less, than 1893 Europeans. The real cultivators of the 335 square miles of alien land under cultivation are of course the fifty or sixty thousand African employees who work for wages, employed, most of them, in growing crops which they could and often do grow just as well at home.[119]

The system was clearly unsustainable, as well as intolerable. The settlers could only increase production by getting more work out of Africans, and the limits to that had already been reached: they could not afford to pay higher wages, and Africans could not afford to do more wage work unless they were paid more. The only question was whether the contradiction would be resolved by a voluntary change of policy on the part of the British government, or by violence on the part of the Africans. Colonial rule bred a demand for freedom, and the Chilembwe rising in Nyasaland had been a portent.

In 1921 a young government telephonist called Harry Thuku had founded the Young Kikuyu Association to agitate for more land for the Kikuyu and an end to the abusive labour system and the high rate of taxation. There was a general shortage of labour and in 1920, in response to settler pressure, the administration increased the hut tax from 12s to 16s, a 30% increase, with a view to making Africans provide more work. On top of this, in 1921 the settlers in some areas decided to cut wages by a third. Unsurprisingly the YKA grew rapidly, and in 1922 Thuku was arrested. Several thousand people, mainly women, gathered outside the police station in Nairobi to demand his release. The police fired into the crowd, killing 25 people and wounding many more. Thuku was exiled to Kismayu, in British-controlled Jubaland (now in Somalia), and remained detained without charge in a series of similarly remote locations for the next eight years. The hut tax was reduced back to 12s. Leys asked: '...will Africans in Kenya always submit passively to the system of life we have imposed on them?... Was the Thuku affair a precursor of larger movements perhaps even now fermenting in Kenya...?'[120] The lesson he invited his readers to draw has often been quoted:

> If, some morning, the readers of this book open their morning paper over their breakfast coffee and read of some other Chilembwe or Thuku they must not expect that some particular act of policy or the unwisdom of some Governor is the cause. They should look on the rising as a by-

product of the system under which the very coffee they are drinking is produced. Nor must they blame Governor and Colonial Secretary for repressing the rising with slaughter. That is the kindest way of dealing with native risings. The fact that most of the people who engage in them are in no real sense criminally inclined makes it no less necessary to shoot them. Those who object to the shooting must go deeper. There would be no native risings in Africa if most of the money raised by the taxation of natives were spent on native education, if every family had as much rent-free land as it could use, and if those Africans who prefer to live and work at home were left undisturbed by Europeans who think Africans ought to work for them instead of developing land of their own.[121]

This was the key question Leys wanted MPs, officials, editors and the like to confront, and to recognise their own complicity in what made a rising likely. It sounds preachy, yet it wasn't. It's hard to put a finger on the reason. It has a good deal to do with Leys' spare style, combining a clear recounting of facts with engaging historical comparisons and analogies: sprinkled with irony and satire, *Kenya* delivered unpalatable truths in a way that made them hard to deny. The liberal-minded reader was assumed to be with the author from the start: he or she would naturally share his feelings and values, and feel obliged to shoulder the responsibility of doing something about what was described. There was never an obvious point where they could say no. They were even trusted to accept mild teasing. In the chapter on missions, for instance, Leys remarked that 'the people who first become Christian in a tribe are apt to be of a type the very opposite to the commonest types of Church member found at home. They are people with unusual independence of mind and with unusual appetites for new ideas and ideals'. What good English liberal was going to take offence? The settler leadership was introduced as merely 'a much more important minority' than the big game-shooting element, which 'may be disregarded'. They were 'the public school and ex-officer type':

> They provide the country with horses for racing and polo. They also impart the pepper and ginger which form so large an ingredient in colonial politics. A number of them are very rich, and probably most have incomes from property outside the colony. To the earlier arrivals of this group the whole government of the country has gradually fallen. To them belong the largest and the best estates. This kind of man is the lineal descendant of the old gentlemen adventurers, who colonised Virginia,

singed the King of Spain's beard, exacted homage from those people who are compendiously called 'natives' and ended their careers, some in Westminster Abbey, some at a yard arm.

Thus the settlers' leaders, whom the British press represented as the most eminent of the farmers wresting a difficult living from the bush, were put precisely in their place.

Kenya had its final revision in August 1924, and was published in October. Leys being Leys, the production process saw a few prickly moments. He was probably the first Hogarth Press author to whom money mattered a great deal, and he found Woolf's attitude to reporting sales and receipts, and what was due to himself, unacceptably casual. He himself was very particular. For example, in November 1924, just after publication, he wrote to Woolf saying that 'On Tuesday morning you will receive from an uncle of mine in Glasgow – a real uncle, not a pawnbroker – a cheque which together with the enclosed will bring my payment to you to £10 more than the sum you mentioned'.[122] But in March 1925 he managed to give Woolf some offence over the accounting. 'Why suggest that I called you a liar or wrote anything suggesting that you might be?', he wrote.[123] All he had complained of, he said, was that Woolf had used 'inconsistent and to some extent ambiguous language on a matter of great importance to me. I won't refer to the matter any more'. But then he added, characteristically: 'I hope you will not regard my still unanswered questions as so unreasonable as to refuse to answer them. For example did you or did you not send copies for review to the papers of which I sent you a list, in particular...[etc]'. But as with Ross, he didn't see the incident as standing in the way of friendship, and Woolf remained a good friend to the end. He had learned why money mattered to Leys and in 1943, when Leys was sick and had hospital bills to pay, he wrote to ask whether he had enough to live on, in a way that made Leys grateful.[124]

Three years after *Kenya* first appeared Ross published his own book, *Kenya from Within*.[125] It was a more orthodox and more detailed account of recent Kenyan history, well documented and well written, and raised the same issues of justice and fairness. On topics especially close to Ross' heart, such as taxation, and the scandal of the Uasin Gishu branch railway line, built at the expense of African taxpayers to benefit two of the richest settlers in Kenya, it was outstanding.

Ross's narrative also added a chilling reminder that while the settlers were, as Leys insisted, just ordinary people living in a system that gave them an incentive to behave badly, it was not just a few who behaved badly. In *Kenya* Leys had explained that the colony's main sources of revenue were the hut and poll tax levied on Africans, and customs duties, of which the government said imports bought by Africans accounted for half (Ross said it was much more than half); while virtually all the revenue spent on health and education, and on railways and roads, was for Europeans. In *Kenya from Within* Ross showed this in greater detail, and described how the settlers continually pressed for increases in the hut and poll tax, while successfully resisting the imposition of an income tax on themselves. To make up for the shortfall in revenue that was to have come from the income tax an increasingly embarrassed Colonial Office insisted that import duties must be raised, so they were – but largely on items mainly consumed by Africans. What Ross's first-hand accounts of the debates in the Legislative Council bring home is the racism of the Europeans who elected the Council's 'Unofficial' members, and of the Official members (the senior administration) who went along with them.

In many ways Ross's book was a good complement to *Kenya*. It differed from it in two main respects, besides being less compellingly written. First, it implied that the problems posed by settler colonialism were due to the greed and racism of the settlers' leaders, and could be gradually overcome by a government that firmly resisted them. It didn't see it as an unsustainable system that must be abolished or would otherwise be overthrown. Second, its tone was narrative and reformist. It said: this is what is happening, and it is obviously wrong. It didn't ask, what are you, a voter responsible for what happens in Kenya, going to do about it? It lacked the unsettling ethical undercurrent, and the wide historical perspective, of Leys' writing; and it showed sympathy for Africans, as opposed to identifying with them as fellow human beings. But *Kenya from Within* was very good in its own way. It makes one wonder: if it had come out first, would Leys have embarked on writing *Kenya*? And if he had, would it have gone to a second edition, let alone a third?

7: The problem of Phariseeism

In 1920 Leys seemed much more optimistic that a change of policy in Kenya could be secured than he had been a year earlier. 'Things are moving splendidly', he told Gilbert Murray.

> The Labour Party is committed to the right African policy. The Churches and missionary bodies are combining in a really useful way to attack the new slavery in Africa – I really believe they may succeed… And now the League of Nations Union group [its Mandates Committee, of which Leys was a member] seems three-quarters converted to sound doctrine. It is most astonishing to watch all these almost separate sets of people taking the same course and saying the same things in different phrases.[126]

And for a few years after the unexpected success of *Kenya* he still thought that 'the settler system' might be ended by a change of policy in London. A cheap third edition of *Kenya* came out in 1926, and McGregor Ross' *Kenya from Within* was published in 1927. No other part of the Empire, not even India, was getting so much attention. But the scale of the obstacle to be overcome proved even greater than Leys had originally thought.

Writing *Kenya* was demanding, but campaigning was a very different business and had to be done in the time he could spare from his practice. He faced the usual campaigner's problem of organisation and resources. An even bigger problem was that people didn't support the campaign as readily as he had imagined they would. He continued to think that if people knew the facts they would insist on change. But he found that many people who had read *Kenya*, and said they were convinced by it, were not ready to back his call for action. He wrestled with the problem in his letters to friends and allies, and his reflections on it are some of the most interesting things he wrote, and as relevant today as they were then. For several years he thought of it as the problem of 'Phariseeism'.

One of the first influential contacts he made in London was with the secretary of the Conference of British Missionary Societies (CMS), J. H. Oldham, who had read a copy of his letter to the Colonial Secretary and was impressed by it. He commissioned an article from Leys for the CMS magazine, which he edited. Commenting on the draft he was sending him, Leys wrote:

> When I think out Africa the facts… force me to find the source of so much evil and misery in two classes of men, the rich whose comfort comes from what Africans do, and religious teachers and leaders who refuse to face both the facts and Jesus' programme. These last do not consider the Kingdom of Heaven on earth as in heaven a practicable programme. They try to carry out an easy part of it, the preaching of a message… I believe you agree that the church has no real external enemy worth fighting. Its enemy is Phariseeism, a common, subtle, all-pervading sin, in Jesus' eyes the worst, and the commonest, scarcely ever referred to by religious writers and preachers.[127]

The tone of this statement is not typical. Leys had been steeped in the Bible at home and at school, and Oldham was a trained theologian, so to both men 'Phariseeism' had a specific historical and religious meaning.* Leys rarely used the term in writing to anyone else, although the parable of the Pharisee and the Good Samaritan figured in *Kenya*. But the statement summed up concisely his view of the missionary leaders' attitude towards settler colonialism in Kenya: while preaching Christianity, they failed to demand that the enslaved should be freed, as Jesus' precepts required.

And just as in common usage a 'Pharisee' has come to mean (no doubt unfairly to the Pharisees) any kind of self-righteous hypocrite, Leys soon found himself using the concept, though not the word, in relation to other people who professed to be on the side of the Africans: successive Colonial Secretaries and civil servants, of course, not to mention Governors, but also MPs and peers, editors, academics and others – including many people who saw themselves as being progressive on 'the native question' but were unwilling to do what they could – even just signing a letter for publication – to end the injustice being done to those natives. He struggled to get such people to say publicly what they were willing to say in private, and it exasperated him. Even McGregor Ross came in for mild criticism

---

* The Pharisees were a Jewish sect formed around 200 BCE who laid special stress on ritual purity (see e.g. Rebecca Denova, 'Pharisees', *World History Encyclopaedia* 2 February 2022 https://www.worldhistory.org/Pharisees/).

because he was not always ready to put his name to statements that called a spade a spade. Ross and his wife were 'great on tactics', Leys told Winifred Holtby, 'and think me a blundering fool because I always say exactly what I believe and have seen, while Ross will write that something is slightly defective when he means quite wrong'.[128]

Leys' relentless demand for people to stand up and be counted made them uncomfortable and led to him being called 'unrealistic', 'extreme', and 'fanatical'. He understood this perfectly well. What made him unusual was that he didn't care. He knew it was a lot to ask. Very few people – himself included, as he often acknowledged – lived up to their professed ideals ('What a pity it is', he observed to Holtby, after criticising someone else, 'that you and I are the only quite perfect people we know').[129] And he compounded the crime of making people feel uncomfortable by also refusing to say either that he loved Africans or that he hated the settlers. In another letter to Holtby he confided: 'I don't know if I ever told you that I don't particularly like Africans… Occasionally some pious old woman tells me I must have a great love for Africans. When he or she hears my answer she moves swiftly to the other end of the room and I become "that dreadful man".'[130] (His use of the word 'particularly' here is liable to be misunderstood. He meant that he didn't like Africans more than any other kind of human beings, not that he didn't like them. He said the same about the Maasai, in whose interest he had sacrificed his career, telling the Liberal MP Edmund Harvey: 'I don't care a rap for the Maasai, particularly'.)[131]

At the same time he insisted that the settlers were just ordinary people. Writing to Oldham in 1921 he said of them: 'These 2000 souls [the approximate number of land-owning settlers at the time] to my mind matter no more than 2000 Kavirondo* … when I come to think straight I find that they are 2000 humans … I have always defended their characters. They are just ordinary men.'[132] But their profits depended on a modern form of slavery. What was pharisaical was recognising injustice and not doing whatever you could to put an end to it.

---

* The Kavirondo were the peoples of western Kenya, most of whom are now known as Luo or Luhya

Missionaries and the church

The Protestant missions played a central role in the lives of Africans in Kenya, making Oldham, as the secretary of the CMS, potentially a key figure for Leys in his campaign. As John Cell pointed out, the two men, born within a year of each other, could hardly have been more different. Oldham was educated at Oxford and had aimed to be a missionary in India, but was prevented by ill-health. While Leys was in Kenya, Oldham had been a rising star in the world missionary movement, and by 1918 he had become famous as an organiser with unmatched connections within the establishment. Leys' letter to the Colonial Secretary moved and disturbed him and led him to commission the article mentioned above. Somewhat to Leys' surprise he published the article, even though it was more forthright than the letter to the Colonial Secretary. Although Leys realised how different their politics must be, the possibility of a collaboration was hugely attractive: 'Oldham had all the resources the poor and unknown country doctor lacked. He had a powerful organisation, money, an established and respected organ of propaganda, an office with secretaries, a network of influential contacts, and easy access to the government.'[133]

A test case of what this could mean arose the following year. Unlike the church in Britain (here Leys lumped together Anglicans and non-conformists), which had long given up any ambition to see Jesus' teaching realised in everyday life, in Africa the church was a newcomer, independent of the colonial state, and its message was revolutionary, like that of the early Christian church in Europe. 'It is hard for people in Europe,' Leys wrote in *Kenya*,

> to realise how great and various are the effects of the publication of the New Testament in the language of the common speech of a people with no other literature... Most people regard the Bible as a classic, which all the best judges say is written in beautiful English ... In Africa the book is roughly done into the commonplace language of everyday affairs. Its central character is the only figure clearly seen beyond the horizon of village, plantation and mission station ... We cannot see Jesus apart from haloes and dogmas and ceremonies. What is set before Africans is the Jesus of the early records. The response that thousands of them make is simply what people always feel about an extremely attractive person... They often apply to their case the contrast of the poor with whom he was so lenient with the rich and powerful whom he cursed.[134]

The missions taught that Jesus' principles should govern all of life, and the best mission stations practised what they preached (there is a touching pen-portrait of one of these in Leys' last book, *The Colour Bar in East Africa*).[135] The contradiction between this and settler colonialism in Kenya was acute. Missionaries could try to ignore the contradiction, but their leading figures were increasingly confronted with issues which forced them to take a position, and they invariably ended up accepting and sometimes even endorsing government policy.

In 1919, to meet an acute shortage of labour on settler farms, due to the disruption and loss of life caused by the war and influenza, an ordinance was proposed that would have required all African men of working age to work for wages on settler farms for two months a year, adding legal force to the pressure imposed by the hut and poll taxes, and by the threats of the chiefs. The mission leaders in Kenya reluctantly endorsed the plan. When Oldham learned of this he mobilised a successful campaign in Britain against the ordinance, and partly as a result of this pressure it was eventually dropped. Leys was delighted.

At the time Oldham was still strongly influenced by having read Leys' letter to the Colonial Secretary, and by having talked and corresponded with him. But whereas Leys saw that the settler economy depended on forced labour, so that freedom and justice for the Africans required an end to it, Oldham was constitutionally unable to think in such radical terms; he also, as Leys was well aware, had different priorities, above all the building of an international missionary organisation, for which a readiness to compromise was of the essence.

He became deeply concerned with the situation in Kenya, but he gradually came to think that the settlers were too powerful to challenge. He thought that they would eventually get 'responsible government', as the Southern Rhodesian settlers did in 1923, and that the interest of the Africans lay in changing the settlers' attitude to them before that happened in Kenya. In the long term, Oldham now declared, the interests of the Africans and the settlers coincided. To help get the settlers to share this view he thought that the missions needed to influence government policy, not to distance themselves from it; and a principal means of doing this was to involve the government in funding the missions' provision of education for Africans, which was needed on a scale far beyond the missions' financial resources. He also saw that this would be easier for the government to agree to if it was the kind of schooling advocated for Africa by the influential Welsh-American educationalist Jesse Jones, who had recently led a mission to East Africa and greatly impressed Oldham: schooling oriented to practical skills that would equip students for the kind of jobs that were open to them in settler society.

All of this Leys found unrealistic and dangerous. The trend of government policy in Kenya, he pointed out to Oldham, was towards steadily increasing the settlers' control of policy; and as for expecting a change of settler attitudes, 'As well expect publicans to reform licensing laws and wait until they are convinced of their necessity'.[136] Government-funded education would mean settler-controlled education, and he also considered Jesse Jones' model of education to be racist (although that term was not yet current, and Leys never used it). He had met Jesse Jones, who had admitted to him that he thought African-Americans were 'different in nature and capacity' from Europeans, and that he expected them to have 'a different kind of future'.[137] Oldham didn't go this far in his endorsement of Jones' ideas, but he did think there were politically important differences between Europeans and Africans. Leys, in contrast, believed that a fundamental element of Christianity was Paul's teaching that there were no such differences. African children needed and deserved exactly the same education as European children.

Eventually, in 1926, Leys broke publicly with Oldham. The last straw was a memorandum on policy for Kenya that Oldham sent to the Colonial Office. In it Oldham called for research into the facts of the Kenyan economy while avoiding any reference to the system of forced labour and the Africans' lack of legal rights, or to the incompatibility of all this with Christian principles. Worse still, he deprecated 'public agitation' of Leys' kind. His tone and argument expressed clearly what Leys was up against. Calling for research, Oldham declared that it was

> not desirable that the perfectly legitimate endeavour to make available for the good of all mankind the potential wealth of our East African territories should, through lack of a policy which takes account of all the factors, give rise to abuses which are incompatible with our declared aims and which can be redressed only by public agitation. Such agitation is an unnecessary and wasteful expenditure of energy, and our national reputation is apt to suffer discredit as a result of the exposures which have to be made. These undesirable results could be to a large extent prevented

by the adoption of a constructive policy based on all the factors and giving to the human element that primary consideration which is demanded as much by sound economics as by the dictates of morality.[138]

The familiar assumptions in terms of which settler colonialism was – and always is – justified were all there: the priority was to 'make available for the good of all mankind' the riches of the land which the Africans were incapable of doing themselves – but paying attention, of course, to the 'human element'. It was a classic 'within-system' document, which would, Leys thought, if it achieved anything at all, help to legitimise the setter system, while deprecating his own work as washing dirty linen in public. In a letter to the Scottish press Leys called it 'the policy of the priest and the Levite in the parable' – the epitome of pharisaical behaviour. In the preface to the third edition of *Kenya*, without naming Oldham Leys described Oldham's position as reflecting a new and different spirit from that which had previously inspired the missions:

> The older ideal was that the Church's agents... should offer all they had to give. The new assumes that there are elements in our life in Christendom which we enjoy but which are unsuitable for Africans to enjoy. It would have certain Europeans in positions of importance, such as Colonial governors and the secretaries of missionary societies, form and act upon judgements as to what it is wise that Africans should know and do... What they would have withheld from Africans are... what we ourselves most greatly prize, great literature and political liberty.[139]

Leys had recognised early on that Oldham was an instinctive compromiser who 'persists in attempting to reconcile incompatible views'; but, he added, in a letter to John Harris, the Secretary of the Anti-Slavery Society, in 1923, 'as nobody with my view could hold his job and do his very useful work I am not altogether sorry'.[140] What changed this was Oldham's eventual opposition to campaigning for changes that would antagonise the settlers, which he thought risked making things worse for Africans. Leys saw that the settler economy was unviable without forced labour, and that Oldham's idea that the settlers' interests and those of the Africans were identical 'in the long run' was dangerous nonsense; it was clear to him that the only way to get the system changed peacefully was by arousing a demand for the change in Britain, telling the British public the facts and calling for Africans to be given equality before the law, sufficient land, and freedom to work on it. 'Nothing could be more injurious' to this aim, he told Oldham, than Oldham's memorandum, which instead of highlighting the oppressive nature of the settler regime urged only measures the settlers would not oppose.[141]

As far as I know Leys never charged anyone else with Phariseeism, unless it was the Archbishop of Canterbury himself: in November 1918 he told Leonard Woolf that he was 'firing off a letter to his Grace of Canterbury reminding him that the church played the part of the priest and the Levite to the Africans 100 years ago [by not opposing slavery in the West Indies] and suggesting that similar inaction now will wreck its influence with the African race.'[142] (He added: 'It is an amazing world in which men like me instruct archbishops on the duty of the church!') Church leaders in Kenya who compromised with the system were the most obvious Pharisees, but Leys didn't say so. He knew them and sympathised with their position. John Arthur, the head of the Church of Scotland's Kikuyu mission, kept conceding to settler interests because, Leys thought, he was someone who had 'never been trained or trained himself to think for himself, suddenly faced with an alternative without steady principles to guide him. Inevitably he decides in accordance with prejudices until then unperceived by himself. Then he perceives them and is distressed and bewildered.'[143] Archdeacon Owen, in western Kenya, whom Leys especially admired, made concessions to settler interests in some of his public statements because he was susceptible to settler audiences and wanted to be liked – at least this was McGregor Ross' opinion, which Leys thought had 'some truth' in it.[144]

In the end both Owen and Arthur came round to Leys' position, although some church leaders were stalwart Pharisees: 'You won't get any change out of Bishop Willis [of Uganda]', he warned Oldham in 1920, when Oldham was mobilising support to resist the new labour ordinance. 'Four hundred years ago he would have burned heretics at the stake with a good conscience, out of a sense of right.'[145] But even Willis must have had a change of heart because Leys' daughter, Nanice, remembered that he had once stayed with them in Brailsford.

The wider problem

It was when people unconnected with the church fell short of defending African interests, while professing to support them, that the scale and breadth of the problem that Leys first called 'Phariseeism', and the reasons for it, became most interesting. For example, Sir William Ormsby-Gore, the Under-Secretary of State at the Colonial Office, was an unusually progressive Conservative minister. He made a speech in parliament saying he preferred the West African policy of development by the indigenous population to the settler system in Kenya. The settlers were furious. To pacify them, the pro-settler Secretary of State Leo Amery sent Ormsby-Gore on a mission to Kenya, where he was effectively captured by Lord Delamere, the settlers' leader, and made a speech in Nairobi before he came back praising the settlers and attacking their critics. Leys was angry, and couldn't stop himself calling Ormsby-Gore 'a traitor to the people of Kenya'. If Ormsby-Gore had read *Kenya*, he knew the facts, he told Oldham: 'And yet he repudiates the one means of getting justice done and publicly defends those who are determined to prevent its being done. You hint that he agrees with me in private while condemning me in public. How utterly futile!'[146] But he added a more charitable postscript: 'Traitor wasn't the word for O.G. When a man of fair intelligence, great kind-heartedness and average moral courage comes into close contact with an abler and more determined man [the settlers' leader Lord Delamere] his amiability proves his ruin.'

As for governors, and the men in the Colonial Office who advised on appointing them, their Phariseeism was in a class of its own.

> A definite type exists of men who in London and in the company of missionaries profess the strongest sympathy with native rights, but in Africa emulate, before the hardy settler, the behaviour of the maiden who 'swearing she would ne'er consent, consented'... Astonishing as it may seem, the first consideration in the choice of governors in East Africa is a man's ability to satisfy and serve financial interests in London and in Kenya. That inevitably follows from the conviction held by those who appoint them, that the prosperity of the people of a country like Kenya mainly depends on the degree and rapidity of its absorption of European capital. Other guiding principles are regarded as applicable when circumstances allow.[147]

Most governors were not very intelligent, he told Oldham: they were usually military men, with no knowledge or understanding of Africans. Sir Percy Girouard was intelligent, but he was 'an unscrupulous adventurer who thinks he can play Clive's part without his brains and do what Rhodes did without his money'.[148]

Senior officials in Kenya were necessarily committed to trying to make a success of the settler economy and were not normally required to profess enthusiasm for African interests, but lower-level officials who did, and who were unhappy with official policy, put their careers at risk if they criticised it, as Leys knew to his own cost; they were understandably nervous, he said, and even 'object[ed] to have attributed to them in writing [he meant, even in some private letters he had written] statements far more moderate than they habitually make in conversation'.[149]

But what about people in Britain who ran no such risks but were no more outspoken? Lionel Curtis, a former lecturer in Oxford and editor of *The Round Table*, the leading Commonwealth journal, commissioned and paid for an article by Leys but then didn't publish it because, Leys was sure, it was too radical for his readers. Vincent Harlow, the professor of Imperial History in London, gave a series of lectures on the empire which never mentioned the nature of settler colonialism in Kenya; and Margery Perham, the leading British authority on colonial administration, while arguing privately with the settlers' advocate, the Kenya-born writer Elspeth Huxley, never called publicly for the fundamental change of policy that Leys saw as necessary if bloodshed was to be avoided. Leys didn't mention Harlow or Perham publicly by name but in his last book, *The Colour Bar in East Africa*, published in 1941, he reproached them anonymously. It was useless, he wrote, to blame previous generations of policy-makers for the evils of settler colonialism:

> That chapter of Imperial history is closed. Who then are the men who are responsible for what is being done today, that will be history tomorrow? In our democracy, the British electorate. That electorate expects to be informed and is informed... But in the many books that have recently been published that deal with East Africa, some in seats of learning, by men and women endowed with chairs and out of trust funds, only the fringe of truth at best is lifted. It is to such men of position and influence, who often admit in private what their readers would never suspect, that the public rightly looks for the truth. Their silence is the reason why the wrongs are not righted.[150]

As with Ormsby-Gore, he was realistic and quite charitable about the reasons why so many people who saw themselves as 'pro-native' shrank from supporting his campaign as fully as he wished. McGregor Ross himself, for example, was 'utterly regardless of what people think about him'; but 'for too long [he] was a part of the system'.[151] Ross fought against greedy and unscrupulous settlers, but he thought most settlers were honest and didn't see that even the best of them were caught up in a system which made oppressors of them all. Moreover Ross, like Bishop Willis and Archdeacon Owen, who had also long been part of the system, 'never imagines a situation in Africa that can be more than a slightly modified existing situation'.[152] Leys himself, by contrast, had studied enough African history to understand that he and Ross had arrived in East Africa at the lowest point in the region's history. It had undergone two centuries of social, economic and cultural destruction by outside forces, from slave-raiding and imported diseases to the mass loss of African lives, livestock and crops in the East African campaign during the First World War and the flu epidemic that followed it. Before the ravages of the slave trade in the eighteenth century, Leys thought, Africa had been 'roughly, as civilized as Xth century Europe'. So he had a faith in Africans' future capacity that Ross and the others lacked; on top of which he was confident that a social-democratic revolution was coming in Europe 'as a consequence of which the exploiters in Africa will have the same fate as the slave owner 100 years ago'.[153] For these reasons he imagined something very different from 'a slightly modified existing situation'. He was right about the coming of social democracy, but not about what it would do for Africans.

The missionaries, he recognised, 'breathe the air of the secular society they live in. In Kenya Colony the air is so thick that people cannot see across the ocean – and across the centuries'.[154] Similarly in England: he warned Winifred Holtby, when she undertook to organise a protest letter about the BBC in 1930, that 'people you would never dream might get cold feet do, in African affairs. At this stage you will find disappointment at every corner'.[155] 'Respectables', he reported, 'have told the Rosses that it would be wiser to say nothing [about the BBC]'.[156] Gilbert Murray himself moved, like Oldham, in 'respectable' circles, and so was unlikely to sign, Leys thought, although 'Lady Murray, who is an angel, will probably sign even if he won't.'

By this time Murray had become something of a national institution. While the Liberal Party was rapidly shedding its progressive wing to the Labour Party, he remained a staunch Liberal, a leading humanist and supporter of the League of Nations and other benevolent causes. He had always been concerned about race relations and was troubled by what Leys had revealed about Kenya;

but he never adopted Leys' radical position on race, or his model of political change. He turned down a knighthood, but accepted an Order of Merit, and was plainly a pillar of the establishment. In the event Murray refused to sign, telling Holtby that he thought 'his old friend Leys' was 'now a little out of touch with the prevailing opinion among reformers'.[157] For his part Leys thought that Murray was 'hamstrung by the failure to realise the world he belongs to is dying', which indeed it was.[158] Nothing shows more clearly that Murray was the closest thing Leys had to a father than the fact that this did not alter his respect for him.

Even Lionel Curtis, the editor who had suppressed Leys' article 'when he realised how it would offend his powerful and wealthy friends in politics and industry', was judged, in retrospect, not altogether unkindly: ' ... everyone I know who has had dealings with him gives him the character of a sympathetic man with a keen sense of justice who always draws back when he counts the cost of action ... there are plenty of nice people in the world who are quite useless at getting things done.'[159] He told Oldham, who had complained that Leys called friends who didn't agree with him 'unfaithful':

> I doubt if he [Curtis] will ever... advocate what I advocate. But I don't call that being 'unfaithful'. His aims aren't mine. That's all there is to be said. It's true I expect little help from him. I have many friends from whom I expect no help at all. Why should I complain?'[160]

Immediate reform versus ultimate aims

Some of the reasons Oldham and others gave for not supporting the call for an end to settler colonialism look a bit like rationales for doing nothing. For example Oldham's call for more research, echoed by the Archbishop of Canterbury and by Margery Perham, could be seen as an excuse for not acting on the basis of the ample evidence that Leys and Ross had already produced on what was happening in Kenya, a version of the pretext for inaction which agrees that something needs to be done, but not yet.[161] Oldham claimed to see the achievement of justice for Africans as his 'ultimate aim', while not being willing to back Leys' call for change now. Leys commented:

> I don't think it is ever of much consequence to work for right measures to be taken when the time is ripe for them. The work is done by then. Fox passed the Act abolishing the slave trade. But the achievement was not his... The real work was done by thousands who with common conscious aim ripened public opinion. That is what is needed for Kenya.[162]

But Oldham genuinely wanted to do something. The question he repeatedly put to Leys was what could he do in the here and now? Leys understood that Oldham's job meant that he couldn't call publicly for all the measures that in private he acknowledged were needed: equal rights for Africans before the law, security of tenure on their land, freedom to grow whatever crops they wanted to, freedom from obligations to do work that Europeans were not also required to do, an equitable system of taxation and expenditure. But he could choose one thing, Leys suggested, such as taxation, and concentrate on that. 'Why is it so hard to know what can be *done*?', Leys asked.

> What *you* can do is simply your share of making the facts known and of encouraging people to think out for themselves the course the facts prescribe… The real difficulty… is that the right course is too simple for compromisers to believe in, too unpopular for the respectable people to adhere to, too hard for people who like you and me, want to do the right thing without depriving ourselves of any comfort.[163]

But Oldham was unwilling to call for any one change that would be incompatible with the settler regime. He said society needed 'both the radical and the conservative type of mind', just as an army needed, besides 'pioneers', 'camp followers', among whom he classed himself, who 'may be able, by doing our bit, to contribute something to make advance possible'.[164] 'Publicity with a view to ultimate reform, certainly', Oldham was ready to agree. 'But in addition to this, is any immediate action by the present Government within the range of practical politics?'[165] A call for immediate, as opposed to ultimate, reform, would provoke the settlers to a rebellion, such as the one they had threatened two years earlier if Indians in Kenya were allowed to vote; and, Oldham argued, 'unless in the last resort you are prepared to send out troops, which this Government won't do, you are shut up to getting as far as you can without antagonising local opinion or at least driving it to extreme lengths.' The Imperial Government

> must use the powers it possesses to the full. Unless, however, it has made up its mind that it is prepared, if necessary, to send out troops to enforce its views, the pace at which it can introduce reforms will depend on the extent to which it can get its way without forcing things to the point of rebellion.[166]

It followed that publicity to arouse public opinion in England should be tempered to settler opinion in Kenya, a conclusion that eventually led to the break with Leys. Leys knew perfectly well that the Conservative government would never send troops to Kenya to face down the settlers, but he didn't think the dilemma was a real one, perhaps because he understood better than most how completely dependent the precarious settler economy was on the government in London.* Nonetheless he chided Oldham for being too ready to rule out the use of force: 'Do you find more tolerable the continuance of the injustices suffered by the Africans in Kenya?'[167] Leys also had no faith in the good intentions of some senior Colonial Office officials which Oldham claimed to have discovered; nor did he believe that any well-intentioned despatches that the Secretary of State might send to Nairobi would not be neutered by settler opposition. The record showed that 'Nairobi will always win. Nothing can be done until a new *kind* of governor is sent out'.[168] The need was to get public opinion to force the government in London to act. Without public understanding and strong feeling there was no hope of reform, and the result would be a rebellion followed by repression. Ceaseless publicity was the only answer.

In steadfastly pursuing this strategy Leys had also to contend with the fact that most middle-class people in Britain had an innocent view of the state, closer to Oldham's than his. This even affected McGregor Ross, who had spent his working life inside the Kenyan state and was willing to believe that instructions from Whitehall would be implemented in Kenya if a Labour Colonial Secretary issued them. Leys had no illusions that this could happen without powerful public pressure in Britain.

It makes little sense to ask whether Leys or Oldham had the more realistic conception of how to bring justice to Kenya. As Leys recognised, it was not Oldham's primary aim anyway, and the obvious fact is that both failed. The end of settler colonialism came about as Leys had predicted it would if there was no reform, with half a decade of grotesquely brutal repression. In that respect, Leys was the more realistic. He was more keenly aware than Oldham of the cost of failure.

---

* Leys said he would 'shortly explain' why he didn't think the dilemma was real, but he broke off without explaining and failed to return to the point in a further draft. In 1930 or 1931 he said that 'in the last two years or so 'he had come to the conclusion that without their subsidies and cheap labour 'the only plantation industries [he meant settler farms] that might survive would be tea and sizal' ('Statement for the Advisory Committee by Dr Leys', n.d.). In 1952, in response to an African rebellion, five battalions of the British army were deployed in Kenya.

Pharisееism and racism

In 1929 a second minority Labour government came to power, with Sidney Webb, elevated to the House of Lords as Lord Passfield, as Colonial Secretary. Webb had been at the centre of Labour Party policy-making since 1918 and his *Memorandum on Native Policy in East Africa*, issued in 1930, reflected the efforts that Leys, Ross, Woolf and others had made to get the party to adopt a progressive policy. It seemed to call for several key changes in the right direction and the settler leadership immediately denounced it. But it had fatal flaws. It explicitly endorsed the policy of limiting land ownership in the Kenya highlands to Europeans, and its language on reforms was vague on detail and full of 'as far as possible' clauses. And to Leys' disgust Passfield did nothing to see that any reforms at all were undertaken in Kenya.

Leys was used to governments in London surrendering to settler interests, but he felt Passfield's failure to act as a huge blow. He concluded that he must write another book. *A Last Chance in Kenya*, published in 1931, was partly a criticism of Passfield, who had not even ensured that his Memorandum was published in Kenya, let alone acted on. 'He has acted, during more than two years of office, as if he were perfectly free to choose his own policy', Leys wrote. Passfield's White Paper of 1930 was

> far less downright than the statements on the same subject made eighty years ago by former British governments. But it did say that Africans were to be allowed to grow coffee; it did say that they might have land on individual tenure; it did direct that taxation should be graded according to wealth… If it had been acted upon, this White Paper, though halting and often vague, might have been perhaps as useful a check to the long drift in the wrong direction as a more direct and definite statement would have been.'[169]

But in face of settler opposition, which was supported by the Governor, Passfield had done nothing. Leys' reaction was an early (and no doubt naïve) expression of the division between the Labour Party's radical and conservative elements that would wrack it throughout its existence:

> Do the responsible leaders of the Labour Party agree with the view that Labour Ministers are under no obligation after an election to do as they told the electorate they intended? … If the Labour Party is merely a piece

of machinery for getting more money for its supporters, the sooner it disappears the better. But if it has any real principles to keep it alive, it will be as determined to have justice done to voteless Kavirondo as to improve the lot of the British workman.[170]

A Last Chance was also a response to something more profound: it had become clear that the overt racism of the settlers and most of the administration in Kenya was paralleled by a deeply entrenched racism in Britain which affected even 'pro-native' liberals. In *Kenya* Leys had already summed up the evidence against the existence of different racial capacities:

> Judged by language, art, folk-lore and every other branch of anthropology, there is nothing specifically African about Africans' minds. The more one knows them the more obviously they are 'just people', and the more obviously any special racial 'psychology' is an assumption based only on superficial dissimilarities and on the fact that various human societies have had unequal opportunities of social development. There is no basis in fact for the theory of special racial mentalities.[171]

Now he saw that this needed restating more forcefully. As early as 1919 he had complained to Gilbert Murray that 'the greatest enemies of Africans were 'not the selfish exploiters but those who want the African to be taught to be clean, moral, industrious, happy, grateful, fat, but not free'.[172] *A Last Chance* included a long chapter dealing with what he now realized underlay all forms of Phariseeism, including among 'pro-natives'. Entitled 'African Mentality', it showed how the conditions of servility and poverty to which Africans were subjected in Kenya naturally gave rise to the impression among the Europeans who lived there that Africans were inherently inferior; but it went on to show how this assumption was also held, consciously or not, by people in Britain too. Enlivened by some of Leys' characteristic satirical barbs the chapter can still be thought-provoking. For example, in a passage that might even be a teachable text in relation to 'decolonising' education today, he noted that 'one of the Commissions that have recently visited Africa [the Phelps-Stokes Commission, chaired by Jesse Jones] referred to the "absurdity" of teaching African children, in a translated school-book, about Mary's little lamb'. 'Why', he asked, 'should it be of less educational value to teach African children about English lambs than to teach English children about African elephants?'[173] The chapter demolished one racist myth after another and ended with a conclusion that in 1931 was still very much a minority view in Britain, let alone among whites in Kenya:

> In short, there is no evidence to suggest that race is an important factor in human affairs, and a good deal of evidence to indicate that it has no importance whatever. There is no reason, therefore, to doubt that Africans, once given opportunity, will both share generally in civilized life, and contribute to the world their quota of men of genius.[174]

Leys' last words on the subject of Phariseeism were written in 1942, at the lowest point in the war, in what was probably his last letter to Gilbert Murray. He said he had been ill and was sorry he had not written sooner to thank him for his kind words about his last book, *The Colour Bar in East Africa*.

> But since then the whole country has learned that the Malays refuse to dig trenches for our troops and that according to the BBC the Burmese peasantry are traitors in preferring Japanese lordship to ours. Facts of that sort hit me far harder than military defeats or the exposure of incompetence in Whitehall. I don't claim to have foreseen them. But I did foresee and tried to explain how the state of mind out of which they arise is coming about in the part of the Empire I used to live in. I know you thought I gave certain discreditable facts unfair or at least undue prominence. But I think you will admit that if a dozen other men had written as frankly, and accepted the consequences of doing so, about Imperial policy in countries other than East African, we might now have less to be ashamed of.[175]

8: The difficult years

The break with Oldham in 1926 had felt more like a clarification than a set-back. Leys had then been back in England for eight years. A cheap third edition of *Kenya* was in bookshops, and the following year Ross' book came out. Leys' health was relatively good and his practice was doing well. His often long letters to the press were always accepted and he was in constant demand to write articles. In September 1930, in a long letter to John Harris, the Secretary of the Anti-Slavery Society, he mentioned that he had 'arranged for articles in four papers on the eve of the Imperial Conference' [the predecessor of today's Commonwealth Heads of Government Meetings] that was due to open the following month.

Yet in his letter to Harris there was a note of desperation. He had come to realise that a propaganda war of the kind he was engaged in required a level of dedication and organisation that was lacking. The BBC, which had been created just three years earlier, had announced the series of talks on Africa mentioned in the previous chapter. The list of speakers contained no known supporter of African liberation, but included the director of education at the Colonial Office, who believed Africans had a different 'mentality' from Europeans, and the explicitly racist Prime Minister of South Africa, General Hertzog. Leys saw that this new public medium of communication was going to be hugely important. But it was an additional dimension of the fight for justice in Kenya which was already much more demanding than his friends recognised. In his letter to Harris he wrote:

> I have written to so many people about this terrible B.B.C. danger that I forget if I wrote to you. It seems to me conclusive proof of what I have suspected for long, that the group we belong to that has common aims for Africans, is likely to fail. Even you have to concern yourself with other people than Africans. I am always ready to do what I can but I am tied to my job and am about the only one of the group who has to live out of London. Ross is ill. Buxton [Charles Roden Buxton, a Labour Party

activist and twice briefly a Labour MP], who I wish would make himself our leader and deliberately devote his whole self to the liberation of Africans for the next 12 months, seems to me to have failed to realise that unless continuous watchfulness and effort are engaged we must fail.[176]

Buxton, an exact contemporary of Leys, had travelled extensively in Africa and was genuinely committed to African liberation; but he had many other political commitments, including the Union of Democratic Control (i.e. for the democratic control of foreign policy), of which he was a founder member, the Fabian Society, the Quakers, and the promotion of Esperanto, among other causes, and was not inclined to make Kenya his priority. This was of course true of most of Leys' and Ross' allies. The fact that many of them, like Buxton, also had independent means, and could have devoted time and resources to the Kenya issue that Leys could not, was a constant source of frustration to him. 'Barring yourself', he added in his letter to Harris,

> I doubt if there is a single man on our side who works for it as hard, seeing editors, M.P.s and all sorts of influential people such as these B.B.C. people – as a score of the settlers do. When these settlers come home they don't loiter about and enjoy themselves. They are taking every chance they get, urging their case on every man they meet. They know that if they win this round they will win the campaign, which means until Africans get to the stage of rebellion. They think, though I don't, that they are safe from that for fifty years. The fact is that if there aren't half a dozen people who work on our side as hard as many more work on the other we deserve to lose.

By 'this round' Leys meant a round in the ongoing fight between the settler leadership and their opponents in Britain. The settlers were hoping, as their numbers grew, to win 'responsible government' – i.e. independent political control in Kenya, as the settlers in Southern Rhodesia had done in 1923 – while the critics, spearheaded by Leys and Ross, tried to prevent it.

The first round had been fought in 1921-23. The war had put the settlers in an even stronger position. The requirements of the East African campaign had put overall control in the hands of the British military, superseding the Colonial Office. All able-bodied natives were conscripted into the British army's Carrier Corps, with the result that exports from African peasant output in the reserves, which before the war had accounted for 60% of all exports, fell drastically;

exports from settler farms came to be seen as ever more important, and a pro-settler Governor conceded more and more political power to the settler leaders. His successor, General Northey, appointed in 1918 (the one Leys called a 'barbarian'), was also firmly pro-settler. In 1921, however, the powerful criticism of the proposed compulsory labour ordinance that Oldham, prompted by Leys, had mobilised from the Archbishop of Canterbury and other eminent and respectable people had jolted the officials in the Colonial Office, who were also shaken by the Thuku affair that year. They realised that they needed to get a fresh grip on policy in Kenya. For once they even grudgingly paid serious attention to Leys' own criticisms of the proposed ordinance, and it was withdrawn.[177]

The settlers' dream of 'responsible government' was also threatened in 1921 by a demand for equal rights from the Indian population in Kenya, who dominated the commercial sector and also did most of the government's clerical work.* Their demands included the same right to elect members to the Legislative Council as had recently been given to the Europeans. The India Office in London, concerned with the rise of nationalist feeling in India, supported the Kenyan Indians' demand. The settlers were outnumbered 3:1 by the Indians, and were violently opposed. The Colonial Office backed the settlers. In 1922 a compromise was reached in London, the so-called Wood-Winterton Agreement, between the senior officials of the two departments, which gave the Kenyan Indians part of what they wanted. The response of the settler leadership was to organise a rebellion: with the support of most of the whites in the country they threatened to detain the Governor and dared London to use force against them.[178] The government in London backed down, abandoning the Wood-Winterton agreement. In its place, in 1923 the government issued the so-called Devonshire Declaration which tried to appease Indian feeling by declaring that what trumped the interests of all the immigrant minorities in East Africa, European as well as Indian, were the interests of Africans. Although a concern for African interests had in fact played no part in the conflict, the Declaration said that if the interests of any immigrant community conflicted with African interests, African interests would be 'paramount'. This seemed to mean that the settlers could never hope to get control.

---

* A large Indian workforce had been imported to build the Uganda Railway. Most had returned to India at the end of their contract, but some remained and were the principal founders of the colony's Indian trading and clerical workforce.

Of course, that meaning could change, and the settler leaders were determined that it should. As already mentioned, they 'turned' William Ormsby-Gore, the Under-Secretary of State for the Colonies, when he led a visiting commission to Kenya in 1924. Ormsby-Gore changed from someone who had publicly favoured the West African model of peasant agriculture into a keen supporter of the settler model – the turnabout that had led Leys to call him a traitor.

The way this was done was very characteristic of the formidable Lord Delamere, who had settled in Kenya in 1903 and whose lifelong aim was to make Kenya a 'White Man's Country' – as passionate and all-consuming an aim for him as saving it for its African population was for Leys. Although Delamere was rich and had added enormously to his wealth by selling to later arrivals parcels of the land that he had been granted for next to nothing, he kept borrowing up to the hilt to experiment with every possible kind of crop and livestock. He was intelligent as well as charismatic, and was close to every successive governor. The Europeans in Kenya, a small, mixed and – as Leys always insisted – ordinary collection of people would have been unlikely to get as far as they did, politically, under the leadership of anyone else. The Ormsby-Gore coup was characteristic. Shortly before he and his fellow commissioners arrived,

> Delamere mortgaged his last unencumbered farm to buy a new car. Then, with the consent of the Government, which was conveniently short of transportation, he and a few companions acted as official chauffeurs. Riding in Delamere's bright yellow Packard, the three commissioners saw little more than what the settlers wanted them to see. Moreover, in honour of their visit to East Africa, Delamere at his own expense put on a lavish dinner. Held at the Muthaiga Club, a recreation centre for Europeans, the dinner was attended by more than eighty settlers. When they arrived in London, the change in attitude of Church [a Labour MP, one of the other two members of the commission, who had previously been sceptical of the value of white settlement in Africa] and Ormsby-Gore was remarkable. Church at once began to write a book in praise of European accomplishments in Africa. It appeared in 1927 under the suggestive title *East Africa, a New Dominion*.[179]

And in Leo Amery, the Conservative Colonial Secretary from 1924 to 1929, the settlers had a strong ally. He redefined the Devonshire Declaration as meaning 'equal' development for whites and Africans – the so-called 'dual policy' – and tried hard to ramp through 'closer union', a federation of all the Central and East African colonies – Northern and Southern Rhodesia (Zambia and Zimbabwe), Nyasaland, Tanganyika (Tanzania), Kenya and Uganda – with the implication that the whole area would eventually achieve 'responsible government' under white control. But in this he was thwarted by his more cautious cabinet colleagues. The Labour Party had already been briefly in office in 1924, and was gathering more and more support. Opposition to 'closer union', led by two undeniable Kenya 'experts', Ross and Leys, had begun to make the issue electorally risky.

At stake seemed to be the entrenchment of the settler system or its abolition, and the election of a Labour government in 1929 seemed, at last, to offer a chance of abolishing it. In October 1930 the Labour Colonial Secretary, Lord Passfield, issued the *Memorandum on Native Policy in East Africa,* mentioned in the previous chapter, which seemed to portend a radical change. Ross wrote to Leys saying it meant that their task was done. Leys was thunderstruck. In his view the slippery language of the *Memorandum* showed that even under a Labour Colonial Secretary the Colonial Office was as far as ever from seeing settler colonialism in Kenya as 'the slavery issue of a century ago in modern form', and had no intention of dismantling it. His reply to Ross was blunt:

> So we are now at this pass. As has often happened in the past, a British Government has laid down the right policy. What reason have we for believing that this time, for once, it will be acted upon? ... I hope I don't need to prove to you that wherever in Africa Europeans have been granted land the Hertzog-Delamere policy has always won, in spite of directions from Downing St. much more uncompromising and downright than the terms of this White Paper [Passfield's Memorandum]. Our opponents know that and are confident that they will repeat the victories won in the Union [of South Africa] and Rhodesia [i.e., eventual independence under settler control]. They have sent their best men here, have unlimited funds, have the instinctive sympathy of all who admire pioneers struggling to introduce sweetness and light in darkest Africa. Practically the whole upper and middle classes naturally assume that English gentlemen who live in Kenya must be the best judges of what ought to be done there. On these foundations, these men begin an organised propaganda. And you propose... to meet this emergency by the cessation of what we have been doing![180]

Winning the battle for public opinion meant continuing to work as hard as ever 'to get the facts into the public mind'.

I have been trying to for 12 years and I cannot see a scrap of reason to stop. How have former first-class political victories been won? Emancipation from the older sort of slavery – the Factory Acts – the enfranchisement of women? By their advocacy, by stating the facts that persuaded people these reforms were wise and right, as often and to as many people as their advocates could reach, without ceasing. No main issue has ever been won otherwise except of course by bloodshed.

But the Governor of Kenya, Sir Edward Grigg, who had taken over in 1925, was another keen supporter of white control and declined to implement any of the policies that Passfield's Memorandum appeared to call for. Instead of confronting him, Passfield gave in. He accepted the view of the senior Colonial Office officials, who had, Diana Wylie noted, 'a "kith and kin" sympathy for the settlers', that Leys and his allies on the Advisory Committee were 'militant radicals', a species Passfield particularly disliked.[181] The historian Robert Gregory summed up Passfield's peculiar unfitness for the problem Kenya presented:

> ... his peculiar temperament made him reluctant to undertake any drastic reform ... Steady by nature, a plodder in some ways, he never attracted attention in his long political career by a display of rabid enthusiasm for any measure. Instead he was famed for instilling in the Labour program his own philosophy, 'the inevitability of gradualness'. Webb was also not deeply interested in his work at the Colonial Office.[182]

Leys was justified, Gregory thought, in seeing Passfield and his deputy, Drummond Shiels, as having betrayed Labour's stated principles, whether intentionally or not. Passfield even invited a joint select committee of both Houses of Parliament to debate and make recommendations for future native policy in East Africa, and allowed it to have a large Conservative majority, with the result that in due course it endorsed the status quo in Kenya. The BBC dropped Hertzog from its list of speakers, but the rest of the series was eventually broadcast as planned. The settlers seemed to have won the 1930 'round'.

But as Diana Wylie has argued, the settlers' aim of responsible government was actually defeated at this point, and Leys and Ross had played a central role in their defeat.[183] The Hilton Young Commission, appointed by Amery in 1927 to report on his scheme for closer union, failed to endorse it; Oldham had been a member of the Commission and Leys had certainly influenced him. Leys' and Ross' influence on the Labour Party's official policy on Africa was also significant, because as electoral support for Labour rose, so did the political risk to the Conservatives of supporting the settlers. The two men had, moreover, played a leading role in raising concerns about Kenya among humanitarians more widely, because no one could challenge their expertise.

But material factors were equally if not more important. The worldwide drop in agricultural commodity prices in the depression stalled the Kenyan economy and pushed the smaller and medium-sized settler farms towards bankruptcy; the British Treasury was forced to make a £10 million loan to stave off a collapse of the settler economy and was unlikely to support conceding political control to the settlers so long as it remained to be repaid. And 'closer union', linking Kenya politically with the settler-ruled colony of Southern Rhodesia, had never seemed practicable since between them lay Tanganyika, a League of Nations mandate territory with almost no settlers, and a Governor, Sir Donald Cameron, who, to the Colonial Office's discomfort, backed peasant production and opposed 'closer union'. Above all, perhaps, was the fact that in 1931 the white population of Kenya still totalled just 16,812, manifestly too few to be allowed to rule over three million Africans.*

The settlers' dream of winning 'responsible government' had in reality never been very realistic. In 1931 Delamere died. In 1933 the new Conservative Colonial Secretary, Lord Cunliffe-Lister, bluntly

---

* Why there were still so few settlers in 1931 is a complicated story in which the class character and prejudices of the first settlers to arrive, and of the Governors of the time, played a key role. Of the 16,812 Europeans in Kenya in 1931 a small minority were farming, and as agriculture was the basis of the economy this determined the overall size of the white population. The number of farmers was small because the titled and well-connected early arrivals had been determined not just to keep the highlands white, but also to ensure that the whites who bought land there were rich, reproducing in Kenya the landed class hierarchy that was disappearing in England. They successfully resisted attempts to limit the size of individual landholdings and defended a free market in land, which led to the accumulation of vast landholdings by a handful of people: 'By the end of 1912 Delamere, the two Coles, Grogan, the East Africa Syndicate and East Africa Estates, held one fifth of the alienated land in the Protectorate. In the Rift Valley, at the same time, half the alienated land was held by two syndicates and four individuals.' (M.P.K. Sorrenson, *The Origins of European Settlement in Kenya*, Nairobi: Oxford University Press, 1968, p. 146). One result was to make themselves even richer. In 1902 Delamere was granted 100,000 acres leasehold, at an annual rent of a half-penny an acre; by 1926 he had sold 82,000 of them, mostly undeveloped, to later arrivals, for a total of £212,043, equivalent to about £16 million in 2024 (McGregor Ross [1927], p. 85) . His ally Colonel Grogan was granted fifty acres of harbour shoreline in Mombasa. In 1925 he sold them to the government, with some adjacent land, for a net sum of about £250,000, equivalent to some £19 million in 2024 (McGregor Ross [1927], p. 162). A second result was to discourage settlement by anyone who wasn't fairly rich. Not only were Indians prevented from owning land in the highlands; whites with limited capital were discouraged by the high cost of land resulting from the market power of the early arrivals, and by the volatility of export prices – settlers without deep pockets could easily become

told Delamere's successor, Lord Francis Scott, that 'no government in this country would ever agree to the claim on the part of the White settlers to govern on their own'.[184]

But to Leys, 1930 seemed like a lost opportunity, and a betrayal. And then in 1931 the Labour government split over the issue of how much support should be given to the fast-rising mass of unemployed workers and their families. Ramsay MacDonald, who twenty years earlier had, at Leys' prompting, raised the Maasai issue in parliament, formed a 'National Government' coalition with the Conservatives to implement a policy of austerity, and called a general election in which the Labour Party was reduced to a mere 52 MPs. Leys resigned from the Advisory Committee.

As he had feared, the formation of the predominantly Conservative National Government was bad news for Africans in Kenya. It appointed a commission on land policy in Kenya whose chairman, Sir William Morris Carter, was a colonial judge with a long history of supporting settler colonialism in both Central and East Africa; he was also the judge who had rejected the Maasai's legal case in 1913. The other members of the commission were a former administrator of the Maasai, and a settler. No representative of Africans was included. Predictably, the commission's recommendations reinforced the reservation of the highlands to Whites and did nothing to give security of tenure to Africans in the reserves, or to enlarge the reserves, the two key land issues for Africans.

Meanwhile the impact of the depression on people's standard of living in Britain, and the rise to power of the Nazis in Germany, made it harder and harder to keep the public interested in the problems of Africans in a small colony 6,000 miles away. In a letter to Margaret Hodgson* in South Africa in 1933 Leys said: 'People in civilised countries are too anxious about themselves to have any effective concern about African affairs. All the experts tell them the ground of

bankrupt, as a number of them did in the 1930s. To avoid the risk of having to bail out and repatriate failed settlers the government itself also discouraged immigration by small farmers. If the highlands had been opened up to immigrants willing to live off the land, whether from India or Europe (such as the Zionists, to whom the government in London offered 5,000 square miles of the western highlands in 1903 – an offer which was fiercely opposed by the settlers who had just arrived, and which the Zionists eventually declined), a much larger scale of immigration would have followed. Kenya's Africans would then have faced a situation more like that of the Africans in Southern Rhodesia, who had to endure fifteen years of war to secure majority rule.

* Margaret Hodgson is better known as Margaret Ballinger, who later became the leader of the South African Liberal Party. William Ballinger, whom she married in 1934, was a British trade unionist who had gone to South Africa to work for the Industrial and Commercial Workers Union, paid for by the fund set up by Winifred Holtby.

their XIXth. century "progress" that once seemed solid may slip away from them ... Add to all this the nightmare of Fascism ... there is no hope that the Europe of 1933 can spare energy to intervene in Africa.'[185]

The position of any British advocate of African rights was also becoming complicated by the emergence of educated Africans who could speak for their own people. One of these was Jomo Kenyatta, the representative of the Kikuyu Central Association. Kenyatta first visited Britain in 1929-30 and made extensive contacts with supporters of African liberation, especially McGregor Ross; and in 1931 he came again, this time with another Kikuyu, Parmenas Mockerie, to give evidence on behalf of the KCA to the all-party parliamentary committee set up by Passfield. The Kenyan administration had chosen two Africans to give evidence, and both it and the Colonial Office it strongly opposed allowing the KCA's representatives to be heard. The parliamentarians complied. When the committee asked the Governor, Sir Edward Grigg, what views were held by the different communities in Kenya, he told the committee: 'The African, of course, has no views at all'. (Leys quoted this statement on the title page of *A Last Chance in Kenya*, published later that year.)

Mockerie stayed on in England for two years for further education. Kenyatta stayed for most of the next fifteen years, returning only after the war. He was precisely the kind of educated African who Leys had foreseen would lead a movement to overthrow colonial rule. In 1914 he had wondered 'what kind of men' a generation of commercialism would produce.[186] Kenyatta was a good example: a Kikuyu nationalist more than a Kenyan nationalist, and an adroit opportunist, not a leader with a social and economic vision. Leys met him, but they did not become close, partly because he thought Kenyatta was too dependent financially on the Communists (not because he hated Communists, he said, but because he thought their revolutionary politics were irrelevant in Britain, and because in his experience cooperation with them meant adopting their line).[187] Something Leys had written, presumably disagreeing with him, led Kenyatta to write accusing him of trying 'to ruin his character', which Leys would never have done; but he did not agree with all Kenyatta's political views.[188]

Yet championing the cause of Kenyans now meant trying to work with whoever they regarded as their leaders. By 1938 Kenyatta was writing letters to the *Manchester Guardian* about the forced culling of cattle belonging to the Kamba, neighbours of the Kikuyu, about which Leys had only second or third-hand information; Kenyatta was also writing articles that called for self-government and speaking to a wide range of sympathetic groups – Fabians, the Workers Education Association, the Independent Labour Party and others.[189] Political solidarity work is always delicate, and Leys was temperamentally unsuited for it, to put it mildly. He was surely happy to see Africans speaking for themselves, and philosophical about not always agreeing with them.

But the fear that the campaign against the settlers might fail, that he had felt in 1930, gradually became a conviction that he himself had failed – not only failed to bring about a change in policy in Kenya, but also to change educated opinion in Britain enough to prevent a violent reaction to the rebellion he was sure was coming. Luckily for his spirits, in 1929, just before things started to go dark, he made a new and immensely important friendship with the young novelist, journalist, and feminist peace activist Winifred Holtby. Full of energy, giving lectures all over the country, producing a steady stream of articles for leading newspapers, Holtby also wrote over a dozen novels before her tragically early death in 1935. On a lecture tour in South Africa she met Clements Kadalie, the leader of the country's first African trade union, the Industrial and Commercial Workers Union, and committed herself to mobilising support for it in Britain. She set up a fund and got in touch with the Labour Party and its Advisory Committee, where she met Leys.

There was an immediate meeting of minds, and not just on African issues. She became a confidante of a kind he had never known before. He was slow to recognise how important this was to him. In 1933 he wrote: 'I have just realised that you are the only woman friend I have in the sense of one who shares my mental life – except relations, of course'.[18]

In reality, she probably shared it more fully than anyone else. He wrote to her about Africa, but he also complained about his money troubles and expressed his feelings. In 1934, thanking her for writing to cheer him up when his wife Janey was ill and he was depressed, he wrote 'Yes, I am afraid you are an angel, on the large side no doubt for the heavenly throng. You may pass in fact for an archangel who perform I understand duties corresponding to those of archdeacons on earth'.[191]

What Holtby felt about him is fairly clear. She was twenty-two years younger, and had wide interests, in feminism, socialism, peace, and South Africa, whereas Leys really had only one. But she felt quite close to him. Her close friend Vera Brittain said Holtby's friendship with Leys was 'the most intimate' of all the friendships she made with the men on the Labour Party's Advisory Committee, and she was clearly reporting Holtby's opinion when she wrote that 'His honourable personality... carried passionate integrity to the limit of fanaticism'.[192] Holtby's view of Leys contributed some ingredients, as Brittain put it, to the character of Arthur Rollett in her novel *Mandoa, Mandoa!*:

> His drawback as a journalist was that his conclusions were always foregone, but his asset was a dramatic and scorching brevity of eloquence, as though his ardour had burned out all impurity from his style ... A small, fierce, sensitive, incorruptible little man ... the conflict between his unsleeping conscience and his natural kindliness daily tormented him, for the former drove him to tell unpleasant truths which caused reactions desperately painful to the latter.[193]

Leys was not a journalist, and not very small, but otherwise this is certainly him. In 1934 Holtby wrote to Vera Brittain: 'Dear Norman Leys came into £800 insurance policy last week. As a result he decided to give me a present. He has sent me a little Crown Derby ash tray, & £5 a year for his life time for Ballinger [Holtby's fund in support of Clement Kadalie's union in South Africa]. He really is a love'.[194]

Besides the comfort Leys got from this friendship he had some good moments in the 1930s. One was a visit in 1934 to Achimota College, the predecessor of the University of Ghana, at the invitation of the Principal, his old Glasgow friend A.G. Fraser. He was 'thrilled': 'It is the first example I have seen, and I suppose the only one, of our race doing something really on the grand scale for the African race'.[195] But by 1935 he was depressed. He had lost hope for peaceful change in Kenya, he was tired, his health was not so good, and his medical practice was no longer doing well. He told Holtby:

> The main but not the only reason for persistent gloom is that the practice is slowly but steadily diminishing. My eyesight, my Socialism, my impatience with fools and selfish sluggards, other faults. The fact is I am a hypocrite. I thought I was honest when I told people on coming here that I would ask no one to pay if told payment would mean hardship. But I know now I wasn't honest. I didn't face the consequences.'[196]

The self-criticism was silly. He could not have predicted the Depression, which was why so many of his patients were now facing hardship. But it made him unhappy. Two months later he wrote to Holtby again:

> You should thank your stars that you don't earn your living out of money got from people poorer than yourself. I have just finished the quarter's accounts, a job I hate worse than any other. X women will say when they get what I send them 'no new dress for me this year if I pay this bill'. Y men will say 'no trip with the children to the sea'. An <u>almost</u> equally cursed thing is that since to such people I charge less than my rivals they conclude I am their inferior'.[197]

But Holtby was incurably ill with Bright's Disease, and both of them knew she had not got long to live. In August 1935 she spent a day visiting Leys and Janey in Brailsford. She died a month later, aged 37.

Then, as if to soften this blow, an exciting new opportunity arose. Since Leys' visit to Achimota his friend A.G. Fraser had retired as Principal and had been appointed to run a new college for adults in Newbattle Abbey, outside Edinburgh. In December 1935 he wrote offering Leys a position at it. Leys was delighted: it was 'exactly what I want', he wrote, adding that he especially looked forward to doing something to compensate for the slights and insults the foreign students who would stay there during vacations were so used to receiving. 'If appointed', he wrote (he evidently understood that it wouldn't be solely up to Fraser), 'I would leave here in the spring and spend the summer reading up whatever subjects or periods would be on the winter's programme'.[198]

He expected to be teaching a course on imperialism, and between April and June 1936 he attended lectures and read extensively in imperial history, evidently feeling confident of the appointment. But in July, in spite of supportive references from both Gilbert Murray and W.G. Adams, the Warden of All Souls College, Oxford (another of Leys' talented friends from his student days in Glasgow), the board of the new college rejected his application. Perhaps they wanted a trained librarian (Murray's letter of reference said he had 'nothing particular to say about his suitability as a librarian'), or perhaps they knew Leys' reputation and thought him too 'extreme'. The letter he sent to Fraser in July, acknowledging receipt of this news, is free from any complaint, although it was clearly a shock and a major setback.[199]

It seems likely that he had in the meantime sold his practice, expecting to move to Scotland, or he may have hired a locum to cover the time he spent away from Brailsford preparing for his lectures. His landlord refused to sell them the house in Brailsford, so he and Janey now moved to Yalding, in Kent, another village of the kind that he had once supposed 'existed only on postcards'. It was nearer to London, and so nearer Nanice in London. Their income from savings and his pension was modest but, he told Leonard Woolf, 'we have as much money as a consistent socialist ought to want and far more than thousands of other and more deserving people have'.[200] But as the international situation grew steadily darker, so did his mood. He tended to find his frequent African visitors frustrating, and as his health declined he became 'rather deaf', 'dogmatic and quarrelsome', Nanice told Wylie, and lost his sense of humour.[201]

Worst of all, perhaps, after 1941 he was for the first time at odds with his adored daughter. During the blitz in London Nanice fell in love with Bill Avery, a fellow Air Raid Precaution warden. Avery ran a corner shop that he had inherited from his mother, and was the lone parent of two small children, having been abandoned by his wife. Norman and Janey disapproved of him. Exactly why they disapproved is unclear. For Norman Leys he was probably just not the kind of well-educated, unencumbered, preferably socialist husband that he had had in mind for his daughter. Janey's reason may have been different: after Norman died she stopped opposing the marriage, but she still left Nanice only a 'life interest' in her estate. Nanice did marry Bill, but only after Janey died in 1956, when Nanice was 52. Her response to what seems a tragic case of prejudice is as baffling as the rest of it.

But Leys' political commitment remained strong. In 1938, together with his friend, the journalist Leonard Barnes, and the South African social anthropologist Julius Lewin, he founded a new journal, called *Empire*, which was later taken over by the Fabian Society; and in 1939 he re-joined the Labour Party's Advisory Committee and wrote a paper against the 'colour bar' which was adopted as party policy. And in 1941, at the lowest point in the war, when injustice in Kenya could hardly have been further down anyone's agenda, he turned that paper into a third, very short book, *The Colour Bar in East Africa*. Covering all the Central and East African colonies for which the government in London remained responsible – Northern Rhodesia, Nyasaland, Tanganyika and Uganda, as well as Kenya, *The Colour Bar* aimed to describe the way Africans were discriminated against in each of them, and how these injustices came about.

The book contained some sharp formulations and insights, but it was curiously ill-organised and fragmentary. It didn't provide a systematic account of racial discrimination in each colony, or a systematic analysis of what sustained the discrimination. It seemed to presuppose some general familiarity with the issues, yet it often reads like a primer. Some of its shortcomings no doubt stemmed from Leys' age and ill-health, but its peculiar character was mainly due to its aim. By 1939 his disillusion with Labour had been replaced by a cautious hope that the next Labour Colonial Secretary would be different. Nanice told Wylie that he had conceived a great admiration for Clement Attlee, who became leader of the Labour Party in 1935. On one occasion Attlee had stayed with them in Brailsford after addressing a meeting in Derby. According to Nanice, Leys said that Attlee 'was so quiet that he could bring about a revolution without anyone knowing it.' So *The Colour Bar in East Africa* was indeed written as a sort of primer for whoever the next Labour Colonial Secretary turned out to be. That moment could be several years away, and Leys might not be alive when it arrived. Writing *The Colour Bar* was something he could still do, and seemed worth doing. Leonard Woolf shared his anxiety to find a way to get the next Labour Colonial Secretary to keep the party's promises, and agreed to publish it.[202]

The book ended with a draft dispatch for a future Colonial Secretary to send to the governors of all five East African colonies, imitating 'the dispatches on the same subject that were written a century ago, that were often downright and specific as State papers rarely are these days'.[203] This was a reference to dispatches which the Colonial Secretary Lord Stanley had sent to the Governor of Jamaica in the 1830s. Slavery had been abolished in 1833, but the local laws enforcing racial discrimination remained intact in Jamaica and the other West Indian colonies. Stanley had finally ordered the governors to stop pandering to the resistance of the planters and enforce equal legal rights for all. The draft dispatch in *The Colour Bar* was meant to do this for modern slavery in East Africa. It ordered an end to all discrimination on grounds of race, colour or religion, and the provision of education equally for all within 5 years.

The Colour Bar was very slight compared with *Kenya*, but even if it had been a much better book it was not likely to have achieved its aim. From 1946 onwards the Colonial Secretary in Attlee's post-war government was Arthur Creech Jones, who had been one of Leys' and Woolf's main allies on the Labour Party's Advisory Committee, and he undoubtedly felt in no need of a primer. But while he was interested in the colonies, and much better informed than Passfield, he too undertook no significant reform in Kenya. The immediate reason was that the British economy had emerged from the war too weak to risk losing any of the support that the country's sterling balances received from colonial exports. No radical disruption of the existing system of production in Kenya could be contemplated.* On the contrary, policies to support settler production intensified, and fresh immigration to Kenya from Britain was subsidised. Overcrowding, especially in the Kikuyu reserve, was responded to not by enlarging the reserve but by 'closer administration' – more and more pressure to do unpaid work on soil conservation.[204] British interests prevailed over African interests and as Leys had long predicted, the 'Mau Mau' rebellion followed.

The weaknesses of *The Colour Bar in East Africa* reflected Leys' declining powers. He still had a chronically weak lung, and he had had two recent attacks of pneumonia. In 1944 he was diagnosed with cancer of the tongue. It was to Leonard Woolf that he sent, in August 1944, perhaps the last letter he ever wrote. He wanted to continue the fight, but knew he was dying. He comforted himself with some evidence that his work had not been wholly in vain:

> I feel so grateful to the Hogarth Press that I would like to make it a votive offering of some sort before I die. Isn't it astonishing how 'Kenya' goes on selling after more than twenty years? ... there is a real but small chance that my new trouble is remediable. If my Panjandrum in London says it is I *might* manage to arouse myself to do something about the answers the notorious Elspeth Huxley was allowed to give broadcast to people who sent questions about East Africa ... One was 'why do the natives get on so badly with the settlers in Kenya?' I purred with joy to hear it, though it wasn't the question I would have chosen, and bethought me 'no one can deny that if I had not lived such questions would never have been asked'. Solely responsible I know, of course, I am not, but I did define and was the first to explain the peculiarly East African situation.
>
> I care even more and wish I could help in a battle that Archd. Owen is fighting [to get forced marriages banned in Kenya] ... Isn't there a woman MP who wouldn't just take this up but make a resounding victory for justice out of it? ...

---

* The economic motives that blocked any change in the 'settler system' in Kenya also prompted the ill-fated Groundnuts Scheme in Tanganyika; see Nicholas Westcott, *Imperialism and Development: the East African Groundnut Scheme and its legacy*, Woodbridge, Suffolk: James Currey, 2020, pp. 17-18 and 35.

Bless you. If sooner than you I reach the fields of amaranth and moly I shall search out and greet your wife'.[205]

He died two weeks later.

9: The outcome

As early as 1919 Leys recognised that it was unlikely that a radical change of policy would happen in time to prevent a rebellion. He told Gilbert Murray that a missionary friend, who had been working in Kenya for fifteen years, a 'High Tory' who didn't share his politics, had just written to him saying that the tribe he lived and worked with were now 'as likely as not to massacre all Europeans within reach in a year or two'. He himself was unsure how soon it would happen,

> but that facts and persons in Africa are sorting themselves out along the single line of being ready to murder and burn, I have no doubt at all. I have no hope, until the general European revolution [he meant a social democratic revolution] and its echoes reach the corners of the world, of stopping anything. But I hope by explaining to a few to check the subsequent orgy to the devils of Law and Order.[206]

Unlike Oldham and other liberals with no experience of Africa, he understood what the response to a rebellion would be like. It was what made him impatient with Oldham's pursuit of 'ultimate aims', and sceptical of Oldham's claim to have found senior officials in the Colonial Office who were seriously interested in change. The truth was that the officials in neither Kenya nor London were paying attention to what Africans were enduring and thinking. In 1950 the rebellion Leys had foreseen duly came, and with it the reaction he had feared.

The immediate cause was no longer taxation and forced labour. Population growth had finally compelled Africans to seek wage labour without being coerced, but it had also led to a crisis of land shortage, especially in the Kikuyu reserve. From the late 1930s onwards, and especially during the Second World War, rising demand for the produce of settler farms had allowed the settlers to invest in capital; they now needed fewer unskilled labourers, and also wanted to bring more of their land into cultivation. This led them to tighten the conditions under which about 250,000 people, mainly Kikuyu, had been living as 'squatters' on settler land, cultivating land and keeping cattle in return for the adult males doing three or four months' work a year for the settler. Now more and more of these workers were told to become virtually full-time employees or leave. Most of those who left, or were evicted, had by then lost any right to land in the Kikuyu Reserve, and were effectively homeless.[207] The trigger for rebellion had shifted from forced labour to landlessness.

In the late 1940s small groups of primitively-armed men started moving to the forested areas on the edges of the Kikuyu Reserve.[208] Most Kikuyu supported them, having sworn an oath of tribal solidarity that was being organised throughout the countryside by a secret committee in Nairobi. People who were reluctant to take the oath were intimidated. In 1952 he government started organising a programme of counter-oathing. This was met by a small but growing wave of murders of police informers or people simply identified as government supporters; by the end of the year 121 Kikuyu loyal to the regime had been killed. In October 1952 a State of Emergency was declared. Soon after this settler families began to be attacked; a total of 32 whites were eventually killed. The police, augmented by settlers in the Police Reserve, the Kikuyu Home Guard and five battalions of the British army launched a violent and largely indiscriminate repression. The administration defined 'Mau Mau' as an atavistic sickness, but also made supporting it a crime. All Kikuyu were treated as guilty unless they could convince their interrogators in detention centres that they were innocent.

Half of all the Kikuyu men in Nairobi were arrested and sent to 'work camps' for interrogation. Between 1952 and 1959 one in four of all Kikuyu men was held in one or more of these camps, which eventually developed into a so-called 'pipeline', through which detainees passed towards their eventual release if they satisfied their captors that they had recanted. They had to confess to having taken an oath, tell everything they knew about other Mau Mau supporters, sing songs denouncing Mau Mau, and work hard. If they continued to comply they were moved from camp to camp towards release. As most people felt bound by their oath, confessions were often obtained through repeated beatings, denial of food, and other forms of torture, on top of hard labour. Infections were rife in the camps and there was little or no medical care. Deaths were common and often not reported. Outside the camps the police and the army beat and shot people with impunity.

On top of this, in 1954, in order to cut off the support that the forest fighters were getting from people the rural areas – chiefly food and information – the government moved the entire rural Kikuyu population of over a million people – mainly women, children, and old men – into 804 Emergency Villages – in effect concentration camps. The camps were controlled by 'loyalist' Home Guards, who were allowed and even encouraged to brutalise the inmates.

A so-called 'hard core' of some 12,000 detainees who were judged 'irreconcilable' Mau Mau supporters were locked up in four permanent 'exile' camps, in remote unhealthy areas, where they were forced to work and from which they were intended never to return. It was in one of these, called Hola, that a mass murder took place in 1959. The administration decided to finally 'break' the inmates' refusal to work by beating them, if necessary, to death, and eleven died. The Hola camp murders could not be concealed and finally made it impossible for the government in London to go on defending the indefensible.

Even the historian David Anderson, in his studiously dispassionate account of the Emergency, felt bound to include some graphic examples of what the repression meant, lest the reality should be too difficult for his readers to grasp. In 1962 a former member of the Police Reserve described how he had treated three suspects:

> While we were waiting for the sub-inspector to come back I decided to question the Mickeys. They wouldn't say a thing, of course, and one of them, a tall coal-black bastard, kept grinning at me, real insolent. I slapped him hard, but he kept right on grinning at me, so I kicked him in the balls as hard as I could. He went down in a heap but when he finally got up on his feet he grinned at me again and I snapped, I really did. I stuck my revolver right in his grinning mouth and I said something, I don't remember exactly what, and I pulled the trigger. His brains went all over the side of the police station. The other two Mickeys were standing there looking blank. I said to them that if they didn't tell me where to find the rest of the gang I'd kill them too. They didn't say a word so I shot them both. One wasn't dead so I shot him in the ear. When the sub-inspector drove up, I told him that the Mickeys tried to escape. He didn't believe me but all he said was 'bury them and see the wall is cleaned up'.[209]

In a later book Caroline Elkins listed the kinds of crime routinely committed against people suspected of any kind of support for Mau Mau:

They used electric shock and hooked suspects up to car batteries. They tied suspects to vehicle bumpers with just enough rope to drag them to death. They employed burning cigarettes, fire, and hot coals. They thrust bottles (often broken), gun barrels, knives, snakes, vermin, sticks and hot eggs up men's rectums and into women's vaginas. They crushed bones and teeth; sliced off fingers or their tips; and castrated men with specially designed instruments or by beating a suspect's testicles 'till the scrotum burst' according to Anglican church officials. Some used a *kiboko,* or a rhino whip, for beating; others used clubs, fists, and truncheons.[210]

Some of Elkins' respondents also described what it meant to be a Kikuyu woman locked up every night in an Emergency Village if you were not an approved 'loyalist': they could be raped and sometimes tortured, while children and old people died of malnutrition and diseases.

No overall figure exists of deaths and injuries of Kikuyu men, women and children in the years 1952-59. The colonial government put the figure of Kikuyu deaths at 11,000. It was certainly many times greater. But even if it existed, no statistic could convey the trauma inflicted on the Kikuyu in those years. Their physical and mental suffering, and their division into 'loyalists' who joined in the repression and were rewarded for it, and those they repressed – were traumas from which Kenyan society has still not fully recovered. No colonial official was ever put on trial for the crimes committed in the repression. One of the leading superintendents of the systematic beating in the camps was awarded the Order of the British Empire.

Leys died six years before the rebellion began. His analysis had proved painfully accurate. Landlessness was just as much a consequence of the 'settler system' as forced labour, and the reaction to the rebellion showed how profoundly racist settler colonialism was. There was not only the overt racism of the settlers who flocked into the Kenya Police Reserve and called for the extermination of Mau Mau, but also the deep-seated racism of the white policemen, soldiers and colonial officers who implemented the repression, the racism of the Governor who ordered it, and the racism of the government in London who defended the reign of terror until the last minute with prevarication and lies.

The scale and savagery of the repression have been largely forgotten in Britain, though not in Kenya. But anyone contemplating it, and Leys' analysis of its causes, cannot help seeing what has been happening in Palestine since 2023 as a similar episode in the history of settler colonialism: the history of the Jewish settlers who founded the state of Israel, of the Israeli settlers who have been gradually colonising the West Bank, and of the Palestinians whose land they are occupying. The Kenya settlers' reaction to the 'Mau Mau' rebellion has been echoed by Israeli ministers' reaction to the Hamas attack in October 2023; the detention and torture of Kikuyu in Kenya has been parallelled by the detention and torture of Palestinians in Israel;[211] and the complicity of the British government in the repression of the Kikuyu has been paralleled by the complicity of successive British governments in the genocide in Gaza.

Since Leys' day the costs of dissent have been raised: he paid a price by being demoted, exiled and denigrated, but nothing worse, and the pages of the *Manchester Guardian* were still open to him. Today, dissenters can lose their jobs, and the *Guardian* no longer publishes forthright criticism of government foreign policy.* Journalists in the West are arrested, ostensibly for writing something that can be construed as supportive of Hamas but in reality because they have criticised Israel.** But Leys would surely not have seen today's more intolerant situation as a reason for staying silent about racism and injustice in Gaza or anywhere else. At the end of *A Last Chance in Kenya* he quoted some 'wise words of Mr Gladstone', which are as pertinent today as they were then:

> I am sorry to say that if no instructions had been addressed in political crises to the people of this country except to remember to hate violence, to love order, and to exercise patience, the liberties of this country would never have been attained.[212]

---

* Examples of dissenters who have lost their jobs include Professor David Miller, dismissed by Bristol University; Jeremy Corbyn, driven out of the Labour Party; and Steve Bell, dismissed by the *Guardian*.

** Cases include Craig Murray, Kit Klarenberg, Richard Medhurst, Sarah Williams and Asa Winstanley.

10: Intellectual legacy

The coherence of the analysis in *Kenya*, its strong moral undercurrent, and its pithy and sometimes poetic style ensured that it would have a big impact. Its example encouraged a retired missionary in India, Edward Thompson (the father of the social historian E.P. Thompson), to bring out a book detailing the unspeakable atrocities committed by the British in India following the Bengal mutiny in 1857, a book he had written but had previously been too nervous to publish.[213] And Leys' account of the Chilembwe rising was lifted and reproduced, as we saw earlier, by C.L.R. James in his *History of Pan-African Revolt*.

Later students of imperialism and colonialism have also found Leys' work rich in insights. George Shepperson, who wrote the definitive study of the Chilembwe rising, thought that Leys 'cast an eye towards' Frantz Fanon's theory of 'therapeutic' violence.[214] Leys didn't see violence by Africans against Europeans as therapeutic, as Fanon did, but as we saw earlier, he concluded his letter to the Colonial Secretary with the observation that there is 'one means that, unfortunately, man can always use to prove that he is not canine but human, not slave but free, the murder of his master'. Thirty-odd years later Fanon wrote that 'the native knows that he is not an animal; and it is precisely at the moment he realises his humanity that he begins to sharpen the weapons with which he will secure its victory.'[215]

An even clearer anticipation of later thinking was the way Leys' focus on the impact of unregulated capitalist development in Kenya was taken up in Karl Polanyi's famous thesis on the impact of 'self-regulating capital'. Leys saw the destruction of the social bonds of African society under settler colonialism, without state intervention to limit it, or to protect Africans from the consequences, as 'the full and perfect expression of the capitalist system'. In Europe the growth of the capitalist system had been offset by the simultaneous extension of democracy, which protected people from its worst effects: but in Kenya, he wrote, the victims of capitalism were 'plunged, defenceless, into the current of social forces which in civilized countries are kept under control, but which in Kenya have burst all their banks.'[216] In *The Great Transformation*, published in 1944, Polanyi wrote that 'robbed of the protective covering of social institutions, human beings would perish from the effects of social exposure; they would die as victims of acute social dislocation through vice, perversion, crime and starvation'.[217] Whereas in Europe states were able to protect themselves against 'the backwash of international free trade', 'the politically unorganised colonial peoples could not'. As a result, peoples in the 'exotic and semi-colonial regions' were subjected to 'unspeakable suffering'.

Given the originality of these and other insights in Leys' work it is rather puzzling that he seems to have arrived at them without any help from earlier or contemporary social science. Nowhere in his books or letters is there any reference to writers on political economy. His training as a doctor, and in public health, will have helped, but the basis of his analysis seems to have been simply his reading of world history, his curiosity, and his strongly-felt need to systematise. In his letters to Murray he mentions Gibbon and Von Hügel and Euripides, and occasionally a contemporary writer on religion or race relations, but not Adam Smith or Ricardo, or even J. A. Hobson's widely-read 1902 book, *Imperialism*. Marx is mentioned only once, in a letter complaining that the journalist and critic of colonialism Leonard Barnes, whom he tried unsuccessfully to persuade the Derby Labour Party to adopt as a parliamentary candidate, was 'a little over-fascinated by Marx, who attracts intelligent people against their will as the sun attracts planets'.[218]

The lack of any other reference to Marx is especially striking because his grasp of the dynamic nature of capitalism was so sure. His insistence that tribal life was already being transformed by capitalism, making it futile to base policy on the idea of preserving it, reminds one of Lenin's criticism of the Russian populists on similar grounds. But there is no indication that he had ever read anything written by Marx, let alone by Lenin. In his letter to A.G. Fraser in 1936 about the lectures on imperialism he was planning to give at Newbattle Abbey College, he summarised the central features of what he called 'capitalist industry' in a few bullet points, and described how it was overwhelming societies all over the world.

By Capitalist industry I mean industry that is (1) highly mechanised (2) productive of huge numbers of identical articles which by their cheapness kill industry organised otherwise (3) conducted with the incentive of making maximum profit to private owners (4) controlled by a tiny minority with immense power in Parliament, over the press etc.[219]

But he ended by asking 'Does a single book give an account of its essential features?' He could hardly have written this if he had read *Capital*, even if he had read and rejected it. I suspect his idea of Marxism was based on the crude version promoted by the Third International between the wars which he will have encountered among some British anti-imperialist activists. His own socialism was Christian in inspiration, and parliamentary.

Another remarkable absence from his writing is Ireland. His brother Kenneth was a specialist on Irish history and the parallel between settler colonialism in Kenya and in Ireland must have struck them both. But the reference to 'the problems of the native Irish' in his postcard to Gilbert Murray (reproduced at the end of Chapter 1) is the only mention I have found that suggests, tantalisingly, that he had indeed thought about the parallel. He also makes no reference to the long history of anti-racist writing, from early writers against slavery in the eighteenth century to Mary Kingsley in the late 1890s; or to the history of the extermination of indigenous peoples in North America and Australia, and the exterminist, survival-of-the-fittest doctrines that were invoked to justify it.[220] This silence is almost harder to explain than the lack of reference to writers on political economy, since when he was living in Northfield, Massachusetts, Leys had been old enough to hear something about the racism and lynchings that were rampant in the post-bellum US South. What is more, the barbarism of King Leopold's Congo was going on while he was a medical student living in the university Settlement in Glasgow, where world events were energetically debated, and the genocide of the Hereros in German South West Africa (Namibia) took place while he was in Chinde. It's difficult to believe that Leys hadn't followed these events to some extent, and hadn't read any of the debates about them; so it is striking that he never mentions any of them, or any other anti-racist writers, even in his letters to Woolf and Murray. It seems as if he developed his analysis of colonial exploitation entirely without reference to these events or the literature on them.

Leys also appears to have had relatively little engagement with other anti-colonial groups. Apart from the Anti-Slavery and Aborigines Protection Society, and the Mandates Committee of the League of Nations Union, hardly any of the other anti-colonial or anti-imperial organisations and groups in Britain that are discussed by historians of the period feature in any of Leys' letters that I have seen.[221] Having a job, and living 130 miles from London, limited what he could do. His consuming aim was to end modern slavery in Kenya, on which he was an expert, and he had little time to spend on wider issues. He grudged spending time and money to attend meetings with people in London, many of whom would not put their name to plainly-worded criticisms of government policy. What he could do was write. His single-minded focus on principle from his home in deepest Derbyshire could irritate people in London who considered themselves serious activists. The Labour MP Drummond Shiels, another doctor, who had been Passfield's under-secretary of state at the Colonial Office, smarted at Leys' criticisms of their failure in *A Last Chance in Kenya*. He vented his irritation in a condescending review: the book's faults, he said, were 'those of a handicapped and somewhat lonely fighter for human justice, who is shocked and dismayed at the apparent indifference to his message of hoodwinked ministers and a callous bureaucracy, and who appeals to public opinion for support'.[222]

The self-made nature of Leys' analysis, based simply on the application of intelligence and a fair knowledge of history to the situation in Kenya, may explain why his predictions about the wider world in the 1930s were no better than those of anyone else who followed the news at the time. He had no general social theory or analytic framework that he could apply. At first he thought a movement as evil as Nazism could not last – there was 'far too much natural decency in mankind to enjoy it for long'.[223] Once it was clear that Nazism threatened to take over Europe, he tried to reassure his sister-in-law by telling her that whether you called it God or something else 'there is a stronger will in action than Hitler's. I am sure of that'.[224]

On the other hand, his method was not naïve. He always said that the facts would speak for themselves, but he was well aware that concepts determine what counts as a fact. When Oldham showed him the outline of a book he was proposing to write on 'interracial relationships', covering the USA, South Africa, West Africa, India, Japan, China, Korea and the Near East, Leys immediately saw the danger. He was afraid, he told Oldham, that Oldham would be 'tempted ... to describe, with conspicuous fairness, the position of various schools and types, and the direction of various currents, using uncritically the terms and conceptions they use'. He went on to illustrate, over several pages, the problem that the concept of 'race' itself presented. Would Oldham always take care to use the term in a way that would make it clear that whatever the people in his survey thought, racial differences were entirely due to differences of context – historical, geographic, etc – and were capable of being changed?[225]

Another example of Leys' awareness of the power of what we would now describe as 'framing' was the doctrine that native interests were 'paramount'. Most liberals were happy to take it as meaning that African interests would have priority. Leys knew it didn't, and rejected it. 'In truth', he wrote, 'No one knows what it means. No African, or friend of Africans, asks that in any respect Africans should be in a position higher than Europeans. All that is asked for is equal justice'. And again, 'The serf does not ask to be made paramount; he asks to be made free'.[226]

In arriving at his own concepts, Leys held that the key was to stay close to what ordinary people experienced and thought, and to be scrupulously accurate about what you saw – a kind of pure empiricism, apparently. But not really. In his letter to Fraser about the lectures he would give at Newbattle Abbey he said that in order to get an understanding of world events he would look for the causes of the two great movements of the day, Russian communism and German fascism, and would find them in the conditions of life of the masses, not in the thinking of elites. A retired administrator from India, Lord Hailey, had just covered 20,000 miles travelling round Africa collecting materials for his monumental *African Survey*, the outcome of Oldham's efforts to establish a researched evidence basis for colonial policy.* 'How can that enable him to grasp the central African problem', Leys asked, 'however many the high officials he talked with or the barazas of chiefs he met?' [227]

> *Live* in a country and get as intimate as you can with its ordinary inhabitants, and one can learn something ... The people to watch for – I don't pretend to spot them myself – are the Pauls preaching in market places and the Lenins pamphleteering in garrets.

* Hailey, a former administrator in India, had no African experience. He rejected the view that there were physical differences between whites and blacks and recommended 'limited' official acknowledgment of African grievances and spending money on African development. His 1,800-page compendium, *An African Survey: A Study of Problems arising in Africa South of the Sahara*, London: The Royal Institute of International Affairs, 1938, became the bible of colonial officials until post-war nationalism consigned it to the dustbin of history.

Underlying Leys' analysis was, obviously, a set of moral values and a principle for selecting what to study based on a view of what drove changes in the world and a wish to help push change in the right direction. If he had read Marx's eleventh 'thesis on Feuerbach' – 'The philosophers have only *interpreted* the world in various ways; the point is to *change* it.' – Leys would surely have liked it. And if he had lived another twelve years he would have been delighted by the publication in 1956 of Thomas Hodgkin's path-breaking study of *African Political Parties*, based on talking with all the Pauls and Lenins he could find in post-war Africa.

In these ways Leys was very modern. But he was also a product of his time. The British Empire was a fact and the inclusion of East Africa in it had been inevitable. It made no sense to him to be opposed to its existence. Part of what made the imposition of European imperialism on Africa inevitable was the superiority of European technology, including firearms; but it was also due to the superiority of European culture. He had no illusions about European culture, but despite its vulgar consumerism he thought that it was superior to Maasai culture, and that this was obvious enough to need no elaboration. He didn't share the romantic view of the warlike pastoral Maasai as a special group of noble savages that settlers like Delamere liked to promote, in contrast to the agricultural, adaptable, and thus threatening, Kikuyu.

Today many people are uncomfortable with the position Leys held. It stemmed partly from his grounding in religious and Greek and Roman history, and his strong feeling for the 'great things' which Gilbert Murray had taught him to see as all-important. Maasai culture – and for that matter all tribal cultures – were, as a whole, incompatible with acquiring access to this inheritance; above all tribal cultures didn't leave people free to think what they liked. Anyone who is tempted to criticise this as colonialist needs to ponder Leys's response to those in his own time who wanted to protect Africans from 'Europeanisation'. 'I am heartily in favour of the revival of all that is distinctively indigenous in African life', he wrote. But that revival would be the work of 'Africans with new minds', i.e. liberated Africans.[228] 'We are detribalised', he pointed out; those who opposed 'detribalisation' were really trying to protect Africans from 'knowledge and liberty'.

Leys used words that are now taboo, like 'natives', 'savages', 'primitive', and others that were in common use in East Africa when he lived there, although rarely in his writing (and there, as Lotte Hughes notes, you can't always be sure he is not being ironic).[229] But while he was in these ways a product of the Empire, he was strongly opposed to the way in which the 'new imperialism' accorded the Empire's subjects different legal rights according to their colour. So while he accepted the British Empire as a given he was never an enthusiast for it, and was increasingly sceptical about its future. In *The Colour Bar in East Africa* he pointed out that in the Roman Empire the son of a slave could rise to the highest rank, and said that 'When Indian coolies and Kikuyu labourers can hope that ability in their grandsons may be as well rewarded we shall have reason to have confidence in the permanence of the British Empire'.[230] As there was no prospect of that happening he clearly didn't think the Empire would survive, or deserved to.

Leys was paternalistic – and indeed patriarchal, in his home life – in a way that also marks him as a man of his time. He was paternalistic in relation to people whom he saw as less able than he was to make good decisions about their lives. A good example comes from Wylie's interview with George Rodgers, mentioned earlier. During the general strike of 1926, a group of miners who were marching to London passed through Brailsford. According to Rodgers, 'Leys refused to give them money because he said they'd just spend it, so he sat them down on his lawn, bought a 40lb. Derby cheese, bought all the bread in a nearby shop and sat them down on his lawn and fed them'. This kind of paternalism clearly extended to many of his Derbyshire patients – 'the peasantry of some backward English county, among whom even now the traditions of a servile age survive' – whom he compared with the peasants of Kenya.[231]

John Cell thought Leys was also paternalist in his relations with African politicians of his own generation, such as Kenyatta and Joseph Kang'ethe, the leaders of the Kikuyu Central Association, but this is questionable.[232] Leys had foreseen that capitalist development was likely to produce leaders who didn't share his political opinions and might not even be very scrupulous, and so it had proved. 'We should not be impatient or disappointed to learn that what people [in Kenya] want is better opportunities to get rich', he wrote in 1941. 'You cannot expect lofty ideals in people when the one lesson we have taught them all is that they must earn money to pay tax or go to jail'.[233]

Leys differed from Kenyatta and Kang'ethe on various issues, and argued with them. He was as ready to be as difficult with them as he was with everyone else.

Norman Leys and the author in 1932

11: The man himself

Leys was first and foremost a man of principle, and you can admire him but not feel you would have liked to spend an evening with him. But there was more to him than his principles, and it would be short-changing him not to finish this account of his life with a more rounded picture.

There is no doubt that even those who knew and liked him found him difficult at times. Virginia Woolf's comment, that he was 'not altogether easy company about the house', could well have been made by McGregor Ross, Leonard Woolf, Oldham, his brother Duncan and quite possibly Winifred Holtby too. He was never deliberately rude, but he always just said what he thought. Or as his daughter Nanice told Diana Wylie: 'They always said he would tell a baker how to bake bread but would want the baker to put him right'. That side of Leys was affectionately satirised by Holtby in her novel *Mandoa, Mandoa!*, if one accepts that the character of Arthur Rollett, whom we met in Chapter 8, is partly based on him. In one scene Rollet interrupts a tea-party of complacent liberals, urgently seeking to persuade the host, Lord Lufton, to take up arms against a newly-discovered scandal.

> Arthur Rollett was well aware that he was ruining a pleasant tea-party. But he could not think a tea-party was more important than the Right. He rose to his feet … 'I know I am a tactless man,' he said, looking down upon them. 'But I cannot help it. I am unable. I am simply unable, to understand the point of view of men and women who cannot feel the shame, who cannot wish to prevent – even at the expense of interrupting an agreeable week-end – this evil thing. Don't you see that you and I – the British public – on whom the responsibility ultimately rests for what our government does – don't you see that we are committing one of the most hideous African transactions since the Belgian Congo scandal? I can't understand it.[234]

Anyone who is disposed to think Leys was a tedious nuisance can find entertaining support in the character of Arthur Rollett, but Holtby was close to Leys and found him lovable. It would be nice to know whether Leys spotted the allusion to himself, and if so, whether he found it amusing. I'm not sure his sense of humour was equal to it. He read *Mandoa, Mandoa!* on the RMS Apapa, the ship taking him to the Gold Coast (today's Ghana) to visit Achimota College; his letters to Holtby show him struggling to find positive things to say about the novel, which is rather embarrassingly bad, and quite patronising towards Africans.* He felt bound to tell her that her 'bloodthirsty and sensual' Mandoans were as unlike as possible the Africans he used to know.[235] My guess is that the Rollett character's resemblance to himself simply escaped his notice.

A really keen sense of humour, which requires a sense of the ridiculous, is probably rare among puritans. Leys liked practical jokes, a bad sign; they had been popular at the Settlement in Glasgow. But he did share a quiet sense of humour with those who knew him well, and the barbs of satire and touches of irony in his books and letters can be fun. The American educationalist Jesse Jones, who had chaired a commission on education (the 'Phelps Stokes Commission') to East Africa in 1923, advocated education for Africans focused on 'hygiene, industry and character formation', which impressed Oldham. Leys' comment was that 'one can only say that if the Americans have really discovered any specific means of making boys and girls good, it is a pity that they describe it so obscurely'.[236] Somewhere in-between practical jokes and irony, chiefly in his letters to Holtby and occasionally to Woolf, was a mildly amusing form of self-mockery. This was often about money. 'I have a confession to make', he told Holtby.

> There is something I want more than justice for Africans, more than fame, more than the affection of my neighbours, more than a front seat in Paradise, and that is MONEY, pots and pots of it… I would do anything for money. But as in fact I know of no way of getting it in quantity big enough to be worth while I do nothing at all about it. If only somebody would come along and offer me a bribe. They offer them to other people. Why not to me?[237]

---

* *Mandoa, Mandoa!* was written against the clock in an effort to compete with Evelyn Waugh, who was writing his racist but funny novel, *Black Mischief*, at the same time, as both of them tried to capitalise on the publicity given to the same event, the crowning of the Emperor of Ethiopia in 1930.

In another letter to Holby he said he was thinking of kidnapping the daughter of a local landowner for ransom; he thought he could keep her hidden for a week. He worried about not leaving Janey enough money to live on comfortably, saying she had paid the price of his political opinions.[238] He also felt that his lack of money, relative to people with private incomes, prevented him giving all he could to the cause of justice in Kenya – 'my one job that may redeem my life from failure', as he once put it to Oldham.[239]

In the 1930s, after the disappointment of the 1929-31 Labour Government, and as the Nazi threat to Europe grew and his health declined, Leys tended to get depressed, and his political isolation and his lack of close friends, didn't help. The two friends with whom he felt intimate, Leonard Woolf and Winifred Holtby, were epistolary friends whom he rarely saw. Someone with a different personality might have remedied this, but Leys couldn't. He had been shaped to be a loner.

That doesn't mean he enjoyed being alone. In 1936, when he thought he was going to join the staff at Newbattle Abbey College, he wrote to A.G. Fraser, the College's Principal, saying his lectures would be based on studying what ordinary people were thinking, not on official reports or the views of people in authority. But the thought made him sad – 'annoyed' was the word he used – because it would once again make him 'a heretical minority'. 'In Africa I didn't mind. I was young and can honestly say I sought the true and the real. But now I want the kind of mental ease that comes from working with people one agrees with. I do expect partial agreement from you.'[240] But almost by return of post he learned that his application had been rejected.

The Christian dimension of his thought, which had led him to go to Africa, and which infused his writing, was never far below the surface. He tried hard to live according to the Golden Rule, to treat others as he wished to be treated himself. In Brailsford he and Janey went to the Anglican church in the village, to be part of the community, and sometimes they went to the Presbyterian church in Derby, six miles away, but he had little time for organised religion. He told Oldham: 'At heart I am a Quaker. They have kept the idea of a corporate conscience. I don't believe in a man's trusting entirely to conscience, or to what he considers the voice of the Spirit in his heart. I want guidance from my fellow Christians.'[241]

But where were fellow Christians to be found? Most people who saw themselves as Christians didn't see Jesus' teaching as a practicable guide to daily life. In 1932 he told Holtby: 'Fraser and Owen are among the very few Christians I know.* I am thinking about trying to be one again. If only everyone around me would try too I am sure I could manage'.[242] In his last years he became increasingly preoccupied with Christian ethics and was working on a book-length interpretation of the New Testament for the twentieth century. A letter to A.G. Fraser in 1942 shows him struggling to clarify his understanding of what recent scholarship had shown Jesus' position to be in relation to both belief and morals, as opposed to what church leaders from Paul onwards had said it was. Leys wanted another Reformation, but this time based on Jesus' revolutionary ethical principles unencumbered by residues of the customs and doctrines that prevailed in the years immediately after Jesus' death.[243]

Leys was, in short, a thorough puritan, in the original sense of the word. With regard to sex, he disliked 'lust', and 'vice' but he was realistic. African men who were forced to work away from home for months on end could not be expected to be celibate: 'Among a pure proletariat regular marriage is incongruous with economic circumstances'.[244] What concerned him were the consequences of short-term alliances and prostitution for family life and the transmission of venereal diseases. As regards the personal behaviour of fellow Europeans he was matter-of-fact. In Chinde many of the Scottish, English and German men he looked after as patients had lived 'quite openly, and as a rule quite happily, with African concubines'.[245] What seems to have mattered to him was whether they did so openly, 'in the front veranda', or 'furtively'. When the exotic Dutch novelist and socialist Odette Keun (remembered by the Brailsford pub landlord as 'some kind of princess') stayed with them in Brailsford, disabled by misery, having been abandoned by H.G. Wells after a twelve-year relationship, Leys was sympathetic, not censorious.[246] He was inhibited, but not prudish. He told Holtby he had been 'brought up to be afraid of women, by two maiden aunts. I think I am still afraid of them, but not so much'.[247]

His brother Duncan knew him better than anyone except Janey and Nanice. In a letter to Winifred Holtby in 1933 Duncan asked her if she had noticed 'a kind of increased sereneness in Norman lately. He doesn't lack energy, but is much easier company and less easily put out – often rather sad, I think, though he's quite capable of bursts of

---

* A.G. Fraser, the Principal of Achimota College in the Gold Coast; Archdeacon Owen, the leading missionary in Kavirondo, western Kenya.

genuine high spirits…He's neither saint nor hero, and I've known him rather cruel at times, and most damnably intolerant, yet he appears to me as a kind of rock of wisdom in a very shifty hard world. Probably the main thing is that he is not afraid?'[248] Forty years later Duncan included a section on Norman in a family memoir, from which I have extracted the most revealing parts:

> Throughout his life he exerted a bare minimum of energy to advance his position professionally. … His attitude was the outcome of a puritan education accepted by a man of high intelligence and active, aggressive temperament, a modern roundhead. But he was a sensitive man, impulsive, generous, powerfully critical when he thought criticism needed, of attitudes and individuals,
>
> He had absolutely no manual skill. He loved practical jokes. He used to claim that he had 'let it be known' that he could not do up parcels. Once [when] I was driving with him in the quiet lanes of his Derbyshire practice, there was a puncture. I changed the wheel and he was lost in admiration; he had never attempted it.
>
> He was less a respecter of persons than anyone I have ever known. His socialism was typically British, growing out of his religion. He thought socialism the necessary modern interpretation of Jesus' teaching. He hated public speaking and adopted a curious aloof manner, gazing anywhere but at his audience, but his lecture would be meticulously prepared.
>
> Janey had pathological anxieties about him, of which the most obvious was that he would become alcoholic or a drug addict … Norman did certainly seem to be somewhat dependent on a medicine bottle of whiskey which he carried on his rounds in his country practice, but I think this was because his wife showed such uneasiness at any over-drinking … He was very gentle and tender with animals: they always had a cat at Brailsford.

Leys' obituary in *The New Statesman* is thought to have written by Leonard Woolf, who knew him better than anyone then alive outside the family. It ended by saying that 'in ordinary life he was the most simple, modest and kindly of men'.[249]

Virginia Woolf did not know him so well, but she was skilled at quickly sizing people up. Leys stayed with the Woolfs once or twice while Leonard was producing *Kenya*, and in September 1924 Virginia wrote in her diary:

Norman Leys was here one night; making it quite plain that only certain sorts of people could pass the eye of his needle; & paring one down very quick; one of these good sturdy uncompromising men, whom M.L.D.* would like, very able, trusty; paying no attention to art of any kind, and enforcing his virtue at every turn – but it is virtue of course. Distrusts Oxford. Wishes to write as clearly as he can, hopes to live in the East end & educate working men. Wife spends £150 on garden; this distressing, but her only pleasure. Doesn't like taking fees, wh. mean that children go without boots. Thought me Thackeray's daughter & was only reassured when I cleared away dinner, and talked of religion, morality, his quarrel with the Colonial Office, how he was besieged; protests too much in short; but a very nice man.[250]

As for Leys paying 'no attention to art of any kind', it is true that his upbringing, and the life he had led, had not inclined him to take much interest in the kinds of art that interested Virginia Woolf. But he didn't lack aesthetic sensibility. He ended *Kenya* like this:

There are two moments in the African day when Nature herself strikes confidence in the heart. Just before sunrise all the night sounds cease. The whole earth is still, and exhales a quiet breath before the sun blinds and smothers it. It was surely then, in ancient times, that Memnon's strains were heard.** At that moment one knows that great things can be done. The other moment one remembers best [is] at the coast, when, just before sunset, the earth seems, after the long day's heat, to be restoring its light to the air from every particle. The palm, the house roof, the fisherman's boat on the reef, bloom in new colours, and shine sharp and clear as if luminescent. In that moment one knows that Africa is beautiful, and will respond generously by greater beauty to the best that man can do for man.[251]

---

* Margaret Llewellyn Davies, the influential Secretary of the Cooperative Women's Guild from 1889 to 1921.
** Memnon was a mythical king of Ethiopia, whose statue at Luxor was said to emit a sound like that of a lyre at dawn.

Annexes

1. The letter to the Colonial Secretary, 1918*
How Leys came to write this letter has been described in Chapter 4. It was a plea to the Colonial Office to end the forced labour, insecure land tenure and lack of legal rights from which Africans were suffering in Kenya, and which were the immediate cause of the 'disturbances' he saw coming, and for which the Kenya administration was preparing.

The letter was divided into eight numbered 'chapters'. If one were to give them titles they would be: I Land and forced labour; II The break-up of tribal life; III Islam; IV Christianity, Islam's rival; V What makes people loyal to a government; VI The Chilembwe rising and its significance for Kenya; VII what policies needed to be adopted to avoid a rising; VIII education and preparation for self-government. Here there is only space for a selection. Chapters I and II are included to show the cool but plain-speaking way in which Leys told the officials in London what life was like for Africans in Kenya – something he suspected, correctly, that they did not learn from the reports they received from Nairobi. Chapter III on Islam is included because it was so prescient: Leys thought that when East African Islam eventually reconnected to the wider Moslem world it would be dangerous to interests seen by Moslems as Western, as it has proved to be in the shape of Al-Shabaab. Chapter V, on loyalty, with its echoes of John Locke and Edmund Burke, shows Leys appealing to the Colonial Office officials' sense of themselves as honourable mean trying to rule the Empire well; and the final chapter VIII, ending with his warning of what would happen if nothing was done, is included because it called for Africans to be prepared for self-government at a time when the Colonial Office saw that as something too remote to be worth contemplating.

---

* The original copy of the letter is in the Gilbert Murray papers, Box 149, in the Bodleian Library in Oxford. It is reproduced, with one sentence inadvertently omitted, in John Cell (1976).

The Right Hon. The Secretary of State for the Colonies,
Downing Street, 7 February 1918

Sir,

I have the honour to request your acceptance of a statement descriptive of the existing situation in the Crown Colonies of East Africa. I write in the belief that civil disturbances are to be expected, disturbances that will eventually prove to be widespread and will in any case be destructive to the life and property of Europeans. I presume that you will already have received warnings from the proper authorities. My apology for making a statement of my own is a residence of sixteen years in British East Africa, Nyasaland and Portuguese East Africa, during which my position, while it has given me no claim to write with the authority due to your ordinary advisers, has permitted me to keep my ear close to the ground, and to study the facts and opinions of native life. These facts and opinions I shall attempt to describe and interpret. The mere discovery of unrest and of the danger of its expression in sedition reveals nothing that can serve for guidance. The unrest can be removed only by a policy rightly informed of its causes. Its various manifestations arise out of common origins, out of common currents of thought and ideas within a wide area that includes much diversity, and out of common industrial and economic conditions.

I *[Land and forced Labour]*

Analysis reveals the simplest factor of unrest, although not probably the most important in the end, to be economic. Superficially regarded the unrest appears to be due to economic grievances which, however greatly due to misconceptions, act with the force of reality. In Eastern Africa industrial and economic conditions are indeed the most uniform of all the conditions causing social change. They are also everywhere the most consciously felt of these conditions. The grievances arising out of them are easier of definition and easier of removal than the others. Their prompt treatment would at least postpone for some years seditious attempts.

These economic grievances arise out of the conditions of land tenure and of labour for Europeans. No detailed description of the varying conditions under which land is held and cultivated is necessary. It is sufficient to mention the fact that nowhere except in the ten mile strip on the coast – and there almost all the land has passed out of native ownership – has any native individual, family or tribe legal title to any land, and the equally important fact that besides thousands of natives who are entirely dependent for food on land held under Europeans, land for which they often have to pay rent either in money or in unpaid labour, there is a much larger number of natives who have merely just enough ground on which to grow their necessary food, to whom it is quite impossible to grow crops for sale, wherewith to pay the tax money and to buy trade goods. It is an immediate necessity that Governments in Eastern Africa should ensure for every family rent free land as secure in law as the land that the Crown has granted to Europeans. This rent free land must furthermore be situated in the area of the tribe to which the family belongs, and it must be adequate to the cultivation of crops for sale. These conditions are each strictly necessary if the general suspicion natives have that they are being squeezed out of the free occupation of land in their own country is to be dispelled. And if it is the case, as is to be feared, that the one difficulty in the way of such a policy is the existence of large tracts of land, mainly unimproved, granted by the Crown to Europeans, it is most necessary that no further land should be sold or leased to Europeans until the natives of the country are provided for. Unrest is probably nowhere else so great in Eastern Africa as it is among those who pay Europeans every year in rent several times larger than the purchase price paid to the Government by the Europeans for the land so used, land in many cases which natives regard as the property neither of Government nor of individual Europeans but as their own.

A still more potent cause of unrest can only be removed by making labour entirely and universally free. There is no slavery under our flag. But labour is performed under conditions which produce and even exaggerate some of the evils of slavery. These evils are certain to arise, unless actively prevented, whenever a race without civilization and without political rights comes into economic relation with members of the race that controls it. I say economic relation because the active cause is hope of profit. It is most important to recognize that we are dealing with men as moved by impersonal economic forces and not by either philanthropy or by cruelty. The motive of the West African slave trade was not race hatred but profit. The same motive operates now in Eastern Africa. Three generations ago it was believed that by preventing the ownership of the person slavery would be abolished. Servile conditions of a new type have arisen, in consequence of new and unforeseen factors. These new factors are the ownership of immense areas of land by Europeans in tropical Africa, the adoption by Government of the duty of helping European owners to develop their land, and the system of direct taxation. All these are new in our generation. The tax operates by compelling the earning of money. Money can be earned by the sale of commodities or by labour for others. Lack of sufficient land, absence of markets and ignorance of what to grow are causes generally operating to prevent production for sale. In Nyasaland, however, the system of differential taxation whereby the native who stays at home pays double the tax paid by the employee ensures most effectively the sale by natives of labour rather than of commodities and stimulates the flow of labour to plantations. In British East Africa the tax is uniform, so that other means have been necessary to supply the enormous demand for labour that has so rapidly arisen in the last fifteen years. There the size and situation of the land-grants themselves have been a powerful cause of migration of labour. In the Kavirondo plain and in the Kenia group of tribes the population is so thick that there is no room to do more than grow food, and the areas of natural overflow for the native population are in European occupation. In the Kikuyu Country in fact, where individual tenure of land is the tribal custom, land granted in freeholds to Europeans by the Crown is the ancestral home of thousands of natives.

Some six years ago, however, taxation, land restriction and the normal growth of the demand for trade goods among natives proved insufficient to supply the rapidly growing demand for labour. In a really free country wages would have risen, thus restricting industry to the more profitable channels. Wages did rise slightly from about 6 or 7, to 7 or 8 shillings a month, but little if any effect on supply resulted. The settlers demanded that the influence of the Government with the natives should be used to induce them to leave their homes to work for Europeans. The demand was acceded to. Magistrates were instructed to 'encourage' labour migration. 'Moral suasion' was to be used. These instructions were variously carried out. Some magistrates ignored them and were vigorously attacked in consequence by the settlers and their representatives on the legislative council. Others took the straightforward course of sending police or tax collectors to get men. Such means were officially disapproved. But I doubt whether labour, if it must be got, can be got with less friction and hardship by any other means. Most magistrates tried honestly to carry out their instructions and get the labour somehow without compulsion. Their usual procedure was to summon the chiefs and tell them to get the labour. That course seriously affected friendly relations between magistrates and chiefs and still further undermined the position of the chiefs themselves in the opinion of their own people. That method was, however, in general effective in producing the labour.

It is of the greatest importance to realise the authority carried by a magistrate's advice in most districts. Chiefs are summoned, roads and bridges kept up, food brought for sale, and a hundred other things are done or got, not by legal process but by administrative order. Government in these countries depends for its very existence on obedience to advice, directions, orders – call it what you will – of particular application, and not of the general application of law. To natives indeed a magistrate's orders have superior authority to law. Breaches of the law bring definite measurable penalties. Disobedience to Government orders is essentially sedition. Thus when magistrates tell chiefs they are to advise their men to work for Europeans, the 'advice' reaches the individual as something he dare not resist though he may try to avoid it. To call the system forced labour, to say that compulsion is used, is no abuse of language. Whatever may be the intention of those who sign directions to magistrates, compulsion is the form in which they reach the people concerned. The law indeed provides a safeguard. But, apart from the fact that natives, in British East Africa, though not in Nyasaland, are too ignorant to know how to appeal to it, the law only enables the individual to refuse any particular offer of employment. It cannot prevent a chief from worrying him because he prefers not to go to work for Europeans at all. Further, it is a gross breach of etiquette in the minds of natives in British East Africa, except the minority of the mission educated – and to natives manners, morals and law are in general indistinguishable – to take a European to court. A native never expects to get a verdict against a European. To prosecute a European is an unseemly way of trying to get revenge for some real or fancied wrong. To rob him, or even to murder him, is to natives not only a more natural, but a less offensive and less disgraceful way of getting even with him than a public accusation.

Such is the contrast, accordingly, between the picture given by the text of the law and the terms of administrative directions, and the picture given by the facts of native life and opinion. It is, of course, only the extreme docility of the African that allows the system to work at all. The harm to Government is the fact that natives consider Government and not the settlers responsible for their having to leave home to work, and for the specific injuries incidental to existing conditions of labour; for the food they get, inevitably inferior to what is available in the villages; for the diseases so prevalent in many plantations; for the punishments they receive from employers. The Government from time to time appoints an inspector to see that labourers receive their contract rates of pay. No attempt is made to fix or enforce a standard of hygienic and other conditions of life among employees. It is very doubtful if an attempt to do so would have results of any value. Improvement of these conditions can only be produced by other means which I shall refer to later. I here merely mention the important fact that the physical condition of unskilled labourers when they return home is markedly inferior to their condition on leaving home. One can always tell in which direction men are going when one meets a gang resting on the road from the appearance of the men.

The economic results of forced labour are important. Most of it is extremely bad in quality. The complaints by the settlers of deliberate idling are perfectly true. Many go to work with the intention of doing as little as possible, and how little that is no one without experience can imagine. Hence frequent fines and floggings and general bad feelings, felt by no means continuously by natives but always ready to be excited, an abundant fuel for seditious notions.

I have never met anyone in British East Africa familiar with native opinion there who knew of any tribe that would not prefer to see all Europeans leave the country. Of that fact the labour system provides the principal explanation. By itself it would not explain sedition. But it prepares for it in the general mind.

Compulsion affects the price of labour as well as its quality. Free labour in the conditions I have described is difficult to define. But if one calls labour free, when it seeks work without pressure from magistrates or chiefs then most of it is free. The wages of all are kept at a low level by the compulsion of some. Voluntary labour seeks work to get money for use. Forced labour has little or no use for the money it earns. Hence, in the Kenia province superabundance of cash more than doubled in a few years the price of sheep which are the real currency in that province. Scarcity, due to the withdrawal of labour from cultivation in the villages, also caused a rise in the price of all food.

A third result of compulsion is the practice of desertion, so bitterly complained of by settlers. Many natives in obedience to the orders of chiefs engage to work for Europeans with the deliberate intention of deserting. Natives commonly invent special means for entry on labour sheets so that they may not be traced when they reach home. Desertion is in British East Africa a heavily punished criminal offence.

I have drawn no complete picture. If I have emphasized the worst features it is because they exist and because I believe they will cause insurrection. On the top of these pre-war conditions came the immense demand for porters for the military forces. These porters were compelled to serve, explicitly so. In our opinion the occasion abundantly justified compulsion. In native opinion with few exceptions the war is merely the result of rivalry between two conquering races. Tens of thousands of porters have died of disease and privation. The war has destroyed for ever our claim to be the protector from wars of natives with one another. Even in Nyasaland, where five years ago most tribes would have by no means wished us to leave the country, the feeling is now in many parts very different.

I am convinced that if serious trouble is to be avoided in the next few years it is necessary at once to make labour free in fact and everywhere; to forbid and strictly to enforce the prohibition of every kind of influence by magistrates and other government agents over the free choice of natives. Natives must not only be told but be convinced that whether they do or do not leave home to go to work for Europeans is no concern whatever of Government. Furthermore, public departments must themselves treat labourers as entirely free. They must raise wages when labour is scarce and lower them when it is plentiful. In a really free market price will affect supply as it does everywhere else. The first result of the withdrawal of the influence of Government over labour supply will be to make labour scarce and dear. The next result, developing later and more slowly, will be to increase the output of the average labourer. In a very few years, I believe, increased output will more than compensate for increased wages. Whether, ultimately, free labour will prove actually more abundant than forced labour will depend entirely on the attractions offered by the employers on the one hand, and on the other upon the opportunities provided to natives for earning money at home.

I have described the most obvious, the simplest, the least mistakeable causes of unrest. The remedies I have so far defined are purely negative. Alone they will do nothing to increase the production of wealth. And a maximum wealth production is not only highly desirable in our own interests. It is an unqualified necessity to the prosperity of the African race. The race will only become productive to the fullest degree when stimulated by an active Government Policy to industry in the village homes of the people. Such a policy is the natural and necessary complement to the policy of free land and free labour. And it would stimulate rather than hinder production in the estates of Europeans.

II *[The break-up of tribal life]*

A prosperous peasantry is a necessity in Eastern Africa for other and greater than economic reasons. The unique condition of native society in these parts in our time makes the preservation and development of village life necessary as nowhere else. That society has undergone, in one generation, a revolution of unprecedented rapidity. Not merely have the extremes of barbarism and civilization met. They have met and mingled so hastily and so violently as to cause widespread destruction of the fabric of native life. Never before has a primitive society been urged at such a pace to change its whole scheme of life. Broadly speaking, the old order of native society no longer performs its functions. It may seem the case that in a primitive society no government should concern itself with social and ethical changes. On the contrary it is only in the presence of stable institutions of a civilized people that the state can afford to ignore them. When barbarians are turned by the hundred thousand into a vagrant proletariat, when not only the deliberate influence of Europeans, in religion, in government, and in industry, but even every meeting point between men of different tribes and traditions destroys superstitions that gave security to property, when the new conditions of life make thousands every year forget their homes and families forever, the cement that binds individuals in a common ethic and belief, the cement that makes government of any kind possible, is being dissolved. There are indeed sheltered corners where the disintegration has hardly begun. In other parts the old worship, the old sanctions and reverences are quite gone. The fragility of the old system can hardly be exaggerated. Isolated beliefs and prejudices generally persist but the restraints upon individual appetites and lusts snap at the first strain. Conduct in an African tribe depends on an artificial code bound up with an imaginative explanation of both the outer and the inner world. The first few breaths from the world of European ways and thought blow both code and the explanation to fragments. Society becomes atomic, a mere aggregation of individuals enslaved by instincts and appetites, and the social virtues which alone make men good subjects of the state disappear. That is why crimes and vagrancy are rapidly increasing in British East Africa, why perjury is becoming almost the rule with native witnesses, why chiefs complain they are no longer respected. The whole mechanism of Government is hindered by this social and ethical decay. Labour needs more and more expensive European supervision. Relations between individual Europeans and natives become harder to keep frank and friendly.

In no other part of the world is society in a similar situation. In the East as in Europe the subject is an individual embedded in an integrated society. It needs an effort of the imagination to realise a people without even the embryonic forms of institutions so familiar to us that we never think of the life they convey to us. The church, the school, the town, the trade or friendly society, the newspaper, the sports club, the public house, form with us a living framework in which the individual subject of the state grows through maturity to decline. They are the only channels of human life, and often its very sources. Through them the national will reaches the individual. The state up to recent times has been little more than their co-ordinator and protector. They seem, to the individual, to give far more than they demand, while the nation claims, in means and in life, much more than it gives. They rather than national energies and activities are civilization, and in their health liberty consists. With us so tough is the tissue of society that change whether religious or political or industrial only reaches the individual through adaptations of these the vital organs of society. In Eastern Africa such a fabric does not exist. Changes have been so rapid and so violent as to give no time for protective adaptations. The individual stands naked. His childish guesswork of a working theory of life can no longer guide him. He is the slave of the appetites, lusts and instincts which even the most barbarous society when intact controls, and at the mercy of economic forces as incomprehensible to him as they are irresistible.

Governments in Eastern Africa recognise the danger of social disintegration. They have hitherto attempted to meet it by attempts to preserve the tribal system. They give chiefs power that old tribal custom never gave them, they forbid individual families to live in villages of less than a certain size, they forbid religious propaganda unless invited by the chiefs, whose interest it is to prevent it. It is to be feared that conservatism of that type is both useless and harmful. Chiefs are already in many tribes an anachronism. The very support Government gives them, and still more the duties Government lays on them, add to their unpopularity. The old order is already in many tribes moribund, and is everywhere doomed. It deserves a euthanasia. That only a slowing of the rate of economic change can achieve. The system itself, the world of old fears, old obediences, old loyalties cannot be carried over into the future. Any policy built on its preservation whether from its supposed suitability to native character or from its necessity to European Government is bound to fail. Apart altogether from the presumption, a very large one, that a primitive tribalism can so develop as to serve human needs in the future, it is futile with one hand to give the system artificial support and with the other to stimulate economic and industrial changes that destroy it.

The analogy that inevitably arises in the minds of those of our own generation is with the economic revolution in England a hundred years ago. Its disasters and miseries were due, not to any weakness of the national spirit nor to breakdown of the national government but to the partial collapse of the less obtrusive but vital institutions of society before the stress of rapid economic changes. If we imagine the effect of that industrial revolution aggravated by the removal, under pressure, of most of the factory operatives by journeys of days or weeks from homes and families, by the breakdown of municipal government, by the abandonment of the old worship, and the dissolution of old sanctions for respect to persons and property, and if we suppose both factories and government in the hands of an alien race, we have no unfair analogy to what is happening in Africa.

I do not suggest that Governments should attempt the creation of a new social fabric in Africa. In that sense no race can possibly govern another. The new fabric will most certainly come into being. No human creatures ever rest in anarchy. Already indeed new bonds between individuals are in formation, new restraints are winning recognition, new institutions the corporate expressions of the new order are coming into life. These and their proper relations with Governments I shall describe later. In the economic sphere here discussed production of wealth within the circle of village life alone will permit the new order to grow up in place of the old. All that is possible should be done to preserve the tenuous ties between the social system that is passing away and the one that is struggling to life. The true conservative policy is to cherish the new growth while the old is dying. Economically, opportunity must be given to the individual to produce what our world demands of him without wholly cutting himself off from old habits and traditions. It is only in the villages that family life can be preserved, and tribal life can survive until replaced by institutions suitable to new conditions. Thus alone can the state be given a stable social foundation.

The trouble with village life now is sheer poverty. Nothing occurs in the villages but the growing of food. The householder has to work away from home to earn even enough to pay his tax not to speak of the purchase of the material needs of the first stage of civilized life. When at work on plantations or railway he is worse fed and housed than at home. Unions for a month or a day take the place of family life. The tone of plantation life, especially in East Africa, is lower by far than in villages. Most of the work is as monotonous as a treadmill. A large proportion of the workers work as slowly and as carelessly as they dare. Not by such means are the habits of industry taught, and hand and eye trained for wealth production. Many natives indeed have both gained for themselves and enriched the community by work for Europeans. But where many have gained far more have lost. Not that it would be wise to discourage wage earning, except where enquiry shows special prevalence of disease. Its main defects and abuses can be cured by making labour everywhere entirely free, and by giving opportunity for livelihood in the villages. Family life with better food and housing would then be offered to natives by employers, and the output of labour for Europeans would be multiplied several fold, when willingly undertaken as the alternative, not to stagnation and poverty at home but to the life of a prosperous peasantry. What would be thought at home of a policy which compelled, by differential taxation and administrative pressure, the English or Irish peasantry to leave their villages for labour in mine and factory?

There need be no fear as to the effect, on either revenue or production, of a policy of economic development in the villages. The principal reason of its absence in British East Africa and its small result in Nyasaland is that native industry has been deliberately deflected from the villages. For that reason the mere cessation of efforts to make natives leave their homes for work will not suffice. Definite encouragement of production in the villages is necessary, if only because it is an imperial interest that total production should not diminish. The fact must further be faced that such a policy will arouse opposition. European employers in Africa still believe that it is the duty of Government to get them labourers and to keep their wages down. And it is probably the case that the whole population of these parts that can be spared from food growing is insufficient for the full development of the millions of acres already granted to Europeans by the Crown. Actively to discourage natives to leave home to work would be to break faith with these estate owners and concessionaires. But their opposition to the positive policy which I describe as both a necessary justice to natives and as a means by which maximum wealth production and trade activity can be reached, must frankly be recognised as interested and fallacious.

An even greater difficulty will lie in the attitude of some of those who have been carrying on the existing policy. It is only natural that even opposition should be met with. Yet unless the policy here advocated is genuinely accepted by the local authorities and encouraged by them, it will have no real success. In many parts the new idea that money can be earned by work in the villages will need implantation. And I need not labour the point that bad methods may ruin the most hopeful of schemes. It would be easy, for instance, by giving a price for cotton lower than European planters can get, or by failing to provide markets and transport, to prove that cotton production is only practicable on large estates. But if a small proportion of the money and energy that have been spent by Government on European settlement, on surveys, police protection, imported stock, experimental farms, entomological experts, veterinary inspectors, were to be wisely spent on the encouragement of production by a native peasantry, the results would be astonishing.

III [*Islam*]

Islam and Christianity are the two rival heirs of tribalism. Both offer a complete way of life. Both give precisely what tribal life in decay can no longer give, a bond transcending the tie of blood relationship, a bond, moreover, that, once formed, holds fast and constantly grows closer. Both these systems cover a far larger part of life than the part covered by the administrative system. Their influence is, judged by any measure, far deeper than Government influence. The attitude of Government to them is of far greater importance than their attitude to Government.

Mahomedanism in Eastern Africa is often described as being nominal. A better word for it is undeveloped. It owes its underdeveloped character to the prohibition of translations of the Koran, to the absence of other religious writings, and to the absence of authorised teachers. There is in fact, in most places, no deliberate propaganda at all. It spreads by the mere attractiveness of a simple creed and ceremonial. Nothing less simple could spread in the automatic way it does spread. In the simplification both ethic and legal system are lost, because neither seem to be demanded by the needs of the moment. It is not the tribal restraints that the detribalised native misses but the loss of tribal solidarity: not the claim his tribe made on him but the support his tribe gave him. It is just that solidarity which the embryonic Mahomedanism of Africa offers. Thousands of even those whose homes are still in their native villages will when asked their tribe call themselves Mahomedans. Further enquiry elicits that they know nothing of Islamic law, and ethic. They know merely some ten words of creed with some half dozen ceremonial practices. Some call the system a freemasonry, but it is really much more. It gives without requiring fee or exertion or restraint nothing less than a fatherland. The ceremonies and the formula of the religion are the symbols of a common patriotism. The entire absence within its pale both of actual Europeans and of Western ideas makes the religion in Africa essentially racial. Its racial character is emphasised by the treatment the religion receives from our Government and their agents. Most Government servants believe that Mahomedanism is a 'very good religion for Africans'. I have heard two Governors say so when addressing Africans. The reason of this attitude is perfectly plain. Mahomedans have no appetites for Western ways of thought and habits of life. They never want to learn to read English. The religion teaches, not the brotherhood of man but the brotherhood of Mahomedans, at first sight a much less inconvenient doctrine to administrators to whom racial superiority is a fundamental axiom of Government. If Government servants were free to follow the policy they think the wisest most of them would give active encouragement to Islam. As it is, Government in British East Africa spends public money in teaching it. The police and the Kings African Rifles are almost wholly recruited from among Mahomedans, who form in no Protectorate a majority of the population. In Zomba,* during the war, Christian worship was forbidden and Mahomedan worship was encouraged among the natives in the military camp. In Nyasaland the compulsory levy for carriers was not enforced on many Mahomedan villages, while it often took every available man from Christian and pagan villages. The great majority of Government officers, civil and military, choose Mahomedans as personal servants, while most of the domestics of non-official Europeans are Christian or pagan. The general impression thus prevails all over British East Africa that the authorities wish natives to become Mahomedans. (The Germans, on the contrary, avowedly gave the preference in Government appointments in the interior, though not on the coast, to Christians.)**

In attempting a judgment on the situation I have described it must never be forgotten that Mahomedanism in the interior of Eastern Africa is embryonic. Whatever its future may prove to be it will not have the same character as at present. It will either develop or decline. Introduced as the religion of Arab slave raiders and of the Africans who took their part, Arab influence has since died away with the cessation of the traffic to the coast. But with the disappearance of educated men and of schools the time of rapid spread began. Enough of its early association with a conquering caste, mainly African in race, survives to give the religion

---

* Zomba was the capital of Nyasaland and of Malawi until 1975.
** According to John Cell Leys was mistaken on this point.

something of the prestige of an aristocracy. But the movement as a whole consists of an untaught multitude, conscious only of unity and awaiting some inevitable development. Its almost involuntary spread is a sign of so perfect a satisfaction of temporary needs, that when these needs change – and society in East Africa is certainly not static – the type of Mahomedanism will also change. A short ritual and a cryptic creed will not remain its sole expressions.

Not that Mahomedanism is ever or can ever be merely a natural response to human needs. It is the most rigid of all religions. Historically its seeds have always developed true to type. The only unusual thing about it in Eastern Africa is the long delay in full development due to political severance from the Mahomedan world. African Mahomedans know that world exists. In hundreds of mosques they pray weekly for the Sultans of Turkey and Zanzibar. It is certain that in future contact will be re-established with Islam as a world religion. The development of Mahomedan thought and practice is certain to follow historic lines. A new Mahomedan political philosophy is an impossible growth on African soil. In one important direction indeed growth is certain to be stunted. No development of the legal system of Islam is possible. Not only in criminal but also in civil law, it is from Rome and Westminster rather than from Mecca that the African will learn a rule of contractual relationship. Educated Moslems in the interior complain that Africans will not follow the Moslem rule in marriage, divorce, inheritance and so forth. Nothing but confusion, of course, would follow the competition of Moslem law with our system. Unfortunately such a prospect removes the main cultural value of the religion to barbarous people. Its sole historic justification is that it was the law-giver to lawless tribes and discordant sects. And if the introduction of the Moslem theory of social rights is impossible, the code of private rights and duties is deprived of validity. The two are indistinguishable in Islam, just as church and state are. (The position of the religion in India offers no analogy. There we found it established long since, with both legal and private codes in actual operation, and persisting, as is natural, in spite of political decay.) It is safe also to predict that African Islam, divorced from its own scheme of social and private rights and duties, will develop in a direction that may be called nationalistic. Historically always more of a political scheme than a religion, it has never developed except as a political system. And in Africa already this character is plain. Mahomedans feel themselves one people, a people that of necessity excludes Europeans. The Moslem world is self-sufficient. It has never from Mahomed's day to our own shown any wish to come to terms with the Western plan of life, to share in any but its material accidentals. I have never met an intelligent Mahomedan who did not know that he was right and I was wrong. I have never got any distance into the mind of any Mahomedan – except some Arabs who are thoroughgoing agnostics – without discovering that he actually did consider all Europeans his inferiors, usurpers for a time of empire, and destined either to conversion or to conquest here and damnation hereafter. The Mahomedan does not believe the religion a good one for Africans. He believes it to be the only truth for all, and that it is one of his first duties to ensure its supremacy in every walk of life.

The wisdom of the policy of encouraging Islam is thus to be judged according to whether it is to develop or not. If its spread in Africa proves to be only a temporary fashion due to its peculiar affinity with a transient phase of African life, official encouragement will prove to have been a comparatively harmless mistake. If on the contrary the religion is going to live and grow, it is idle to expect from it the submissive virtues of a consciously inferior caste. In that case its encouragement will prove a policy only one degree more disastrous than its persecution would have proved.

V [Loyalty]

I have investigated the operation of economic and industrial forces, and the prevailing currents of feeling and opinion which issue in unrest. There remains to view the subject from its opposite end, to discover the means, whether by the direction of these currents or otherwise, to right relations between governments and their subjects.

The view is hindered by a presumption in the political thought of our time which must be deliberately set aside. We are accustomed to the control of industry by the state. All governments freely manipulate economic forces. In Africa they are even more completely under control than elsewhere. A whole tribe is transported to a new home, or the labour of a hundred thousand men at a time is diverted, by the stroke of a Governor's pen. And no state, least of all in Africa, is likely to lessen its control over the material means of life. By contrast, modern governments profess to have abandoned control over opinion and belief. 'A free church in a free state' represents a principle commonly believed to be universally valid. I suggest that it cannot be considered so, and that in tropical Africa in particular its application is impracticable. I believe it has been accepted in Europe only in consequence of the transfer from ecclesiastical to civil authority not only of many of the functions of society, such as education and the care of the insane and of the sick, but of the transfer also to the state of the feeling of religious reverence formerly conceived of as due to the church alone. I suggest that these changes in Europe are coincident with and mainly dependent upon the changes which have identified states and governments with nations. The separation of church from state does not with us, as might appear, imply the withdrawal of civic and national aims and activities from the influence of the individual and corporate conscience. The bond between state and subjects has become a religious as it has become a national bond, so that the life of the modern state now depends less on obedience than on active loyalty. The religious nature of that loyalty is shown by its dominance. Far more citizens in our time would die for their country than for their faith. Separation of church and state is accordingly natural only to those states in which active loyalty is felt by the general body of citizens to be the supreme religious duty.

In Africa this natural and active loyalty does not exist. Loyalties there indeed are, but no loyalty is given to the state because none is felt for the state. Sedition in Africa is thus due, not merely to causes in economic and religious life, but to the absence of resistance to their force. At present the African cannot or dare not rebel. Western education and the contact with world religions will enable him and make him dare. The future will depend on whether before he ceases to say 'I dare not' he begins to say 'I ought not.' The heart of the question has been reached.

Solutions applicable elsewhere are here inadmissible. Over the rest of the empire the question has been or is being settled, for our generation, by the extension of political liberty. In Africa the problem is for us unique. Rome like us governed races with creeds and social systems in decay. To her, as to us, the problem of their loyalty arose. She solved it partly by sharing such political rights as the age conceived with all her subjects who sought them. She shared these so fully as to make the children of barbarians feel themselves to be Romans; so that citizens of the third and even of the second generation from barbarism gave to the empire generals, statesmen and emperors. These ties of equal status and opportunity for the fulfilment of advantage and ambition were, however, regarded as insufficient. Every subject was in addition explicitly bound to the state by a religious tie. From all Rome demanded the worship of the state. She could conceive of no empire without the devotion of religious worship. It is ominous that the religion that refused all terms except her own with the Roman Empire, and that other creed which finally overthrew the empire, are the only militant creeds in Africa to-day. We need that warning that such problems never settle themselves. We ourselves have moved so far from the old ground of conflict that the compromise in which the old quarrel issued is no longer real to us. With us it is not the divine unction upon the head of our king but the identity of the state with national feeling that is the source of loyalty. But wherever that identity has not been reached we are faced, as even the war in Europe reveals, with the same problem of that older empire. How is loyalty to governments in Africa to arise? Can it be taught? Can it be designedly made to grow? We cannot ask Africans to worship King George, as the early Roman Emperors required worship of our ancestors. Nor can we with Constantine and his successors enforce conformity to a church from which the secular ruler derives reverence and authority.

Loyalty is a kind of affection. It is not given, in gratitude for past nor in hope of future benefits, nor is it withdrawn because of misfortune or disaster. It is felt by people whose government is their own, seldom or never by any others. People indeed may feel loyalty to a government not of their own making. In such cases the sense of ownership is derived from peculiar qualities in the Government, from its adaptation to and service of special institutions and feelings, rather than from general qualities of wisdom and disinterestedness. The loyal are those who feel their government, even if they think it a bad government, to be their own, whether made by them or for them; the disloyal those who feel they are governed by strangers, however wisely they may govern.

It is not that loyalties do not already exist in Eastern Africa. They are inspired, notoriously, by many individual Europeans. In addition, loyalty is evoked in perhaps its purest form by two widely differing relationships. There is a great deal of real loyalty in converts to their missions and there is an even greater devotion shown by the rank and file of the King's African Rifles to their regiment. I believe that the nature of these two particularist loyalties provides the key to the problem of general loyalty to Governments. Both regiment and mission offer leadership, and the leaders in both bridge the gulf of racial difference by sharing always their special knowledge and often their fortunes and their lives.

If that is so, the aim of governments in Eastern Africa must be one of acclimatization, of adaptation to feelings and beliefs widely different from those natural to a governing race or caste. Governments must do more than take directly upon themselves the duty of sharing the knowledge and the arts and the instruments of civilised life according to the measure of the capacity of their subjects. All that they must certainly undertake. But in addition the spirit of government must be African, not in the sense that Imperial problems have an African aspect but in the sense that there must be as instant and intimate a response to the states of mind of the governed as in the case of governments by the governed themselves. If governments cannot be by the people they must be with and in the people. We must leave it to them to set the problems, even if it is we who must decide them. An instance of my meaning is found in the prohibition of the export of Indian labour to Natal. In decreeing the prohibition I suppose Lord Hardinge acted in accordance with Indian sentiment rather than with Indian, not to speak of Imperial, interests. The danger here is not so much one of conflict between Imperial and local interests as from the kind of minds that govern as wisely as they know, without being moved by what the governed think or feel.

Government by consent is an ambiguous phrase. It must of necessity be a temporary phrase turning either into government by cooperation or into government in the face of dissent. At the moment passive consent is in Africa turning into dissent, which, however fitful and purposeless, is the sign of an unguided and untaught life. Unrest, however inconvenient to us, is less the sign of a social disease than the disordered appetite of a social pregnancy.

No purely alien bureaucracy has ever inspired gratitude or loyalty. Yet without such a basis of loyalty government is in a condition of permanent estrangement from its subjects. Elsewhere, in the result, the bureaucracy is superseded. In Africa, so far as our vision goes, it must persist. It must find its own escape from the riddles of nationalism, an apparition that always takes a bureaucracy by surprise. It is certain that a common national feeling will pervade all the tribes from Kenia to the Zambezi during the next generation. Presuming that the solution of self-government is impossible, how are we to meet that African nationalism? To the objection that the prophecy is gratuitous, I would answer by asking what other result can be expected to follow the introduction of a uniform administrative system that pays no respect to tribal boundaries: a precocious economic development rearranging individual status everywhere in accordance with the ability to earn money: the rapid spread of two religions, the notorious unifiers of the past: all these acting on a people with a consciousness of race even while in undisturbed tribalism, now strengthened and defined by the unbridged gulf, political, social and economic, between black and white, and by the knowledge that in all the rest of the world national aspirations are either already satisfied or likely soon to be satisfied? To state these facts is to postulate rather than to predict nationalism. If we cannot satisfy it in the natural way, how can we meet it at all? Certainly not at any rate by relying on the existing title of governments in Africa, on bargains with other European powers: or on treaties with chiefs, treaties the terms of which the people know nothing of, and chiefs, many of them, whose authority is derived from their signature on the treaties.

In proof of the version of history I have given I would refer to one instance from Nyasaland and one from British East Africa. The Kikuyu and other tribes of the same ethnic group which form about a third of the population of the East African Protectorate never had any chiefs at all. There is no such institution among the Kikuyu. The natives who, a generation ago, signed treaties on the tribe's behalf, were mostly not even members of the tribe. One of the most important of them is to this day prohibited under tribal law from owning land because of his foreign birth and descent – and that in a tribe in which practically every able-bodied man is a landowner by individual tenure. Not one of the Kikuyu chiefs has any authority except as a government agent.

I would also instance the case of the North Nyasa administrative district. The soil of the whole district is the freehold property of a financial corporation. How the corporation came to own these thousands of square miles on which some sixty thousand natives live I cannot here narrate. The points I would emphasise are that the corporation pays an annual tax on the land of about £3000 a year to the Protectorate Government, a sum which it can only hope to recover in the future either directly from the natives in rent or indirectly by the profits of their labour: and also that all the enquiry I was able to make in the district failed to discover a single native aware of the facts of the legal ownership of the land. Not even the man who is the successor of the chief who made the original treaty knows that it involved the conveyance of a freehold title to the land occupied by his tribe.

A summary description of the history of our relations with the different tribes in Eastern Africa is impossible, and the instances I have given are not typical. No single instances in fact would be typical. The single common political category under which all the tribes in the East African Protectorate fall is that they are 'protected'. That status in law is one which gives the protecting power complete sovereignty in practice, while it withholds from the inhabitants every one of the rights of subjects. The natives are neither in law nor in fact British subjects. They are foreigners over whom we exercise administrative authority; whom we tax as we think proper; whose land we take when we think it can be spared for giving to our own countrymen. The treaties with native chiefs are not even cognisable in our courts of law. The law presumes that these treaties are in force as between equally sovereign states, that the subject of the protected power may find redress for wrong complained of by appeal, not to our courts but to those of his own government. It is needless to remark that these native governments have no shred of existence. Protectorate governments legislate and administer without pretence of regard to any such imaginary authorities, and, most reasonably, never give treaties a thought. The sole effect of these treaties in Africa to-day is to prevent the natives acquiring the status of British subjects which they would have obtained had these regions become British territory by conquest or cession.

The actual relations of natives to Governments are naturally very different from what they might be imagined to have as the subjects of protected powers. These relations may be stated in a sentence. To the average native, government is the recipient of taxes, the demander of labour, the arbiter in disputes between Europeans and natives, and the court of appeal for natives themselves. That is literally all. The old claim of governments to be the protectors from inter-tribal warfare has been swept away forever by the miseries and destruction of the present war.

As a governing race we are apt to regard ourselves in the light of our honest intentions. We like to think ourselves as the liberators, forgetful that for every hundred freed under the flag by the cruisers in the Mozambique channel there were thousands who sailed the middle passage in chains under the same flag. Most of us have more of the blood of the slavers who built the prosperity of modern Bristol and Liverpool than of the Clapham philanthropists. We should not forget if only because the African has not forgotten. Not that the African knows anything of the history of the past as we know it. Hardly any African now alive has heard tell of Livingstone, except from missionaries, and certainly none have heard of Hawkins. But the racial memory lives. Children each generation learn our reputation. We have still the name of being exacting. We are still the wonderfully clever people who take men from their homes and villages to work for us.

It is of the utmost importance to recognise that in such political relations loyalty does not grow. In all the tribes taxes are paid and obedience is rendered, not from loyalty nor from a sense of duty, but because of the disasters that would follow refusal. Our government in these parts rests on the obedience the ignorant and barbarous always give to the stronger and cleverer. So long as it has no other foundation, education and civilization will weaken its authority. They are weakening it now. One lesson, furthermore, this war has certainly taught many natives. They believe now that they can fight as well as Europeans. They know they have sometimes fought better.

There is no country in the world where grievances are not widely felt. In a free country the subject has the means of expressing them and of himself attempting their removal. In Africa native opinion has neither the means of expression nor the means of action. And when grievances are laid at the door of an alien government, when its demands fall on all and its services are felt by none, education enables growing numbers to reflect upon and nurse their grievances until some way of resistance offers, however foolish or criminal or hopeless it may be.

VIII [Education and self-government]

The touchstone of educational policy, and through education of all policy in Africa, is the relation of governments with the class of educated natives. In Nyasaland that class has the very greatest influence, in British East Africa it is only now emerging. The importance of these men lies, not in their being a necessity, as clerks and so forth, to the machinery of Government, but in their being taken as models by an increasing number of their countrymen. They, not the chiefs, are the real leaders of opinion.

The educated minority of the subject race is never popular with their governors. Nevertheless, to guide the thought and ambition of these men, and to gain their sympathy and co-operation, should be part of Government's deliberate policy. A place must be given them in the state comparable with their influence on society. Otherwise they inevitably pass into opposition – and all opposition is potentially sedition – which is merely the reflection of the common attitude of Europeans to them. If 'the withholding of knowledge is the greatest of all injustices,' then surely the discouragement and repression of those who have received it is the greatest of political crimes. The guilt of disloyalty and sedition falls at least equally on the officer who condemns and discourages natives because of faults inevitable in the first generation of mental emancipation as on the natives themselves who, with hope of intellectual and social advancement repulsed, become Ishmaels. A certain officer once told me that he had had a correspondence with John Chilembwe. Misled by the style of the letters, he at first answered them as he would have answered the letters of a European. But, as he told me, when he learned who his correspondent was, he soon put him in his place. That officer had his share in the rising. There are few of us who have lived in these parts who have not some share.

It is most necessary that when in future new chiefs and head men come to be elected or appointed, Governments should, whenever possible, recognise the candidature of none but men of good education. In many tribes the chiefs with their special friends and followers form a party opposed to Christianity and education. Unfortunately that party is generally looked upon as a kind of pro-Government faction. Governments should be careful to avoid special alliance with what is already in many cases the diminishing minority of harmfully conservative and illiterate pagans, and the standing order under which a chief can forbid his people to build a school should be abolished at once. The position of the chiefs, difficult enough in any case, is not improved by Government support of their opposition to inevitable changes.

It is finally of the utmost importance to face with the greatest frankness the fact that opposition to any educational policy of real value will take the form of a professed inability to find the money. The real meaning of those who cite that reason for delay is that in their view there are other more necessary objects of expenditure. There is a mycologist in Nyasaland with the duty of the prevention of diseases that affect the economic products of the soil. There is no officer whose duty it is to teach or to supervise teaching. There is not even an officer employed in the work of preventing disease in man. In German East Africa there are more than twenty doctors employed by Government in the prevention as distinguished from the treatment of disease, in Nyasaland not one. In British East Africa especially every department spends large sums upon the protection and encouragement of wealth production by European capital, in surveys, experimental farms, a veterinary service, police, means of communication, and in many other ways. I can learn of no other country where Europeans are so lightly taxed. There is certainly none where so much public money is spent on them. I submit that in comparison education, education covering the whole area, is a necessity and that expenditure on these objects is, as a whole, less necessary and in some cases at this stage of growth in society even harmful because premature. The natural order of growth in society has been reversed. We have cared for production, not for the producer.

My argument is based on no presumption of what the future may bring. The African may or may not prove to be capable, in the phrase of the day, of self-determination. He is certainly capable of protest by insurrection against what he conceives to be wrong determination. Both the religions he is absorbing teach him that he is capable of more than a mere political equality with Europeans. I hold, indeed, that there is one view that is essentially false to the facts, and fundamentally incompatible with the purpose of our country. In a standard book upon Nyasaland the native is described as a person most wisely treated like a dog to which one has the friendliest of feelings, wayward, quarrelsome, but happy when fed, obedient under discipline, submissive to direction because incapable of self-direction. It would be hypocrisy to pretend that such a conception of native mentality has not been influential and even prevalent among those who have hitherto had the direction and shaped the policy of our governments. In permitting it to continue to influence events our country encourages the one means that, unfortunately, man can always use to prove that he is not canine but human, and not slave but free, the murder of his master. To that expiation the war has brought our countrymen in these parts very near. It is in that conviction that I have ventured to address you.

I have the honour to be,
Sir,
Your most obedient servant,
Norman Leys
Medical Officer, Nyasaland

2. The Problems of East Africa (1919)

This statement is undated but was probably written in mid-1919 for the attention of Leonard Woolf and a few other activists.* It marks the opening of Leys' campaign to educate the Labour Party and looks forward to the appointment of a Labour Colonial Secretary who would be willing to bring settler colonialism to an end, something he was still hoping for in 1941 when he wrote The Colour Bar in East Africa. *It shows him facing up to the difficulty of preventing the settlers from getting 'responsible government', and the even greater difficulty of actually abolishing the 'settler system'. He wants sympathisers in the party to understand what is happening in Kenya and take up the challenge. It reads as if it had been written in a hurry; it is obscure in places, and sometimes reads almost as if he was thinking aloud. The contrast between its tone and that of his letter to the Colonial Secretary is striking. There, as in all his published work, his anger was tightly controlled. Here, writing privately to political allies, it was not.*

STRICTLY PRIVATE AND CONFIDENTIAL
THE PROBLEMS OF EAST AFRICA**

The real difficulty is not the discovery and adoption by public opinion of a terso [terse?] policy.† It is scarcely too much to say that such a policy is little more than the application of the axioms of elementary political arithmetic of universal validity. The real problem is to relate our policy to events.

I cannot illustrate the problem better than by referring to the enclosed cuttings, all taken from a single month's issues of the principal newspaper in East Africa. From these cuttings certain crude facts may be gathered.

(1) There is a famine in Eastern Africa, caused or aggravated by the forcing of probably two-thirds of the able-bodied men to leave home to work for Europeans, in industry and for the military.††

(2) The Government is importing foodstuffs into the most fertile country in the world. That policy is opposed by those who wish labour kept cheap and abundant. Among them is at least one public servant of

---

* It is among Leonard Woolf's papers in the Sussex University archives, but not listed in the records of the Advisory Committee on International Questions which had been set up the previous year.

** By 'East Africa' Leys mostly means the British East Africa Protectorate, as Kenya was called until 1920.

† The meaning of this sentence is obscure. The next one perhaps says that spelling out what needs to be done in East Africa is easy, but finding a way to do it is another matter.

†† The reference is to the conscription of Africans as porters in the war.

high position, the Chief of Customs.
(3) Famine has led to thefts of food. Two Europeans are under trial for flogging a food thief to death.
(4) In another case a European successfully punished a native whisky thief by poisoning the whisky and so killing the thief. Apparently no legal proceedings were taken against the poisoner.

Any other month's issues of the same newspaper would provide a similar number of snapshot photographs of the social condition of the country. In such a mental climate political and social principles that seem ordinary and natural to us are incongruous and unreal. A Governor who wished to give security of land tenure to natives, or to provide schooling for one in a hundred of the children would be actively opposed by every European of social position. The few Europeans in favour of such measures are debarred by their opinions from positions of influence. The whole scheme of government is planned upon quite other ideas, which are supported by the press in London and Africa, by those in authority in the Colonial Office, by the rank and file of the administration, and by the European population with which Government officers have common daily intercourse. A governor with our ideas would find his task almost impossible even if he had the Colonial Office behind him. How could he break the conspiracy to keep wages to threepence a day when a free labour market would spell permanent ruin to much, and large loss to all of the industry directed by Europeans?

All the land (the reference is to British East Africa proper)* belongs to or has issued from the Crown. Some of it is occupied, without a shred of legal security, by the natives. Those so called native reserves are only just large enough to grow food for the population in good years. The great bulk of the rest of the fertile land is owned as freehold or held on 99 and 999 year leases by about six hundred Europeans and corporations. It has been acquired from the Crown for less than a hundredth part of its present market value. On that land there work the largest proportion the whole European community can persuade and coerce to work for an average wage of less than threepence a day. Compulsion is variously contrived. (In Nyasaland the employees pay half as large a tax as the stay-at-home). It is the avowed policy of the government to get the natives to work for the Europeans. The whole scheme of native administration is deliberately planned so that they must. (East Africa was before Europeans administered it a grain exporting country. Now it is imported).

These few hundred Europeans have an actual monopoly of political industrial and economic power. The wages they pay are the sole source of

---

* i.e. Kenya.

revenue.* They themselves are taxed lighter than any other set of men with property in the whole world. They pay (1) a poll tax of a pound, which is levied equally on all non-Africans, on the Indian coolie with two shillings a day and the big planter with ten thousand pounds a year, and (2) their share of the 10% general import tariff. Their exports are carried at a loss on the Government railway. Their machinery is imported free. Their Stock has been and still is largely provided for them at prices specially cheap, by auctions in which Indians and Somalis are not allowed to take part, of cattle confiscated from natives as punishment for tribal misdemeanours that are due to compulsory labour and loss of land for the benefit of these same European landholders. The whole circle of life is for them and by them. Shops, hotels, shipping are directly dependent on them. They control and direct, consciously and avowedly, life in all its phases, from its material sources through all its channels.

These few hundred men, with their agents and dependents in trade, form a highly organised body, represented on the legislative and acutely conscious of their position. They are making large fortunes. Their former demand was for land. Now that they have it their sole remaining requirement is abundant cheap labour. It will seem incredible to you but it is the case that the Government has publicly accepted the duty of getting the labour for them, not for individuals but for the class.

Nominally, of course, policy is directed by British public opinion. It is difficult to prove a negative. I can only say that I know of only two occasions on which Parliament was appealed to. The more important effort failed. In spite of Mr Ramsay MacDonald's freely given help the Government took half the land agreed on by a 'treaty' made only six years previously as the property 'for ever' of a certain tribe, and gave it to the settlers. The other instance is instructive. A settler murdered a native. He was tried, admitted the murder, and was acquitted by a jury of fellow settlers. Mr T.E. Harvey called for papers.† On their arrival there was a small storm that even fluttered the pages of the Spectator. The man was deported. I was in the country at the time. No one would have dared to express approval of the deportation in any public place. The Governor of the moment, by far the most humane the country has ever had, had proposed no action in regard to the murder and acquittal. The sequel is instructive. After war broke out the murderer was allowed to return to the country. He returned to his large estates, to his greatly multiplied flocks and herds, multiplied by the care of the relations of his victim. He is now the president of the provincial settlers' association. He gives and receives

---

* Because almost the only reason Africans worked for wages was to pay the hut and poll tax. These taxes were not in fact the sole source of revenue. Import duties, which Leys mentions later, accounted for about a third.

† Edmund Harvey MP called for the facts of the case to be laid before Parliament.

hospitality and is treated as an equal by those in high official position. So much for the lion's roar.

The point is that people at home wake up over a scandal. But they exert no influence whatever over policy. And I don't see how they can, except through Colonial Secretary and Under-Secretary, in Parliament.

A third instance. A magistrate was found to have raped the wives of native policemen. There was some kind of enquiry by a judge of the high court, and he was reproved. A visitor to the country wrote to *The Times*. There was a scandal. The man lost a year's seniority and was transferred to another Colony. Public opinion at home thought the punishment disgracefully light. European opinion locally thought it too heavy.

Beyond these three instances I know of none in which British public opinion has attempted to influence events in British East Africa or Nyasaland. There has indeed been agitation against the persistence of the status of slavery in German East Africa [Tanganyika]. Only their ignorance protects those who conduct the agitation from the guilt of the most naked hypocrisy. Our industrial slavery is ten times worse, kills ten times more, indoctrinates ten times more with hatred and 'disloyalty' than any domestic slavery of the Arabs, an evil though it be.

A bureaucracy that obeys neither the British nor the African public must obey somebody. It must service some idea. It must be harnessed to some purpose and have a 'policy'. It is too honest to follow its own aggrandisement, and too efficient to be difficult to manipulate. Up to a point the bureaucracy in East Africa is highly efficient. It has done nothing for public health. It has not put one child in school for every hundred the Government in German East Africa educated. But its political and economic control over its subjects is perfect. It could build pyramids cheaper and better than the Pharaohs. It has managed tribal migrations – in order to find land for its friends – better than Moses managed the Exodus. Furthermore, the rank and file of the service is perhaps the least active mentally of any in the world. In the administrative branches mainly, it is recruited from the class that is always called on to fill vacancies in nominated service.* But in the case of East Africa it is never a man's first choice. The cream of the small class in England that gets higher education lives mainly in London or India. To Africa go men whose first demand from the world is a gentlemanly occupation, carrying with it leisure, opportunities for sport and authority over others. Most have private means, all have richer and better gifted relations. They go out on £350 a year, and with careful attention to means of preferment, may rise in twenty years to £600, when they retire with a pension of £500. From these men, almost always honest, humane and tolerably efficient,

---

* i.e. not by competitive examination.

the Colonial Office can find few with brain adequate to the position of Governor. Most Governors of Crown Colonies in tropical Africa are not drawn from the Colonial Service. These posts, the only plums in the service, are given to military men and others. I imagine the reason to be partly that it is known that 'risings' are never far off. And also, the Colonial Office wants Governors who will be firm with the small minority of native sympathisers who always seem to turn up in an English Service. General Northey was made Governor of British East Africa a few months ago. He has been fighting native troops under German leadership for two years.* He is one of the men who like Lord French believes in stamping on a rebel as one would crush a noxious insect. He would as soon think of going to a Quaker Meeting as think of reading Burke. He is as unfit for the uniquely difficult task of governing five million ignorant, docile, bewildered people, goaded to the edge of rebellion that even they know to be suicide, as an Irish peasant. We are back in 1918 to the day of Governor Eyre.† The government, accordingly, that I allege to be under the control of those engaged in 'economic development' for private profit, is an unusually suitable instrument for the purpose. Its rank and file is composed of men conservative in politics, believers in the religion that enjoins labour on the many, and the enjoyment of its fruits by a minority of a superior race, sportsmen rather than readers of books, unaffected by any wind of doctrine since the Tariff Reform Campaign, as loyal to the code of their caste as any hero of Kipling's, and as contemptuous and ignorant of the feelings and wishes of those who never went to a public school. These men are directed in Africa by men chosen by the Colonial Office staff from a class that thinks in terms of command, considers obedience the eternal duty of the subject race, believes in 'discipline' as in a God, and sincerely thinks that the last word in political wisdom is to keep those who are born to labour in their place.

Africa is governed by the less intellectual public school man, directed by the more energetic than ordinary military officer. No honester or more patriotic set of men is to be found in the world, and none stupider. Only such men could believe that to put wealth into the pockets of a few hundred exploiters (and the usual widow and orphan shareholders at home) can strengthen or even increase the wealth of their country. They cannot even imagine that if Africans were given liberty and knowledge their capacity for wealth production would enormously increase.

I would particularly beg you to realise that personal cruelty, whether in British, German, or Portuguese territory is a comparatively unimportant matter. It would be easy to make the country ring with stories of

---

* Northey had commanded British forces based in Nyasaland and Northern Rhodesia from 1916 to 1918. He became Governor of the British Africa Protectorate in February 1919.
† Eyre was infamous for his savage suppression of a revolt in Jamaica in 1865.

atrocities. They have been more common and more heavily punished (by Dernburg a very able man), in German than in British East Africa.* The worst I know of happened in Natal and Rhodesia. They certainly contribute to rebellion. But they are irrelevant to the main political question. Given existing political, economic and social relations, you will find a larger or smaller minority of men in every race whom authority over their fellow men turns into brutes.

The problem is not to 'curb . . . government of its bias in favour of exploitation'. It is to substitute in the minds of the governing the aims we have in the place of exploitation, which has been and continues to be the sole aim of government.

The mention of the possibility of insurrection is to many ears an indecency, like the telling of a dirty story in a drawing room. To the settlers indeed and their political friends at home a native rising is a calculated stage in the process of the training every tribe should undergo. One hears settlers, and even many officials, refer to such and such a tribe as one that has never been smashed and it is quite generally, and probably correctly doubted whether any tribe will finally settle into the bosom of civilisation without trying first to kill every European within reach and losing in consequence most of its land and cattle and a number of its members by fire, lead and hemp.

I admit that native risings will be peculiarly filthy, the work of men who seek escape from what they hate, to what they know is destruction, who prefer death by bullet and rope with some revenge, to death in labour camps without revenge. No European is ever likely to help them. But I can't think of such people as wicked, and I wouldn't think a European who encouraged them as wicked as the statesmen who egg on Japanese to kill Bolsheviks.† I am afraid I think that 'who would be free themselves must strike the blow'.‡ I mean that no race or class gets liberty from those who withhold it without the act or threat of violence. (The American Civil War is an exception). I don't believe Self-Government in India would be 'practical' politics unless Bengalis and Punjabis had indulged in 'unrest'.

There are really three alternatives. We in can go on, with recurrent outbreaks, precipitated by anything, famine for instance, caused by oppression, punished by slaughter. We can attempt without diminishing production for Imperial interests to supplement old by new policy, educate, stimulate industry in villages, and still keep up the same. I fear such a compromise policy would prove in practice impossible, and in particular that bible and school book will merely lower the flashpoint of combustible material. The third course which I don't expect to see any

---

* Berhard Dernburg was German Colonial Secretary from 1907 to 1910.
† Japan intervened in support of the White Russian counter-revolution from 1918 to 1922.
‡ 'Who would be free themselves must strike the blow' (Lord Byron, 'Greece Enslaved').

home Government bold enough to compel the local Government to follow, is to take the screw off for a few years, let production fall, let most of the settlers be ruined, and begin cautiously to make children buy slates and earn money to buy them by growing cotton at home. That is the only course that will save life but it involves too big an admission of wrong doing and folly in the past to be followed. The Germans followed the second course. They flogged men both for not working and for not sending their children to school. The crime soonest punished in Africa is hustling.

What you want is a policy for the first Labour Colonial Secretary. His real task will be to ensure that the men he directs share his ideas and aims. That task may be analysed as follows.

(1) He must cut himself free from the ruling idea that because a scheme will be profitable it must have Government support. I imagine that to previous Colonial Secretaries there came, to Lord Lansdowne (while East Africa was under the Foreign Office), the Duke of Westminster, who said, give me 600 square miles where my agent says the soil is most suitable, and I will import sheep, produce wool, and make the Empire flourish; to Lord Harcourt, a Mr Samuel, who said, give me several thousand square miles of barren wilderness containing millions of tons of washing soda which I will bring home to Europe.* I know that Lord Lansdowne was told that the land the Duke wanted was the best land the Maasai had, and I feel sure Lord Harcourt was told that digging soda rotted the labourers' feet. I want the Labour Secretary of State to tell peer and Jew alike to go away.** He must reckon on a storm in the capitalist press. He must expect the furious and dangerous hostility of the local Europeans. But he won't do any good otherwise. His work can't be done without large loss to a few hundred wealthy people who will fight like cats in a corner. It won't do for him to enquire if the soda-diggers can't be given boots. The kind of production now going on can't be done at a profit under decent conditions, most of it.

(2) The Labour Colonial Secretary will fortunately have a free hand in appointing Colonial Governors. The good Governor is the Governor who conceives and carries out the programme defined. He will have a devil of a time. He will be surrounded by expert advisers, heads of departments brought up under the old regime. Unless he has local experience he will be helpless in their hands. And it will be very difficult to find men with local experience with our ideas. Remember that promotion has for years gone to those who serve Moloch most faithfully. It is literally true that the

---

* See Lotte Hughes, 'Mining the Maasai Reserve: The Story of Magadi', *Journal of Eastern African Studies* 2/1, 2008, pp. 134-164. Samuel actually rescued the project when the East Africa Syndicate, which had begun it, ran out of funds.

** This reflects the casually pejorative usage of the time. Leys greatly admired Judaism (see the last part of his chapter on 'African Mentality', below).

men chosen for the higher positions are those who help capital get the largest profit, although it is also of advantage to men to be occasionally accused of being interested in native life, of supporting schemes of industrial education, of making patriotic speeches over foundation stones for churches. I believe that until the Service is reconstructed, governors should be men brought up to public life at home.

(3) The administrative and technical staff of the governments in Crown Colonies should in future be recruited by public examination. The rank and file now have two serious faults. They belong to one political party, almost to a man. (When an officer gets a daily paper at all from home, which is seldom, it is almost always the Morning Post). And they haven't active minds. To find a man who knows an African language as all missionaries do, is very rare. Few men ever read anything beyond light novels. Practically none of them imagine the possibility of an Africa not just an extension of the scheme in operation now. The kind of men I want to see out there are graduates from W.E.A. classes.*

But as we can't get them we should at least get men who share the opinions and aims of the main body of public life. Fortunately, however, the existing rank and file will be loyal to British authority even if its policy at home is opposed by their class. They are an honest set of men, and among them there is a lot of half conscious dislike of exploitation. They don't think hard enough to seek a remedy for it. But most of them can be trusted to fall in with a new orientation of the governing machine.

---

* The Workers Educational Association, founded in 1903, was led by eminent intellectuals such as R.H.Tawney and has numbered famous figures among its teachers. Karl Polanyi's book *The Great Transformation* began life as notes for his WEA lectures.

3. Preface to the third edition of *Kenya* (1926)[252]

The preface begins with Leys' reply to an attack on him by Lord Delamere for having repeated in Kenya *the charge that Delamere had engaged in 'dummying' – acquiring land in the names of other people to evade limits on how much one individual could get. It seems likely that Delamere had indulged in some kinds of 'dummying', as his carefully-worded denial tends to suggest; he didn't care if everyone in Kenya knew it, but he didn't want it known in Britain. He hoped to discredit Leys and the Colonial Office was happy to help. Leys showed, in reply, that attacking him could be counter-productive.*

The preface goes on to dismantle the official propaganda that was being deployed to promote the settlers' aim of being granted 'responsible government', with interesting reflections on the discriminatory impact of specific kinds of forced labour, and on the significance of the increasing prevalence of crime. It ends with an attack on what he saw as a new willingness on the part of the leadership of the Protestant missionary movement to compromise with the racist character of settler colonialism in Kenya – an implicit criticism of J. H. Oldham, with whom he had just parted political company. He was well aware that in making this attack he risked losing support in church circles, but he didn't want support that wasn't committed to African liberation. (The middle sections of the preface, reviewing recent changes in policies on land, labour and taxation, are of less permanent interest and have been omitted.)

PREFACE TO THIRD EDITION

… Before more important matters are dealt with I shall venture a last word on a personal matter. I quoted in this book some passages from a letter that first appeared in a Nairobi newspaper seven years ago. The writer of the letter accused Lord Delamere of 'dummying' in land. Neither Lord Delamere nor anyone else denied the accusation, and people naturally and justifiably assumed that the statements of fact in the letter were correct. As this letter put the case better than I could put it, I reprinted the relevant passages, with Lord Delamere's name omitted. Eighteen months after my book was published, and when the second edition was half sold, the Government* published a Command Paper of fourteen pages in refutation of the 'unfounded charges' I am alleged to have made against Lord Delamere, who is, in effect, officially canonised in its pages. It contains a statement by Lord Delamere himself, in which he writes: 'The Land Officer

---

* i.e. the British government.

was kept fully informed of the facts so there was no question of dummying in the ordinary sense of the term'. Soon afterwards I wrote to the Press accepting that denial 'as unreservedly as it was made'. Why it was not made seven years ago does not appear.

As the Command Paper deals solely with Lord Delamere's original land grant it gives a very inadequate and misleading account of his activities. But it has real importance as revealing the mind of the Government of Kenya at a time when it professes to follow a policy of greater justice than formerly to the natives of the country. That a European should land in Africa with £50,000 and multiply that sum tenfold, partly no doubt by his own exertions but mainly by the sale for £200,000 of land that he had got from Government for nothing, and by using the kind offices of the Government in inducing the natives of the country to work for him, this still seems to the Government an admirable proceeding. Those of my contemporaries in Kenya who have read my book know how carefully I refrained from quoting statements that would have reflected on individuals even when they would have greatly strengthened my argument. I shall break that rule for once against the combined attack of the Government and Lord Delamere. The Command Paper omits to mention how many hundreds of square miles he has at one time or another had and either sold or kept possession of. Nor does Lord Delamere himself make mention of his views as to how much land it is appropriate that certain other people should be allowed to acquire and to keep. I shall supply the deficiency. In his evidence before the 1912 Labour Commission he said: 'If the policy was to be continued that every native was to be a landholder of a sufficient area on which to establish himself, then the question of obtaining a satisfactory labour supply could never be settled'.

Although I have had the privilege of making free use of the experience of both administrative officers and missionaries with the most recent information, I find it excessively difficult to estimate recent changes in Kenya. These changes are explained by the fact that the Government has been compelled to bow to the partly awakened public opinion of this country. But anxiety to disarm criticism is a bad motive for reform, and a worse guide to execution. The reader should always bear in mind the immense difficulties of carrying out reforms which scarcely anyone in Kenya thinks necessary, while those influences that created the former policy continue in unabated force and are active in rendering nugatory whatever in the reforms might injure already vested interests. The key to the situation of the moment is the desperate desire of the Europeans of Kenya to do nothing that might retard the day on which Parliament, they believe, will give them constitutional as well as practical control of the country. That is what makes them so sensitive to criticism. But once their representatives have a majority of seats on the Legislative Council they could snap their fingers at their critics. They know that the success of that master ambition has been endangered by the exposure in this country of certain things which the Government, acting under their influence, is discovered to have done. They are therefore compelled to approve such reforms as may satisfy British public opinion, so long as nothing is done to diminish the profits which some are making and others hope to make. Reforms with such origins, motives and restrictions are apt to prove a making of the worst of both worlds. It is only fair to add that some, perhaps most, of my informants, remembering the high moral character of many of their friends in Kenya, take a more favourable view. I on the contrary cannot forget what these same men permitted to be done when they had things all their own way, and I mistrust any change of heart that conflicts with people's strongest interests and long-cherished and dearest ambitions. It is also necessary for readers to remember that energetic pursuit of reform by the Government would bring down upon its head revolutionary resistance such as was threatened with complete success a few years ago.* It is only the force of a strong and sustained opinion in this country that will enable the Government of Kenya to escape from an impossible situation.

One change for the better is a very large increase in the sanitary staff and in the expenditure on sanitary services. In the four years both have more than doubled. More is also being spent on native education. One hundredth part of the new ten million pound loan is earmarked for research into matters that affect the health and well-being of Africans. The training of native hospital assistants has begun, and a voluntary fund has been started for an infant welfare centre. An official pamphlet on the care of labourers contains advice which, if it is followed, would immensely improve their diet and housing. All this is to the good. But schoolmasters and health officers cannot work miracles. Health, whether of body or mind, is impossible to people in the tropics with incomes round about sixpence a day. And again, it is ridiculous to spend money on research when long-known and well-tested means of preventing the commonest tropical diseases are neglected. The reason of their neglect is the poverty both of the Government and of those whom the preventive remedies would benefit, and that poverty is the consequence of the existing economic system. What makes it absurd for a doctor in this country to advise a man who was gassed in the war and in consequence is slowly dying from chronic bronchitis, to go the Riviera, also makes it absurd to expect that malaria and dysentery can be banished from the plantations of Kenya.† Even in British West Africa, where the workers do enjoy the

---

* A reference to the settlers' threatened coup which prevented the implementation of the Wood-Winterton agreement in 1923, mentioned in Chapter 8.
† Leys tends to call all settler farms 'plantations'.

wealth they create, and the standard of living is far higher than in Kenya, efficiency in sanitary services is very hard to reach.

In regard to education there has even been retrogression as well as advance. When, a few years ago, the authorities were first stirred by criticism, the promise was given that some of the money paid in direct taxation by Africans should be returned to them in the shape of equally visible services, notably in educational grants. But the new native councils were used as soon as they were set up to get the tribes to levy on themselves an extra tax, additional to the hut and poll tax, for increased social services; and nothing more is being heard of the promise that some part of what is paid to the Colony's exchequer should be spent on benefits to those from whom most of the money is derived. The Government's educational policy is revealed most clearly by the fact that it proposes to spend on new school buildings alone for the 1500 European children in the country more than its total expenditure on the education of African children during the last five years.

... In many ways the authorities show favouritism to plantation industries. When two years ago the Secretary of State was persuaded to put the compulsory labour regulations into force for the building of a new railway, the men who were forced to do the work were taken, not from the plantations, as they are in the Belgian Congo, but solely from the villages. These men were engaged in growing native foodstuffs, of which in some district or other there is in most years a serious shortage. Yet these, rather than the men employed on the plantations gathering sisal leaves or picking coffee berries, were the men whose work the Government preferred to interrupt. In defending in Parliament this compulsion, Lord Balfour was instructed to say that the men who were compelled were doing no work in the villages from which they were taken. The official apologists for the Government are stating that it was customary for the young men, in the Kenya tribes, to form a military class that scorned honest toil. A standing army of this kind did exist among the Masai, the Nilotic Kavirondo and a few other smaller tribes, comprising at most one-eighth of the population of the country. These standing armies, in the case of every tribe except the Masai, and recently in their case too, were broken up nearly a generation ago. But to say that the Kikuyu, the tribe from which the forced labour justified by Lord Balfour was drawn, had at any time an idle military class, is totally untrue. And the people in Kenya who made the statements on which Lord Balfour relied told falsehoods that are cowardly as well as deliberate.

... Another instance of favouritism is to be found in the administration of the Communal Labour Ordinance. In olden times roads and bridges were kept in repair by the free labour of the people in the adjacent villages. Our Government gave this custom the sanction of statute law.

But this law provides that the twenty-four days of unpaid labour which the tribal authority may requisition in each year, for the less skilled work on these so-called communal services, can only be required from those members of a tribe who prefer village life to plantation life, wage-earners being exempt from the payment of this tax of a month's unpaid labour, which is levied on all who manage to avoid work for wages. In the alienated areas, of course, all similar work is paid for out of the taxes, which, as will be shown in this book, are paid mainly by the natives of the country. It is as if the unskilled labour on roads and bridges in rural England had to be done for nothing by the rural workers, each of them liable to be called out for a week in every quarter at the pleasure of the County Council, while all the navvying in the towns was paid for at market rates, out of taxation borne chiefly by the rural workers.

... Village agriculture will never have a fair chance in Kenya so long as those engaged in it believe that it may be interrupted at any moment, whether for railway construction or for communal labour, at the mere nod of some Government agent. Even the most conservative of my informants agree that the payment of labourers on communal work is of prime importance. In a country where most of the workers are paid sixpence a day or less, the requiring of unpaid labour from a single section of the population, and that section the poorest, amounts to slavery.

... One development of grave import is a large increase in crime in the country ... For years after I first went to East Africa, and before the results of frantic exploitation by European capital had shown themselves, none of us thought of locking his door, and one went on a journey of a week or more leaving not only property but wife and child in what then was always the safe keeping of their African neighbours. To do so now would be madness. The only remedy for lawlessness advocated not only by the European Colony but also by the Government of Kenya, is an increase in penalties already barbarously severe. Thus an Ordinance has just been passed making rape punishable by death. No one imagines that a court would ever hang a European for the rape of a native woman. The attitude of the Europeans of Kenya to the converse case is that the crime would in fact be inconceivable if proper feelings of respect for Europeans were inculcated in Africans, but that since from the lack of firm handling the crime has actually happened, it must be stamped out. Their peculiar position makes it impossible for them to realise the irrationality of that standpoint. It would seem to them quite irrelevant to cite the experience of this country, where all the foulest sorts of crime were far commoner a hundred years ago than now, and diminished only when school learning spread until it became eventually compulsory and free, while hanging people for these crimes failed to reduce their number. Nor does it seem to them to matter that since convictions for rape are nearly always based on the evidence of a single person, the danger of a miscarriage of justice must be greater than in the case of any other crime. This passionate unreason is the strongest proof that the government of Kenya by its resident Europeans would inevitably be a tyranny. Yet we find the present Governor using these words when opening a new school for European children: 'He reminded his listeners, however, that they had a brand new generation of settlers growing up amongst them, in the children of the present settlers ... They were, as Captain Coney had said, the future rulers of the country – the future rulers, he would add, of a great self-governing colony.' This same Captain Coney, who is a member of the Legislative Council, is reported by the *East African Standard* of the 20th February 1926 to have said, in an address to his constituents: 'You will never solve the labour problem until you have control of the country – when you have that you will immediately solve the problem'.

In the text of this book the opinion is expressed that Protestant foreign missions are at the parting of the ways. There are increasing signs that the whole movement is, like so many movements in the past, taking the wrong road and departing with increasing certainty from the plans and ideals of the founder of the Christian religion ... The original Christian scheme was the establishment of a corporate society which was to become the habitation of the entire human race. The motive of that society, the purpose it was to serve, was the sharing to the utmost possible limit of all the boons of life, knowledge, wealth, beauty and service, by each, and with all who were able to enjoy these boons. Freely they had received, and freely they were to give. It is in that spirit of unstinted devotion that many missionaries have spent their lives. It is sometimes said that the world is not worthy of this devotion. That is not true, since only by its means can the world be liberated. Thousands still devote their lives as their great exemplar taught and practised ... But among many of these men's leaders, especially those of them who direct their work from Europe, a different spirit is growing. That spirit would have missionaries limit and measure their services to Africans. The older ideal was that the Church's agents, whatever their own limitations, should offer all they had to give. The new assumes that there are elements in our life in Christendom which we enjoy and value but which are unsuitable for Africans also to enjoy. It would have certain Europeans in positions of importance, such as Colonial Governors and the secretaries of missionary societies, form and act upon judgements as to what it is wise that Africans should know and do. And it justifies this new departure from former missionary policy by the allegation that something unique has been discovered in the culture, or mentality or temperament of Africans, though just what this unique quality may be is never defined. May heaven forbid that we should inflict upon Africans those evils from which we ourselves seek to escape! But as in the view of people of this school the modern competitive system of industry is not an evil thing, they have no objection to its extension to Africa. They find in capitalists and in those who planned and still control the operation of that system in Kenya, their warmest supporters, and themselves belong to that section of the religious world that sees nothing incompatible between the modern system of industry and the ethics of the New Testament. What they would have withheld from Africans are rather what we ourselves most greatly prize, great literature and political liberty.

4. 'African Mentality' (1931)

These extracts are from Chapter IX of A Last Chance in Kenya, *dealing with the racist idea that that Africans had a different 'mentality' from Europeans – an idea universally held by the settlers and explicitly promoted in Britain by some officials at the Colonial Office. By this time Leys had realised that most people in Britain, including many of those who saw themselves as 'pro-native', also subscribed to this idea, at least unconsciously, and that it needed to be confronted head-on. He pointed out that Europeans in Kenya, who never saw Africans in any but inferior roles, found it easy and reassuring to believe that they had inferior roles because they had inferior abilities; and they rationalised this self-interested belief by maintaining that Africans had a special 'mentality'. People in Britain didn't constantly see Africans in subordinate roles but there was a growing popular interest in the tribal cultures that were being described, and sometimes celebrated, by anthropologists, and Leys thought that this was having a somewhat similar effect.*

The middle section of the chapter describes how the concept of an 'African mentality' had been used to justify both inferior education for Africans and 'indirect rule' instead of steps towards self-government. This section has been omitted to make room for the chapter's final section on the idea that significant cultural differences are racially determined. It can only be described as a semi-serious romp through the history of migrations from Central Asia into Europe, showing that wherever they went the migrating 'Tartars' were assimilated into the historically and ecologically determined culture of the regions they settled in. Leys' aim here was evidently not to disprove the idea that cultural differences are racially determined but to show that it was absurd. The chapter ends with a striking tribute to 'the Jewish doctrine and ethic', which he thought had made Jews an exception to the rule that mass migrations always end in cultural assimilation.

When Plato lived in Athens, most of our ancestors were uncivilised people, living in the tribal stage of society. Many of them were less civilised than the Baganda were, when Europe first learned of their existence sixty years ago, but probably all of them were further on than the Kikuyu were then. Yet we have no doubt that these barbarous ancestors of ours were quite as intelligent as their Greek contemporaries, and just as intelligent as we are now. The sole difference between them and us and between them and the Athenians of their time, is that they were denied, by the facts of geography and history, the opportunities the Athenians had, and our even greater opportunities.

Are the inferior average attainments of Africans to-day also rightly so to be explained by their inferior opportunities? Are Kikuyu and Kavirondo children as intelligent as our own, as capable, if put under the same influences, of becoming equally civilised men and women? The answer we get to these vitally important questions altogether depends on whom they are asked of. Practically all the settlers, and the great majority of the senior officials in East Africa, answer them in the negative. And that, of course, is why African children do not, in fact cannot, get the education European children get, although what they do get they absorb far more eagerly.

Now, both settlers and officials, we have seen, have many privileges and advantages over Africans that in their view are the natural reflection of their superior attainments. They have an exclusive right to the franchise, superior rights in land, an advantage of some sort, in short, in every phase and aspect of life. They say they would be 'swamped' if they had not these advantages, if they were extended to Africans, meaning that, if Africans were given the same opportunities as they and their children have, their existing monopoly of high positions, and large incomes and extensive estates, would vanish. Now that is a very natural view for them to take. Indeed, given their circumstances, it is inevitable. No body of ordinary men and women, endowed with all those privileges, dependent for their very existence on the labour of Africans, would agree that the children of their labourers should have the kind of education that would enable them, when they grew up, to control their own industrial economy and to develop their social and political institutions as free nations do. At present, in Kenya, Europeans are masters and Africans servants. The vast majority of Europeans in Africa believe that relationship to be an integral part of the natural order of human society. They not only believe that but feel passionately about it as no one in this country does about any political topic. During three years spent in a 'settled' area the author found that to doubt that white men must always be masters and black men servants was, without exaggeration, regarded as proof of having a criminal mind.

But when people feel passionately they do not think clearly. That is why these men and women, suffering under the curse of privileges – for that is what exclusive privileges always are – cannot see that if, as they claim, they have a natural inherent superiority over Africans they would have nothing to fear if African children were given the same opportunities as their children. How real a disadvantage the privileges of Europeans are is illustrated by the fact shown in the Reports of the Education Department, that European children in Kenya do less well in competitive examinations than Indian children, though the education they get is four times as costly as the education the Indian children get, and though, of course, the examinations are conducted in a language that is spoken in few of the homes the Indian boys and girls come from.

But the foregoing, while a perfectly true account of the attitude of the settlers and of many officials, would, if it stood alone, be a very defective and unfair explanation. It is in large measure explained and in their view justified by certain obvious facts of life. These facts, being what people see and hear and do in Africa, are not easy to explain in a book. The untutored African sees the sun daily move round the earth, and cannot be persuaded that in truth the earth goes round the sun. Facts no less certain, vivid and apparently unsurmountable, as irresistibly convince the European that the African is his inferior.

How sharp the contrasts are in one's very first hour in an African port! Every European one sees, dressed in spotless white, cool, unhurried, obsequiously attended, giving orders at his ease. While the Africans one sees, an ill-clad, jostling, sweating, jabbering mob, obey orders. Their very smell is different. Every day most men spend in Africa reinforces that first impression. But the key to the estimate which, even after years of experience, planters and merchants form of Africans' characters and capacities is that they have never seen and never spoken to Africans whose relations to society are not servile. Most Europeans never see Africans' home life in the Reserves, and few indeed are so enterprising as to get to know, as men and women, the better-educated class in the towns, with whom, more than with any other class, the future of the country lies.

It ought further to be admitted that living in relations so predominantly servile has to some extent produced servility of mind. Its total absence in Jamaican society, among the grandchildren of chattel-slaves, is a startling and delightful revelation to anyone who has lived in either South or East Africa. But this servility is due in no degree to the quality of the minds and characters of Africans themselves. The conditions of life of wage-earners in Kenya are entirely what their Government and their employers between them decide they should be. That part of their lives that is spent in producing wealth, in every country the largest section of men's lives, is entirely beyond their power to control. We as a nation introduced into Kenya the system of society in which there is no place for Africans but the lowest, and contrived and imposed those measures that compelled Africans to enter that lowest place. They have no wish to fill it and, if there were no need to earn the tax-money, the great majority would go home and stay there.

This, then, is the answer to the easy assurance of their own superiority on the part of Europeans generally. If Africans display, as they sometimes do, servile qualities of mind, it is because we, having, thanks to machine guns, the power to treat them as we pleased, treated them and still treat them as slaves, as people unfit to be free, incapable of responsibility, except, of course, for the fulfilment of long labour contracts. For those who have been and are responsible for the Government of Kenya to spend less than 5s. a year on each African child's education, and more than fifty times as much on each European child's, is to brand men as slaves with an iron, and then point to the scars in scorn, saying that since they grew there the men must be slaves by nature. It is this, the general attitude of Europeans resident in East Africa, that makes absurd, and something a good deal worse than absurd, the policy of 'associating them in the discharge' of our country's trust. What are our wards likely to think of us when they find we have handed the execution of our trust over to executors who believe that, if the wards of the trust were given the opportunities they demand, they themselves would be ruined? The honester of the settlers repudiate, as did those of Northern Rhodesia, so invidious and hypocritical a position. They are and mean to be masters, not trustees, and say so.

But there are some Europeans who live or have lived in East Africa who believe Africans have the same natural capacities as themselves. These include the men and women who know some African language really well. Of that small minority, the author never met a single one who regarded Africans as his mental inferiors. In his view, people with such knowledge are the only reliable judges. What value should we put on a Chinaman's estimate of our mentality, if we found out that though he had lived among us for years, he couldn't understand what people say to one another in tramcars and railway trains and teashops?

It is very regrettable that in Kenya it is thought bad form to know an African language really well. Except for some missionaries' children, even people who have been brought up in the country rarely do.

In point of fact, it is an extraordinarily difficult thing, unless one is exceptionally gifted, to get to know the language and life of a tribe really well. The first stage, of collecting a vocabulary of a few hundred words, is easy. But that does not enable one to understand a single actual sentence. And it is often impossible, especially for officials, to get willing help from the people themselves. Their point of view is something like this. They believe all Europeans to be very clever. Nothing is too difficult for them. This man, they say, obviously knows Kikuyu. He knows lots of words, including some quite rare ones, though, like all Europeans, he uses them very queerly. How can so clever a man possibly be ignorant of the answers to the silly, simple questions he asks? He must know perfectly well, for instance, that when a man needs a new hut, every man in his village helps him to build it. How otherwise could he ever get it built? Besides, how can he have any real difficulty in learning Kikuyu, when we learned it without even trying to? And, anyhow, what is he after? (One finds, of course, the same aversion from answering the simplest questions in the poorest in every country, until they know what one is getting at.) So they conclude that this Master either has some nefarious purpose in his endless and confused enquiries, or is just trying to be annoying. Much of what is known as field anthropology is, for the reasons just given, quite unreliable, especially what is got through interpreters. When an assiduous questioner has to be satisfied, sensible people tell him the things that satisfy him.

Until after the war, Christian Missions had the complete monopoly of the education of African children in all East Africa. Even now, not one in a hundred of the African children at school are in Government schools. One reason is that in ordinary European society those who teach Africans are looked down upon, so that, apart from the men and women who have the sense of devotion to a cause, teachers for African schools are hard to get. The much more numerous Government schools in West Africa and Tanganyika are largely staffed by ex-missionaries.

Until quite recently, what was taught in these Mission schools was simply all that the missionaries' knowledge and time and means allowed them to impart. It was assumed that Africans, being normal human beings, would learn the ideas and habits of civilised life as they had opportunity. But in recent years the rise into fashion of the study of anthropology has had the strange result of making some, but by no means all, anthropologists put forward the theory that each race has a special mentality of its own. Strange, because no man could read any work by any of the anthropologists such as Tyler or Fraser, who deal with facts rather than with their own fancies, without being forced to believe that the human mind everywhere, from China to Peru, and in all ages, has the same character, the same pattern, the same potential desires and ideals. For thirty years the author has tried to find, not only the evidence to prove the existence of the differentiæ of African mentality, but also what any two anthropologists agree that the alleged differentiæ are. He has never been able to find a scrap of evidence for this theory, and reputable anthropologists themselves acknowledge it to be baseless. It is not, of course, that people do not differ. They do, endlessly. But one finds the same differences everywhere under the same conditions and opportunities for development.

But it can readily be imagined with what avidity this theory was fastened upon by all those who want to keep Africans 'in their place', that place being one under authority. For years this theory of differentiation has been the orthodox doctrine in the Colonial Office, and is the source of all those question-begging terms such as Europeanising and detribalising. One of the senior officials from Kenya told the Select

Committee that it was the policy of his Government to make the African a good African, not a bad European. When such people are pressed to explain themselves, they say that Africans ought to be encouraged to preserve their own institutions and develop them along 'their own lines'. If then they are asked if a hut tax or labour contracts for a year or more were features to be found in tribal institutions, they have to admit that they are not. Ask them, again, what is to happen if Africans, like the people of other continents, find they want to change their social and political institutions, and we are told they should be discouraged from doing so, which means they must not do so. As the theory of this policy of differentiating Africans from Europeans is intellectually dishonest, so is its practice unjust and oppressive. As we have seen, so far from leaving African life undisturbed, we have forced Africans to become part of our society when it suits us to: that is, in their economic relations with us. In all the phases in which this policy of differentiation operates, it severs the roots of what alone enables men to do justice, by making them assume that Africans are of different clay from themselves. It had in one case the ludicrous result of enabling a man to write a book describing the Christian attitude to the subject, that contained no mention of the circumstance that in the original Christian society not only was it taught that differences arising from the composite racial origins of the Church ought to be ignored, but also that in actual fact differences between European and Asiatic were ignored and soon forgotten.

Anthropology, it is true, has a certain real, if limited, value for those who are entrusted with the governing of people in, or emerging from, the tribal stage of society. But the study of a people's past is no substitute for attention to the urgent problems of their present emergency, and can never give much guidance during what in Kenya is nothing less than a mental as well as economic revolution. An illustration of how it is sometimes used to obscure the essential economic issues is the 'talk' on the wireless given, late in 1930, by Mr. Leakey, the archæologist, who undoubtedly knows more about the Kikuyu than any other European knows about any tribe in Kenya. The thesis of his talk was that everything that goes wrong in Kenya is the result of ignorance – ignorance of the white man's ways on the part of Africans, and ignorance of native customs by European employers. He gave two illustrations. In one he made good his point, and it is significant that the incident occurred in the early days of our occupation. Peace parleys had been held, involving several tribes as well as the Government, and seemed at last to have succeeded, when the representative of one of the tribes turned round and spat, not only upon his former enemy but also upon the British officer who was conducting the parley. This officer, unaware that with Africans spitting on a man is a sign of friendship and confidence, promptly knocked out the man who had spat upon him, when, of course, the war began afresh. That story indicates the kind of occasion on which knowledge of anthropology is of real value. But the second story was of a planter who one day was asked permission by one of his labourers to take a day off, because his wife was having a baby. He gave the permission. Next day, when out riding in a part of his estate miles away from this labourer's home, he saw him carrying a large bunch of bananas. He concluded that the man had lied to him, as so many had before, and swore he would give a day's leave to no more, being ignorant of the fact that Kikuyu law ordains that a husband must provide a wife just confined with a special rare sort of banana. Now, is it reasonable to expect employers in Kenya to study anthropology? They are there to make their living, and with luck, their fortune. Why should they pay a close attention to the lives of their labourers that is customary with employers nowhere? But in any case is the ignorance of the employer the real point of the story? Is it not rather that in Kenya an employer has the entirely arbitrary right to decide when, over periods of as long as a year, a labourer may or may not leave work, and that the law punishes those who leave work without permission by both imprisonment up to one month and a fine up to £5, which is equivalent to a labourer's gross earnings for more than a year. Surely the point is that one cannot expect employers to be studious, but one ought to expect the laws to prevent servile conditions, not to create them.

Here once more one meets the assumption that one ought to have a different standard of judgement for Africans, should think that what is important to them is something quite different from what we in their place should consider important. Why should we assume that the study of Africans' past should help us to solve problems arising from the fact that we have flung them, willy-nilly, into the seething cauldron of capitalist industry, when we should never think of looking for a solution of our own coal industry to its history? In point of fact, its history has some trifling importance, since the system of way-leaves and royalties can be understood only by past history. Just such and no more is the relevance of anthropology to the problems of society in Africa.

The native inhabitants of Eastern Africa, when Europe first became aware of their existence sixty years ago, were, with few exceptions, in the tribal stage of human development. That is why they were so ignorant, and accordingly so easily oppressed, why they were so ill-prepared for the industrial revolution that has overtaken them, and why the present generation, though not of necessity the next, is unfit for political independence. In some things of the mind, the fashion fluctuates from generation to generation. Rousseau's noble savages, worthy of imitation, were succeeded by heathen in their blindness, deserving only to provide raw materials for European lords and masters. Now the pendulum has swung back once more. And it is true enough that people who live in a tribe have virtues we sorely lack. In tribal society there are no paupers, no unemployed, no idle rich, no prostitutes, no prisons. No man goes hungry so long as a fellow clansman has enough. But there is another side to the picture. When all are mutually dependent, none has independent mind or character. And we in our society would not barter our personal liberty for anything. We must be free to believe in God or to deny, to advocate government by a dictator or by a democracy, to eat beefsteak or nothing but vegetables. But in a tribe men are not free so to choose. All must think alike and behave alike. And out of this absence of variety, of what we call individualism, there comes a great poverty of mind. The Kikuyu have no word for grass, but only a score or more words, each for one kind of grass. No purely tribal language has any word meaning 'matter', or for 'idea' or for 'interesting' …

Evidence as to the source of cultural variation is available in the various histories of different branches of the same race. Central Asia has for many centuries been getting more arid and hence less capable of supporting human life. Wave after wave of migration passed east and west out of this region of Tartary. One such wave got as far north as the top of the Baltic where we know the descendants under the name of Finns. The Finns fell under the influence of the culture shared by all the nations in that part of the world. Thus they were converted to Christianity late, and became Protestants when the Reformation arrived. In modern times they have always been in the fashion, so to speak. They are democrats, have women's suffrage, excel in games of physical skill, and many of them are Socialists.

A second wave reached the Danube valley and produced the nation we know as Hungary. Again we see that their national culture is characteristic of the region of the world the Magyars inhabit. They were converted to Western Christianity, and, living on the boundary of the area reconquered by the Counter-Reformation, most of the Magyars are still Catholic, and so, like most other Catholic countries but no Protestant ones, have a Dictator. The arts, specially of music, flourish among them, as among their German neighbours.

A third wave of Tartars got as far as the Balkans, where they were converted to Greek Christianity like all their neighbours, and like them, though unlike their cousins the Turks who conquered them, they resisted conversion to Islam.

A fourth wave, the Turks, for some reason founded a great Empire. Living in that part of the world where nearly all became Moslem, they also did. But after they had lost the last province of their Empire, they decided to imitate the culture of the nations who had been victorious in the Great War and set up a secular State with democratic forms. The Tartars who stayed in Tartary became like their neighbours, Moslems of a more ordinary type. Though conquered by Russia, they resisted conversion to Greek Christianity, but presumably are less able to withstand Communism.

In the case of all these Asiatic nations there was, of course, much mingling of blood with their European neighbours. But in no case was the infusion great enough to obliterate the evidences of Asiatic origin, in language, folklore and, in some cases, dress, dances and other amusements. These, be it noted, are the sole evidence of the race to which these nations belong. All their important national characteristics they owe not to race but to history and geography. Put your finger anywhere on the map of the world and you can tell, by knowing the culture of the region, what the inhabitants of that spot believe – even what they eat. Nurmi is a famous runner, not because he has Tartar ancestry, but because open-air sports are all the rage in North-Western Europe. The Bulgars resisted Islam, not because the ideas of Greek Christianity are specially congenial to Tartars, but because their Church was, under the Turkish yoke, the bond of their national unity and the symbol of their future liberation. The Persians, though of European race, adopted Islam and are, in fact, typical Asiatics in everything but their race. In short we find that cultures, civilisations, social institutions, religions, do not normally have racial frontiers. And in the modern world, of course, all those regional cultures tend to run together. Individuals, in some parts of the world at least, do have some of the knowledge that enables them to make personal choices.

The history of the nation that has had fortunes more varied than any other, the Jews, is in striking contrast with those we have been considering. Before they entered upon their wanderings and their sojourns among the Gentiles, they were furnished with a lofty creed, a noble literature and a close-knit social order that had given birth to a proud and self-sufficient national consciousness. When each company of migrant Tartars were adopting the religion and culture they found around them, Judaism resisted the attack of every rival. But the Jews themselves suffered a different fate. The paucity of their numbers everywhere resulted, in the course of many centuries, in admixtures of blood that have obliterated every sign of a common distinctive type. What the original type of the Hebrews was when they were a federation of pastoral tribes we do not know. They may have absorbed some foreign blood in Egypt. They certainly mingled for centuries with Canaanites and Philistines. In Babylon they were further recruited, and by the time the remnant returned to Palestine very little Jewish blood can have had its source in the people who entered Canaan under Joshua. Then came the missionary period when the Jews 'compassed sea and land to make one proselyte', and the nation, thus enriched by many thousands who were attracted by Jewish ethic, challenged Imperial Rome. There followed the final dispersion. And now the Jews of to-day display the ethnological character, [not of] any single so-called Semitic type, but of the people among whom they lived in the Christian era. The Polish Jews have the bulbous nose and the broad head of the 'Armenoid'. The Spanish Jews have the hooked nose and the narrow head of the 'Mediterranean'. The contrast between the two main types is complete, but neither has any claim to be called the truly Jewish. So also with the less common types of Jew. Those who have lived long among the Berbers have fair hair and blue eyes. Bombay Jews are black.

So the splendid record of the Jews, their fortitude in persecution and adversity that seemed illimitable, the astonishing achievements that have enriched all humanity, as have those of no other people, are due not in even the tiniest measure to any racial quality. They are due wholly to Judaism, to the fortifying, inspiring, ennobling influence of the Jewish doctrine and ethic.

We are forced to the same conclusion if we follow the economic history of the Jews. They began as a federation of small pastoral clans, living precariously between 'the desert and the sown', moving with their camels, sheep and goats, as the Masai do to this day, to the mountains in the dry seasons, to the plains in the rains. The second period of their history was agricultural. No doubt their conquest of Canaan, after which they learned to live, by cultivating the soil, in houses and towns rather than in tents, was far more gradual than the records that have survived suggest. For many centuries thereafter, despite their many vicissitudes, they remained mainly an agricultural people. It was only after their rejection of Christianity, when, in the eyes of Christendom, they became an accursed people, that they were forced off the land. All over Europe and Western Asia, the rights both to own land and to enter the learned professions were denied them. The law that made it illegal for Christians to lend money on interest to Christians and the similar law among the Jews gave the Jews their sole opportunity. They entered on the business of finance, not out of choice, still less because they had any hereditary aptitude for it, but because Christians used to consider it a disgraceful occupation. Indeed, if they had a hereditary aptitude it would have to be for camel-breeding, since that must have been the chief occupation of the ancestors of the patriarchs for thousands of years.

In short, there is no evidence to suggest that race is an important factor in human affairs, and a good deal of evidence to indicate that it has no importance whatever. There is no reason, therefore, to doubt that Africans, once given opportunity, will both share generally in civilised life, and contribute to the world their quota of men of genius.

Acknowledgements

I have relied on the work of many remarkable historians of East Africa, and especially three: John Cell, who in 1976 published a brilliant edition of Leys' correspondence with the missionary leader J. H. Oldham; Diana Wylie, who in 1977 published two outstanding articles on Leys and his friend McGregor Ross as critics of government policy in Kenya; and Lotte Hughes, who in 2001 published a definitive study of the Maasai affair. But while historians have been mainly interested in Leys' impact on events in his lifetime, I have been mainly interested in the way events shaped his thinking and actions, and I have traced this largely through a close reading of his letters. He got rid of his own papers, but he wrote hundreds of letters to people eminent enough for their papers to have been preserved with many of his letters among them.

For help in researching Leys' childhood I am greatly indebted to Jeanne Dubino and to Peter Weis, the archivist of Northfield Mount Hermon School in Northfield, Massachusetts. For Leys' later life Diana Wylie not only generously shared her 1974 interviews with Leys' daughter and some of his patients in Derbyshire, but also read my first draft with an eagle eye for mistakes and questionable judgements. Lotte Hughes generously shared the correspondence between Leys and T.E. Harvey. (John Cell sadly died in 2001.) I am also grateful to archivists at the Universities of Glasgow, Edinburgh, Hull, and Sussex; at the Bodleian Library in Oxford; at University College, Oxford; and at Scotland's People, the National Library of Scotland, and the Imperial War Museum.

James Curran and Kenneth King encouraged me to try to write the book. David Anderson shared some valuable sources and very kindly gave me the benefit of his expertise on the Mau Mau Emergency. Vron Ware and Paul Gilroy pointed me to literatures I needed to consult, and Vron commented acutely on every chapter. Nancy Leys Stepan and Roberta Hamilton made valuable comments on an early draft. Tom Leys contributed sharp political insights and greatly improved my prose. Cecile Oxaal provided generous hospitality in Hull. Barbara Harriss-White supported the project from start to finish, and was an astute critic of every draft.

Thanks are also due to Tony Zurbrugg at the Merlin Press. Merlin stands out as an independent publisher for whom political principles are as important as the bottom line – a worthy successor, in this respect, to Norman Leys' publisher, the Hogarth Press.

I am extremely grateful to all these people for their help, but none of them bears the slightest responsibility for the result.

Notes

1. 'Kenneth King Munsie Leys', a manuscript note from 1951 by Kenneth's widow, Agnes Leys, in the archive of University College, Oxford.
2. One of the papers submitted to the court by the boys' grandfather, Peter Leys, in the subsequent custody case, said that both children were sent to Mrs Lang. But in the note on Kenneth by his widow (see note 1) which records Kenneth's memories of his time in Dollar, there is no mention of Norman being there with him; it says that when Mrs Lang fell ill Kenneth was sent to stay with Peter Leys, 'where Norman was already'. If the Munsie grandparents had looked after Norman for two or three years it might help to explain why the Munsie relatives were, Peter Leys alleged, so strongly opposed to John Leys' proposal to send them to a Catholic school, allegedly 'forbidding' him to agree to it. ('Answers' 31 May 1886, court archives, Scotland's People).
3. 'Minute' for the petitioner [i.e. John Leys], 9 June 1886, court archives.
4. My brother Adam Leys wrote an insightful account of the social context of the court case, the membership of Peter Leys' household, and the motives of the father and son, which the evidence in the court papers tends to confirm ('How the two Leys boys were stolen from their father for the good of their souls. A Victorian story', typescript, n.d., in the possession of Mrs Dorothy Hughes).
5. Emma Moody Powell, *Heavenly Mandate*, Chicago: Moody Publishers, 1943, pp.136-39.
6. Much of the information on the two boys time at the school cited here was first provided by the school archivist to Kenneth's widow Agnes Leys in 1951, but it has subsequently been greatly enriched by Peter Weis, the present archivist.
7. Lucy Clark to Lester P. White, Alumni Secretary, Mount Hermon School, August 1 1951, in Northfield Mount Hermon School (NMHS) archives.
8. Tom Coyle to Lester P. White, August 2 1951, in NMHS archives.
9. Statement of the Rev. P. Leys before the Court of Session, Edinburgh, Tuesday 20th July 1886, reproduced in Adam Leys (n.d.).
10. Agnes Leys (1951).
11. Leys to Winifred Holtby, 6 July 1932.
12. Leys to Gilbert Murray, 10 October 1902.

13 Jack Lochead (1951).
14 Agnes Leys (1951).
15 Minute books of the Committee for 1892-93, Dep.298/81 & 82, archives of the National Library of Scotland.
16 Jack Lochead (1951), pp. 9-10.
17 Leys to Murray 17 March 1918.
18 Agnes Leys (1951).
19 Jack Lochead (1951), p. 8.
20 Leys to Murray 24 February 1903.
21 Gilbert Murray to Lady Murray 27 January 1899.
22 Murray to Lady Murray 25 January 1899.
23 Leys to Murray 24 February 1903.
24 Leys to Murray 18 August 1930.
25 Leys to Murray 13 January 1900.
26 Leys to Murray 7 February 1902.
27 Leys to Murray 7 February 1902.
28 James Duffy, *Portuguese Africa*, Cambridge, Mass.: Harvard University Press,1959, p.132.
29 Leys to Murray 10 October/5 November 1902.
30 Norman Leys, *The Colour Bar in East Africa*, London: the Hogarth Press 1941, p. 45.
31 Norman Leys, *Kenya*, London: the Hogarth Press, 1924, p. 30.
32 Colin Baker, 'The Government Medical Service in Malawi: An administrative history, 1891-1974', *Medical History*, Vol. 20/3, July 1976, pp. 296 ff.
33 Leys to Murray 18 June 1905.
34 Leys (1924), p. 142.
35 'To all kinds of people', typescript in the Gilbert Murray papers, Bodleian Library.
36 J. M. Lonsdale, 'The Politics of Conquest: The British in Western Kenya, 1894-1908', *The Historical Journal* 1977, Vol. 20, No. 4, pp. 841-870.
37 John Lonsdale (1977), p. 859.
38 Robert M. Maxon, *Conflict and Accommodation in Western Kenya: The Gusii and the British, 1907-1963*, Cranbury, N.J.: Associated University Presses, 1983.
39 Cited in Diana Wylie, 'Critics of Colonial Policy in Kenya', M. Litt., University of Edinburgh, 1974, p. 57.
40 John Cell (1976), p. 12.
41 Extract in the Kenya National Archive.
42 Norman Leys, *A Last Chance in Kenya*, London: The Hogarth Press 1931, p. 117.

43 Richard D. Wolf, *The Economics of Colonialism: Britain and Kenya 1870-1930*, New Haven: Yale University Press 1974, p. 106.
44 Cited in Robert I. Tignor, *The Colonial Transformation of Kenya; the Kamba, Kikuyu and Maasai from 1900 to 1939*, Princeton: Princeton University Press, 1976, pp. 180-81.
45 Leys to Murray from Mombasa, n.d. Cell dates it as 19 March 1911.
46 Anna Crozier, 'The Colonial Medical Officer and Colonial identity: Kenya, Uganda and Tanzania Before World War Two', PhD thesis, University College London, 2005, p. 85: John Iliffe, *East African Doctors; A history of the modern profession*, Cambridge: Cambridge University Press, 1998, p. 28.
47 Colonial Service Recruitment No.3, p.10, cited in Anna Crozier (2005), p. 72.
48 McGregor Ross to his mother, 26 March 1911.
49 Leys to Murray, n.d. Cell gives the date as 19 March 1911.
50 A copy of the Memorandum is contained in the Gilbert Murray papers in the Bodleian Library.
51 Leys to E.T. Harvey 4 March 1912.
52 Leys to Murray 17 February 1918.
53 The story has been told in detail in Lotte Hughes' definitive study, *Moving the Maasai*, London: Palgrave MacMillan, 2006.
54 Norman Leys (1924), p. 121.
55 Norman Leys (1924), pp. 122-23.
56 Leys to Murray 3 February 1910.
57 Leys to Murray 18 June 1910.
58 Leys to Murray 23 April 1911.
59 Leys to Murray 30 June 1914.
60 Bowring to Leys 8 August 1912, cited in Hughes (2001), p. 78.
61 Ross to his mother, 14 August 1912.
62 Leys to Murray 30 June 1914.
63 Leys to Murray 17 July 1912
64 Leys to Borden Turner, 3 May 1921, in John Cell (1976), p. 177.
65 Leys to Edmund Harvey MP, 4 March 1912.
66 'Statement for the [Labour Party's] Advisory Committee [on Imperial Questions] by Dr. Leys', n.d., probably March 1931, in the Holtby papers, Hull History Centre.
67 Leys to Murray 3 Feb 1910.
68 Norman Leys (1931), p. 100.
69 Norman Leys (1941), p. 25.
70 Leys to Murray 30 June 1914.
71 Leys to Murray 17 February 1918.
72 Leys to Murray 13 June 1914.

73 Jane Leys to Mary Donald 22 September 1914, Imperial War Museum, Mrs. J.A. Leys 88/51/1.
74 Government signal from the capital Zomba on 10 September 1914, filed with Janey Leys' letter in the Imperial War Museum.
75 Leys to Murray 24 November 1914.
76 Norman Leys (1924), p. 325.
77 The definitive account of the rising is George A. Shepperson and Thomas Price, *Independent African: John Chilembwe and the Origins, Setting and Significance of the Nyasaland Native Rising of 1915*, Edinburgh: the University Press, 1958.
78 Norman Leys (1924), p. 330.
79 Leys to the Secretary of State for the Colonies 7 February 1918, in John Cell (1976), p. 134.
80 Norman Leys (1924), p. 330.
81 My thanks to Paul Gilroy for drawing my attention to this. See also George Shepperson and Thomas Price (1958), pp. 418-37.
82 Leys to Murray 6 February 1918.
83 Leys to Murray 11 June 1919.
84 Tom Jones to Percy Koppel, Political Intelligence Department, Foreign Office, 12 June 1918. Tom Jones was a student friend of Leys in Glasgow and presumably copied this letter to Leys as a way of telling him what the Colonial Office view was, and that the Foreign Office had been interested.
85 The quotations that follow are from the letter, which is reproduced in John Cell (1976), pp. 91-136.
86 Leys to Murray 26 June 1918.
87 Leys to Murray 17 February 1918.
88 Leys to Murray 11 June 1919.
89 Leys to Leonard Woolf, 14 August 1919.
90 Leys to Winifred Holtby 17 March 1931.
91 Joyce Bellamy, John Saville and Diana Wylie, 'Leys, Norman Maclean, Christian Socialist and Anti-imperialist (1875-1944)', *Dictionary of Labour Biography* Vol XIII, Basingstoke: Macmillan, 1987, pp. 134-143.
92 Leys to Murray 25 February and 19 June 1918.
93 Leys to Borden Turner, 3 May 1921, in John Cell (1976), pp. 170-77.
94 Leys to J H Oldham 8 October 1921.
95 Leys to Oldham, 21 September 1920.
96 Leys to Murray, 2 November 1920.
97 George and Nora Rodgers, interviewed by Diana Wylie, 28 December 1973.
98 Memoir by Duncan Leys, written in 1976.
99 John Cell (1976), p. 17.

100 Leys to Winifred Holtby 6 June 1932.
101 Leys to Holtby 29 October 1930.
102 Mrs Avery (Nanice Leys), interview with Diana Wylie, 1974.
103 Leys to Holtby 12 August 1931.
104 Leys to Holtby, n.d. but probably 1933.
105 Leys to Murray 2 April 1919.
106 Leys to Isabel Ross 7 September 1923.
107 Leys to Oldham 27 June 1925.
108 Leys to Isabel Ross 16 September 1923.
109 John Cell (1976), p. 18.
110 Leys to Woolf 17 July 1924.
111 Leonard Woolf, *Beginning Again: An Autobiography of the Years 1911-1918*, London: The Hogarth Press, 1968, pp. 230-31.
112 Leys to Woolf 10 August 1924.
113 Norman Leys (1924), p. 162.
114 Norman Leys (1924), pp 192-3.
115 Norman Leys (1924), p. 308.
116 Norman Leys (1924), pp. 153-54.
117 Dane Kennedy, *Islands of White: Settler Society and Culture in Kenya and Southern Rhodesia, 1890-1939*, Durham: Duke University Press, 1987, p. 143.
118 Norman Leys (1924), pp. 165-66.
119 Norman Leys (1924), p. 177.
120 Norman Leys (1924), p. 318.
121 Norman Leys (1924), p. 334.
122 Leys to Woolf 29 November 1924.
123 Leys to Woolf 15 March 1925.
124 Leys to Woolf 24 April 1943.
125 London: George Allen and Unwin, 1927; Frank Cass, 1968.
126 Leys to Murray 21 October 1920.
127 Leys to Oldham 7 February 1919.
128 Leys to Holtby 18 October 1930.
129 Leys to Holtby 4 August 1933.
130 Leys to Holtby 19 March 1931.
131 Leys to T.E. Harvey 9 September 1912.
132 Leys to Oldham 10 June 1921.
133 John Cell (1976), p. 39.
134 Norman Leys (1924), p. 239-40.
135 Norman Leys (1941), pp. 139-40.

136 Leys to Oldham 10 June 1921.
137 Leys to Oldham 14 November 1921.
138 'A Note on the Report of the East African Commission', 1925, in John Cell (1976), Appendix pp. 311-12,
139 Norman Leys (1924), Third Edition, 1926, p. 21.
140 Leys to Harris 30 June 1923.
141 Leys to Oldham 1 July 1925. For Oldham's memorandum see the Appendix to John Cell (1976), pp. 295-316.
142 Leys to Woolf 28 November 1918.
143 Leys to Harris 30 June 1923.
144 Leys to Holtby 17 March 1931.
145 Leys to Oldham 10 June 1920.
146 Leys to Oldham 26 February 1925.
147 Norman Leys (1924), p. 138.
148 Leys to Oldham 26 September 1918.
149 Leys to Murray 30 April 1910.
150 Norman Leys (1941), p. 124.
151 Leys to Holtby 17 March 31.
152 Leys to Oldham 23 July 1920.
153 Leys to Oldham 23 July 1920.
154 Leys to Marion Hunter, a secretary at Edinburgh House, the office of the Conference of Church Missionary Societies, 18 February 1923.
155 Leys to Holtby 17 October 1930.
156 Leys to Holtby 18 October 1930.
157 Murray to Holtby 29 October 1930.
158 Leys to Holtby 15 June 1932.
159 Leys to Oldham 23 October 1930.
160 Leys to Oldham 27 June 1925.
161 For 'The Principle of Unripe Time' see M. Cornford's timeless satire, *Microcosmographia Academica: Being a Guide for the Young Academic Politician*, Cambridge: Cambridge University Press,1908.
162 Leys to Oldham 10 March 1925.
163 Leys to Oldham 3 March 1925.
164 Oldham to Leys 2 June 1925.
165 Oldham to Leys 9 March 1925.
166 Oldham to Leys 25 February 1925.
167 Leys to Oldham 26 February 1925.
168 Leys to Leonard Woolf 24 April 1925.
169 Norman Leys (1931), p. 137.
170 Norman Leys (1931), p. 142-143.

171 Norman Leys (1924), p. 69.
172 Leys to Murray 20 July 1919.
173 Norman Leys (1931), p. 113.
174 Norman Leys (1931), p. 123.
175 Leys to Murray 1 April 1942.
176 Leys to Harris 21 September 1930.
177 Robert M. Maxon, *Struggle for Kenya: the Loss and Reassertion of Imperial Initiative, 1912-23*, London and Toronto: Associated University Presses, 1994, pp. 195-56.
178 McGregor Ross, *Kenya from Within*, London: Frank Cass, 1927.
179 Robert G. Gregory, *Sidney Webb and East Africa: Labour's Experiment with the Doctrine of Native Paramountcy*, Berkeley and Los Angeles: University of California Press, 1962, p. 57.
180 Leys to Ross 21 October 1930.
181 'Confrontation over Kenya: The Colonial Office and its critics 1918-1940', *Journal of African History* 18/3, 1997, p. 445.
182 Robert G. Gregory (1962), pp. 143-44.
183 Diana Wylie, 'Confrontation over Kenya: The Colonial Office and its Critics 1918-1940', *Journal of African History*, 18/3 (1977), pp. 427-447; see also Wylie, 'Norman Leys and McGregor Ross: A Case Study in the Conscience of African Empire 1900-1939', *The Journal of Imperial and Commonwealth History* 5/3, (1977), pp. 294-309.
184 Bruce Berman, *Control and Crisis in Colonial Kenya: The dialectic of domination*, London: James Currey Publishers, 1990, p. 184.
185 Leys to Margaret Hodgson 1 August 1933.
186 Leys to Murray 30 June 1914.
187 Leys to Holtby, date illegible; and Joyce Bellamy, John Saville and Diana Wylie (1998).
188 Leys to Holtby 6 June 1932.
189 See Jeremy Murray-Brown, *Kenyatta*, London: George Allen and Unwin, 1972, Chapter 17.
190 Leys to Holtby 4 July 1933.
191 Leys to Holtby 19 June 1934.
192 Vera Brittain, *Testament of Friendship*, London: Fontana and Virago, 1981, p. 240.
193 Winifred Holtby, *Mandoa, Mandoa!*, London: Wm. Collins, 1933; Virago, 1982, pp. 90 and 111.
194 Quoted in Marion Shaw, *The Clear Stream: a life of Winifred Holtby*, London: Virago, 1999, p. 187.
195 Unaddressed note from Achimota, 23 October 1934.
196 Leys to Holtby 10 February 1935.
197 Leys to Holtby 23 April 1935.

198 Leys to Fraser 17 December 1935.
199 Leys to Fraser 2 July 1936.
200 Leys to Woolf 24 April 1943.
201 Agnes (Nanice) Avery, interviewed by Diana Wylie, 14 February 1974.
202 Woolf to Leys, 22 February 1939, in F. Spotts, ed., *The Letters of Leonard Woolf*, London: Bloomsbury Publishing, 1990, p. 417.
203 Norman Leys (1941), p. 152.
204 Bruce Berman, *Control and Crisis in Colonial Kenya*, London: Frank Cass, 1927.
205 Leys to Woolf 1 August 1944. Virginia Woolf had died in 1941.
206 Leys to Murray 11 June 1919.
207 This summary of the squatters' role in the story of the rebellion is drawn from Frank Furedi, *The Mau Mau War in Perspective,* London: James Currey, 1989.
208 The following summary is drawn from David Anderson's comprehensive history, *Histories of the Hanged: Britain's Dirty War in Kenya and the End of Empire*, London: Phoenix, 2005.
209 David Anderson (2005), p. 300. Anderson's main primary sources were records of the trials of over 3,000 Kikuyu on charges carrying the death penalty, which included merely having a firearm.
210 *Legacy of Violence: A history of the British Empire*, London: The Bodley Head, 2022, p. 556. Elkins' main sources were the recollections of Kikuyu victims of the repression, especially women.
211 Details are provided in Jonathan Cook, 'The message of Israel's torture chambers is directed at us all, not just Palestinians', 24 May 2024, https://www.jonathan-cook.net/2024-05-24/israel-torture-prison-palestinians/
212 Norman Leys (1931), p. 170.
213 Edward J. Thompson to Gilbert Murray, 23 January 1925; Edward Thompson, *The Other Side of the Medal*, London: the Hogarth Press, 1925.
214 'The place of John Chilembwe in Malawi historiography', in Bridgal Pachai, ed, *The Early History of Malawi*, London: Longman, 1972, p. 423.
215 *The Wretched of the Earth,* London: Penguin Classics, 2001, p. 33.
216 Norman Leys (1924), p. 364.
217 *The Great Transformation*, London: Farrar and Rhinehart, 1944, p. 73.
218 Leys to Holtby 8 May 1935.
219 Leys to Fraser 29 June 1936.
220 Sven Lindqvist surveys the former in *The Skull-Measurer's Mistake*, New York: The New Press, 1997, and the latter in *Exterminate All the Brutes* (1996), included in his *Saharan Journey*, London: Granta Books, 2012.
221 For example the groups discussed in Stephen Howe, *Anticolonialism in British Politics*, Oxford: The Clarendon Press, 1993, and in Barbara Bush, *Imperialism, Race and Resistance: Africa and Britain, 1919-1945*, London: Routledge, 1999.

222 T.D. Shiels, 'A Last Chance in Kenya', *Political Quarterly* 3/3, 1932, p. 448.
223 Leys to Duncan and Erica Leys, 19 February 1934.
224 Leys to Erica Leys 10 February 1937.
225 Leys to Oldham 14 November 1921.
226 Norman Leys (1931), pp. 137-8 and 161.
227 Leys to Fraser 30 June 1936.
228 'Memorandum on the Land Question in Tropical Africa' for the Mandates committee of the League of Nations Union, 15 February 1922, reproduced in Cell (1976), p. 213.
229 Lotte Hughes, *Moving the Maasai: A Colonial Misadventure*, Houndsmill, Baskingstoke: Palgrave, 2006, p. 19.
230 Norman Leys (1941), pp. 147-48.
231 Norman Leys (1941), p. 148, and Nanice Leys in her interview with Diana Wylie.
232 John Cell (1976), p. 29.
233 Norman Leys (1941), p. 149.
234 Winifred Holtby (1982), p. 116.
235 Leys to Holtby 16 February 1933.
236 Norman Leys (1924), p. 391.
237 Leys to Holtby 17 January 1933.
238 Leys to Holtby 1 September 1931.
239 Leys to Oldham 30 May 1925.
240 Leys to Fraser 29/30 June 1936.
241 Leys to Oldham 23 March 1918.
242 Leys to Holtby 8 September 1932.
243 Leys to Fraser 7 September 1942.
244 Norman Leys (1924), p. 291, note 1.
245 Norman Leys (1941), p. 45.
246 Leys to Holtby 22 June 1933, 4 July 1933, and 25 February 1934.
247 Leys to Holtby 4 July 1933.
248 Duncan Leys to Holtby, 9 December 1933.
249 Quoted in Bellamy et al. (1987), p. 139.
250 *The Diary of Virginia Woolf* Vol II:1920-1924, London: The Hogarth Press, pp. 312-13. Her comment on Leys quoted in the Introduction was in a letter to Lady Cecil in May 1925, cited in J.H Willis, *Leonard and Virginia Woolf as publishers: the Hogarth Press, 1917-41*, University Press of Virginia, London 1992, p. 214.
251 Norman Leys (1924), pp. 393-94.
252 The whole text can be found online: https://archive.org/details/in.ernet.dli.2015.178545/page/n241/mode/2up?view=theater

Index

Aborigines Protection Society, *see* Anti-Slavery Society
Adams, W.G. 114
Administration, Kenyan: criticised by the Colonial Office 34; and flogging in prisons, 35; and the Maasai, 42-49; angry with Leys 42, 51; Leys' class analysis of, 49-50; limitations of, 59; Ross' role in, 73-74; commitment to settlers, 84, 108; racist, 100; opposes allowing KCA to give evidence, 111; and Mau Mau, 120-122
Administration, Nyasaland: Leys' opinion of, 21, 25; racist, 55-56
Advisory Committee on Imperial Questions: Leys active in 66-67; resigns from, 110; rejoins,115; 75, 77, 98, 108, 112-113
African Lakes Corporation 13, 17, 24
Amery, Leo 93, 106, 108
Anderson, David 121, 185
Anti-Slavery Society 26, 91, 103, 128
Arthur, John 92
Attlee, Clement 66, 116
Avery, Bill 115

Baker, Thomas Nelson 8, 10
Barnes, Leonard 69, 115, 126
British East Africa 27, 29, 32, 34, 39, 50, 60
Brittain, Vera 113
Bruce, Alexander 55
Bute 13
Buxton, Charles Roden 103, 104

Cameron, Sir Donald 109
Canterbury, Archbishop of 92, 96, 105
Carrier Corps 104
Chilembwe, John: Leys' analysis of the rising, 55-57; Leys' account widely disseminated, 56-57,125; 61, 73, 81
Chinde: Portuguese racism and cruelty in, 18-20, 23; 13, 17, 25-27, 33, 56, 63, 127, 136
Cell, John 34, 57-58, 66, 75, 77, 88, 131
Churchill, Winston 34, 46
Colonial Office: supports settlers 29-30, 105-109, 111, 119; and moving the Maasai 43-48, 51; fears uprisings 57-60; demotes and exiles Leys, 51; 26-27, 34, 62-63, 75, 84, 90, 93, 98, 103, 128, 138. *See also* Colonial Secretary
Colonial Secretary: 34, Leys' letter to, 56-63, 65, 77; 75, 82, 86, 88-89, 93, 98, 109-110, 116 125
Communism, Communists 78, 111, 129
Conference of Church Missionary Societies 67, 86, 192
Congo 20, 127, 133
Creech Jones, Arthur 66, 116
Cunliffe-Lister, Lord 109
Curtis, Lionel 94, 96

Delamere, Lord 93, 106, 107, 109, 110, 130
Donald, Jane 24
Du Bois, W.E.B. 13, 67

education: as solvent of racism, 20, 22-

23, 25; government fails to provide in Nyasaland, 25; in Mombasa, 38-39; lack of as major factor in risings, 56, 82; focus of break with Oldham, 89-90, 100; 103, 134
Eliott, Sir Charles 29
Elkins, Caroline 121-122
empire: Leys' attitude to, 17, 58, 130-131; 1-2, 17, 29,59, 60-62, 76, 80, 85, 94, 101, 114-115, 122
European, Europeans: and colour bar 38-40; and exploitation in Kenya 78-82, 84; 15, 17-22, 24, 29-30, 32, 34, 46, 52-56, 59-60, 62-63, 67, 77, 90, 91, 93, 97, 99-100, 103, 105-106, 109, 119, 125, 129-130. *See also* settlers

Fanon, Frantz 2, 125
Fiddes, Sir George 58
Fitt, Emma 7
flogging 32, 35-39, 55, 60, 79-80, 166
Fort Hall 34-35, 48
Fraser, A.G. 113-114, 126, 129, 135-136,

Gaza 2, 123
German East Africa 24, 52
Germans 52-54, 67, 110, 127, 129, 136,
Girouard, Sir Percy 43-46, 48, 51, 93
Governors 1, 26, 36, 41, 43, 46, 50, 51, 59, 63, 73, 81, 82, 86, 91, 93, 98, 99, 105, 106, 108, 109, 116, 122; *see also* Eliott, Girouard, Northey, Grigg
Glasgow 5-7, 9-13, 23-25, 66, 70, 83, 113-114, 127, 134
Gregory, Robert G. 108
Grigg, Sir Edward 108, 111
Gusii *see* Kisii

Hailey, Lord 129
Hamas 2
Harlow, Vincent 94
Harris, John 91, 103-104
Harvey, Edmund 35-36, 42-43, 49, 87
Hertzog, General 103, 107-108
Hobson, J.A. 126

Hodgkin, Thomas 130
Hodgson, Margaret 110
Hogarth Press 76, 83, 117, 186
Hola camp 121
Holligan, Ellen 6
Holtby, Winifred: friendship with Leys, 112-114, 135; early death 112; 2, 14, 66, 68, 70, 87, 95-96, 110, 133, 136
Hughes, Lotte 131, 166, 185
Huxley, Elspeth 94, 117

Independent Labour Party 66, 112
Industrial and Commercial Workers Union 110, 112
Ireland 2, 127
Islam 58, 62
Israel 2, 123

James, C.L.R. 125
Jones, Jesse 90-100, 134

Kadalie, Clements 112-113
Kang'ethe, Joseph 131-132
Karonga 24-27, 48, 51-54, 71
Kenyatta, Jomo 11-112, 131-132
Keun, Odette 136
Kikuyu 15, 34-35, 38, 49, 60, 79, 81, 92, 111-112, 117, 119-123, 130-131; *see also* land, labour, Mau Mau
Kikuyu Central Association 111, 131
King, Miss 11
King's African Rifles 57
Kisii 31-33, 56
Kismayu 81
Kisumu 32

Labour Party: 1, adopts progressive policy for Africa, 66-67; Labour governments ignore party policy, 99, 107-108, 117; 75, 77, 85, 95, 99, 103, 107, 112-113, 115-116, 123, 126
labour: Africans' role for settlers 29-30, 35-36, 42, 49; forced in Portuguese East Africa, 18; forced in Kenya 50, 59-60, 77-81, 89-90,105, 119-120, 122
Laikipia 43, 45-48

land: best given to whites 29-30, 78, 80-82, 99, 106-107, 109-110; inequality in Mombasa 38, 40; of the Maasai, 43, 45-48, 51-52; of the Kikuyu, 119-122; 55-56, 59, 73, 87, 91, 97
Lang, Mrs 6
Lewin, Julius 115
Leys, Agnes 1, 6-8, 10-11
Leys, Agnes (née Sandys) 70
Leys, Duncan 66, 68, 71, 73, 133, 136-137
Leys, Eliza 11
Leys, Jane (Janey) 24, 52, 54, 65, 69, 71
Leys, John 5-6, 8, 11, 24,
Leys, Kenneth 5-6, 8-13, 23-24, 70, 75, 127
Leys, Nanice (Agnes Karonga): clear-sighted view of Leys 68-69, 115, 133; chooses wrong sort of husband, 115; 27, 65-66, 136
Leys, Peter 5-11
Liverpool School of Tropical Medicine 13, 17
Llewellyn Davies, Margaret 138
Lochead, Jack 11-13
Lonsdale, John 33

MacDonald, Ramsay 43, 110
Maasai 30-31, 36, 42-48, 51, 73, 87, 110, 130
Mackay, Colonel 33
Magomcro 55-56
Malawi 17, 19, 57
Mandates Committee of the League of Nations Union 67, 85, 128
Marx, Karl 126-127, 130
Mau Mau 2, 117, 120-123
Maxon, Robert M. 34
Mecca 40
Medical Service, Colonial 24-25, 34, 36, 40, 51
Meynell, Mrs 69
Mockerie, Parmenas 111
Mombasa 27, 29-30, 33, 35-40, 42, 45, 48-49, 58, 62, 73, 79, 109
Moody, Dwight 7-10

Morel, E.D. 76
Morris Carter, Sir William 110
Mount Hermon School for Boys 7-8, 10, 13-14
Mozambique 13, 17-19
Munsie, Mr and Mrs 5-6
Murray, Gilbert: Leys' friendship with, 14-15; intellectually influenced by, 23,130; 31, 36-37, assists Leys in the Maasai affair, 43-48; supports the establishment, 95-96; 51, 54, 58, 65-67, 71, 75, 78, 85, 100-101, 114, 119, 126-127
Murray, Lady Mary 14, 95
Muslim 38

Nairobi 27, 30-31, 35-36, 40, 42, 45, 48-50, 51, 58-59, 62, 79, 81, 93, 98, 120
Nakuru 30, 34, 36, 42, 48
Newbattle Abbey 114, 126, 129, 135
Northey, General Sir Edward 63, 105
Northern Rhodesia 115
Northfield, Massachusetts 7, 9-11, 127
Nyasa, Lake 17
Nyasaland 17-18, 21-24, 26-27
Nyasaland African Congress 57

Oldham, J.H.: mobilises against compulsory labour ordinance, 67, 89, 105; relationship with Leys 78, 86-92, 96-98, 128-129; 63, 103, 105, 108, 119, 133-135
Ole Gilisho 46
Ormsby-Gore, Sir William 93-94, 106
Owen, Archdeacon 92, 95, 117, 136
Oxford 13, 23, 58, 70, 88, 94, 114, 138

Palestine 3, 122
Pan-African movement 1, 56, 67, 125
Passfield, Lord 99, 107-108, 111, 117, 128
Perham, Margery 62, 94, 96
Polanyi, Karl 2, 125-126
Portugal 18, 77
Portuguese 18-22, 40
Portuguese East Africa 13, 17, 24
porters 31-32, 35, 49, 54

Robeson, Paul 69
Rodgers, George 69, 131
Ross, Isabel 74-75
Ross, McGregor: collaborates with Leys, 1, 66,104,109; abandons plan to write with Leys, 73-75; publishes *Kenya From Within*, 83-85; differs politically from Leys, 74, 86-87, 94-95, 98, 107-108; 36-37, 48, 50, 99, 103, 111, 133

Salisbury, Lord 41
Scott, C.P. 77
Scott, Lord Francis 110
Settlement, The 12-14, 20, 127, 134
settlers: 1-3; invited to settle Kenya, 29-30; class character, 29, 109-110; exploitation of African labour, 35, 59, 78-79; personal relations with Leys, 35, 49; role in the Maasai affair, 43-46, 49, 51; supported by the administration, 57, 59, 108; supported by the British public, 77, 83; force Ross to resign, 73; subsidised by Africans, 83-85; seek political control, 89-90, 104-106; defeated, 110; role in the Mau Mau rising, 119-120, 122-123; 50, 87, 91, 93-95, 97, 100, 112
Shaw, Mrs. 69
Shepperson, George 56, 125
Shiels, Drummond 108, 128
Shiré River 17, 21
Slavery 23, 59, 92, 107, 116, 127 see also labour, forced
Sorrenson, M.P.K. 109
Southern Rhodesia 18, 27, 89, 104, 107, 109-110
South West Africa 127
Stanley, Lord 116
Strathaven 5-6, 9
Sudan 29, 46
Swahili 38, 40, 42

Tanganyika 52, 107, 109, 115, 117
Tawney, R.H. 58
taxation: hut tax and the Kisii rising, 31, 33-34; hut and poll tax account for most of Kenya's revenue, 78-79, 84; impact on African society, 35; cause of Thuku crisis, 81-82; settlers avoid an income tax, 84; 19, 23, 29, 40-41, 56, 59, 89, 97, 99, 119, 132
Thompson, Edward 125
Thuku, Harry 81, 105
Turner, Borden 67

Uganda 29, 69, 92, 107, 115
Uganda Railway 29, 43, 105

Victoria, Lake 29

Webb, Sidney *see* Passfield
White Highlands 29-30, 99, 109-110
Willis, Bishop 69, 92, 95
Wood-Winterton Agreement 105
Woolf, Leonard: collaborates with Leys 1, 66, 99, 116; publishes *Kenya*, 75-77, 83; friendship with Leys, 76, 83, 135, 137; 17, 92,117, 127, 133-134, 136
Woolf, Virginia 1, 133, 137-138
World War, First 35, 52-54, 95
Wylie, Diana 38, 66, 69, 108, 116, 131, 133

Yalding 71, 115
Young Kikuyu Association 81

Zanzibar 39, 67
Zambezi 17-18, 61

Also available from the Merlin Press:

Life histories told to
Colin Leys and Susan Brown
HISTORIES OF NAMIBIA: Living Through The Liberation Struggle

The stories of eleven Namibians, in their mid-30's when Namibia gained its independence, telling of how a whole generation matured in the struggle, becoming skilled, disciplined, cosmopolitan and tough. 'fascinating collection of eleven life histories... these stories are inspiring testimony to the human spirit.' *International Journal of African Historical Studies*

ISBN 9780850364996 Pbk £18.99

Compiled and edited by Ken Keable
LONDON RECRUITS: The Secret War against Apartheid

This is the story of the foreign volunteers and their activities in South Africa, how they acted in defiance of the Apartheid government and its police on the instructions of the African National Congress. It tells of: ANC Banners that unfurled; ANC speeches that sounded through public places; Buckets that exploded and showered ANC leaflets; Transportation of weapons, communications, logistics; Helping ANC fighters to enter South Africa, and more... Now a film: https://www.londonrecruits.com/
With an introduction by Ronnie Kasrils and a foreword by Z. Pallo Jordan.

ISBN 9780850366556 Pbk £18.99

Paul Joseph
SLUMBOY FROM THE GOLDEN CITY

Paul Joseph grew up in 1930s South Africa. He awoke to political activism as an Indian in the racially segregated schools and slums of Johannesburg, and aged just 15, committed himself to fight oppression. 'an excellent everyman's account of the anti-apartheid struggle' *Morning Star.*

Black and white photos. ISBN 9780850367508 £18.99

Clare & James Currey
FROM SHARPEVILLE TO RIVONIA, JULY 1959 – JULY 1964

A personal view of resistance in South Africa; a book of publishing, politics, and protest. These letters 'shed light on one of the driving forces behind the famed African Writers Series and reveal his early commitment to the anti-apartheid cause and to publishing topical works on Africa north and south of the Limpopo.' *African Studies Quarterly*

ISBN 9780850367584 £18.99